PRICEWATERHOUSECOOPERS 🇮

IFRS and UK GAAP – A comparison

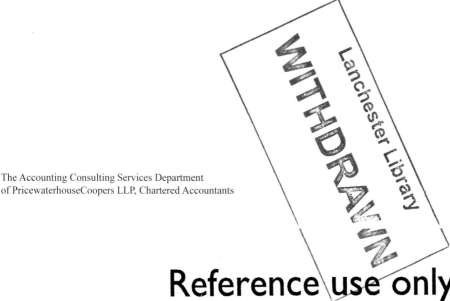

The Accounting Consulting Services Department
of PricewaterhouseCoopers LLP, Chartered Accountants

Published by

 CCH
a Wolters Kluwer business

145 London Road
Kingston-upon-Thames
Surrey
KT2 6SR
Tel: +44 (0) 870 777 2906
Fax: +44 (0) 870 247 1184
E-mail: customer.services@cch.co.uk
Web site: www.cch.co.uk

ISBN 978–1–84140–928–3

Printed and bound in the UK by Bath Press Limited.

British Library Cataloguing-in-Publication Data.

A catalogue record for this book is available from the British Library.

Contents

Key

1	Similar, but minor differences
2	Some differences
3	Significant differences

Contents

This publication does not deal with:

IAS 26, Accounting and reporting by retirement benefit plans.

IAS 30, Disclosures in the financial statements of banks and similar financial institutions.

IFRS 1, First-time adoption of international financial reporting standards.

IFRS 6, Exploration for and evaluation of mineral resources.

Main differences indicator

1	Similar, but minor differences
2	Some differences
3	Significant differences

IFRS	IAS 1, Presentation of financial statements	
UK	FRS 18, Accounting policies FRS 3, Reporting financial performance (part) FRS 28, Corresponding amounts	2

- The main components of a set of IFRS financial statements are broadly similar to those required for UK financial statements and include a balance sheet; an income statement; a statement showing either all changes in equity or changes in equity other than those arising from capital transactions with owners and distributions to owners (a statement of recognised income and expense – SORIE); a cash flow statement; and explanatory notes (including accounting policies).

- IAS 1 incorporates to some extent the UK concept that performance should be measured more broadly than the 'profit' shown in the income statement. However, under IAS 1 the equivalent statement to FRS 3's STRGL can be presented either as a 'traditional' equity reconciliation in columnar form showing all the components of equity (including a sub-total for total income and expense for the period), or as a separate statement of performance in its own right (a SORIE) (as required under UK GAAP), together with a note of other transactions with owners. (The SORIE is required by IAS 19, 'Employee benefits', where an entity chooses a policy of recognising actuarial gains and losses in equity.)

- Unlike UK GAAP, IAS 1 does not prescribe the strict order or format in which items are to be presented in the financial statements. It simply provides a list of items that are so different in nature or function that they deserve separate presentation on the face of the balance sheet and in the income statement. However, the list is very similar to the format line items specified in the EC 4th and 7th Directives and in the UK Companies Act 1985.

- IAS 1 does not require disclosure of operating profit. Under IAS 1, entities may strike a sub-total at operating profit, whereas under FRS 3 this is required.

- FRS 3 identifies three categories of exceptional item ('super-exceptional'), which must be shown after operating profit even though they are often operating items. Under IAS 1, the total of the post-tax profit or loss of discontinued operations and the post-tax gain or loss recognised on the measurement to 'fair value less costs to sell' or on the disposal of the discontinued operation is shown after tax. Other exceptional items, that would be classed as super-exceptional under FRS 3, must be dealt with in the appropriate operating line items.

- IAS 1 requires entities to present current and non-current assets and current and non-current liabilities as separate classifications on the face of the balance sheet, except when a liquidity presentation provides reliable and more relevant information. UK GAAP has specific rules on classification of assets and liabilities.

- IAS 1 requires the disclosure of judgements in the process of applying accounting policies that have the most significant effect on the amounts recognised in the financial statements (for example, management's judgement in determining whether financial assets are held-to maturity investments).

- IAS 1 requires disclosure of information regarding key assumptions about the future and other key sources of estimation uncertainty at the balance sheet date that have a significant risk of causing a material adjustment to the carrying amounts of assets and liabilities within the next financial year. FRS 18 requires a description of those estimation techniques adopted that are significant. For this purpose, an estimation technique is significant only if the range of reasonable monetary amounts is so large that the use of a different amount from within that range could materially affect the view shown by the entity's financial statements.

IFRS	IAS 2, Inventories	
UK	SSAP 9, Stocks and long-term contracts (part)	1

- Both IAS 2 and SSAP 9 require that inventories should be measured at the lower of cost and net realisable value. Cost comprises all costs of purchase, costs of conversion and other costs in bringing the inventories to their present location and condition.

- IAS 2 requires that an entity must use the same cost formula for all inventories having a similar nature and use to the entity. This is not specifically stated in SSAP 9, although the principle of consistency under FRS 18 should lead to a similar treatment.

- Under IAS 2, where there are deferred payment terms for the purchase of inventories, this is regarded as a financing arrangement and the standard requires the difference between the price that would have been paid for 'normal' credit terms and the actual amount paid to be recognised as an interest expense over the period of the financing. SSAP 9 does not deal with this.

IFRS	IAS 7, Cash flow statements	
UK	FRS 1, Cash flow statements	3

- There are some major differences between a cash flow statement prepared under IAS 7 and one prepared under FRS 1. The cash flows reported under IAS 7 relate to movements in cash and cash equivalents (defined as short-term highly liquid investments that are readily convertible into known amounts of cash and subject to insignificant risk of changes in value). FRS 1 requires the movement of cash (defined as cash in hand and deposits repayable on demand, less overdrafts) to be reported in the cash flow statement. Under FRS 1, there is no concept of 'cash equivalents', but cash flows relating to IAS 7 'cash equivalents' would be included in 'management of liquid resources'.

- IAS 7 requires cash flows to be reported under three sections: operating, investing and financing, whereas FRS 1 requires cash flows to be reported in far greater detail under nine standard headings.

- IAS 7 does not require a reconciliation of movements in cash flows to the movement in net debt.

- Under FRS 1, foreign currency exchange differences on cash balances are not reported on the face of the cash flow statement as they are non-cash items. However, IAS 7, requires foreign currency exchange differences on cash and cash equivalents to be reported on the face of the cash flow statement in order to reconcile the opening and closing cash and cash equivalent balances.

- IAS 7 has none of the exemptions that allow many entities not to prepare cash flow statements under FRS 1 (for example, 90 per cent owned subsidiaries).

IFRS	IAS 8, Accounting policies, changes in accounting estimates and errors	
UK	FRS 3, Reporting financial performance (part) FRS 18, Accounting policies (part)	2

- In IAS 8, there is no distinction between fundamental errors and other material errors and all are required to be corrected by retrospective restatement. This differs to FRS 3, which is more restrictive in respect of errors and only restates prior period figures for the correction of fundamental errors.

- IAS 8 requires retrospective application of changes in accounting policies and retrospective restatement to correct all material prior period errors and gives guidance on how this should be applied. In particular, IAS 8 does not permit the use of hindsight when applying a new accounting policy or when correcting prior period errors. FRS 3 does not include guidance on the use of hindsight, but otherwise has similar provisions.

- IAS 8 sets out a hierarchy of guidance to which management refers and whose applicability it considers when selecting accounting policies. Management is required to use its judgement in applying accounting policies that result in information that is relevant, reliable, reflects economic reality and is neutral, prudent and complete. FRS 18 requires that an entity should select the accounting policies that are judged by the entity to be most appropriate to its particular circumstances for the purpose of giving a true and fair view.

- IAS 8 and FRS 18 use different terminology for when accounting policies can be changed voluntarily. IAS 8 only permits a change in policy if it results in the financial statements providing reliable and more relevant information about the effects of transactions, other events or conditions on the entity's financial position, financial performance or cash flows. FRS 18 requires that an entity's accounting policies should be reviewed regularly to ensure that they remain the most appropriate to its particular circumstances for the purpose of giving a true and fair view.

- IFRS includes more detailed disclosure requirements for changes in accounting policy and correction of errors. In particular, under IAS 8, the nature of a future change in an accounting policy when an entity has yet to implement a new standard that has been issued, but not yet come into effect is required to be disclosed, together with details of its impact (where known or reasonably estimable).

- Changes to accounting estimates are accounted for prospectively under both IFRS and UK GAAP. IAS 8 requires disclosure of the nature and amount of a change in an estimate that has an effect in the current period or is expected to have an effect in future periods, except for the disclosure of the effect on future periods when it is impracticable to estimate that effect. FRS 18 requires a description of the change and, where practicable, disclosure of the effect on the results for the current period if material.

IFRS	IAS 10, Events after the balance sheet date	
UK	FRS 21 (IAS 10), Events after the balance sheet date	1

- FRS 21 derives from IAS 10 and is effective for accounting periods beginning on or after 1 January 2005. FRS 21 is almost identical to IAS 10.

IFRS	IAS 11, Construction contracts	
UK	SSAP 9, Stocks and long-term contracts (part)	1

- IAS 11 applies to construction contracts and contracts for services directly related to the construction of an asset. This is more specific in scope than SSAP 9, which also includes contracts for the provision of services. However, contracts for services are covered by IAS 18, 'Revenue', which refers back to the principles in IAS 11.

- IAS 11 requires contracts to be combined when part of a package, or segregated when each contract is part of a separate proposal and revenues and costs can be clearly identified. UK GAAP has similar rules and requires that contractual arrangements should be accounted for as two or more separate transactions only where the commercial substance is that the individual components operate independently of each other and reliable fair values can be attributed to the individual components.

- Both IAS 11 and SSAP 9 use the 'percentage of completion' method to recognise revenue and expenses. Under IAS 11, the stage of completion may be assessed based on, for example, costs incurred for work performed to date, surveys of work performed or completion of the physical proportion of the contract work. UK GAAP allows similar methods, but specifically only permits revenue to be derived from the proportion of costs incurred where these provide evidence of the entity's performance and, hence, the extent to which it has obtained the right to consideration.

- IAS 11 applies the 'percentage of completion' method if the outcome of the contract can be estimated reliably. SSAP 9 places more emphasis on prudence and recognises 'prudently calculated attributable profit' if the outcome of the contract can be assessed with reasonable certainty. Where the above outcome criteria are not met, both IAS 11 and SSAP 9 use the 'zero profit method', under which revenue is recognised only to the extent that costs are incurred that are expected to be recovered. The accounting treatment for loss-making contracts is consistent under IAS 11 and SSAP 9.

- The presentation in the balance sheet differs. Under IAS 11, an asset is shown for the gross amount due from customers for contract work. Under SSAP 9, the asset (net of payments on account) is split between debtors ('amounts recoverable on contracts') and stocks ('long-term contract balances').

IFRS	IAS 12, Income taxes	
UK	FRS 19, Deferred taxation	3
UK	FRS 16, Current tax	1

Current tax
- IAS 12 is similar to FRS 16 in respect of current taxes, except that IAS 12 requires current tax to be presented separately on the face of the balance sheet (there is no such requirement in FRS 16). In addition, IAS 12 requires current tax to be charged directly to equity if it relates to items that are also charged or credited directly to equity. FRS 16 requires all current tax to be included in the statements of performance (that is, profit and loss account or STRGL).

Deferred tax
- In respect of deferred tax, IAS 12 is conceptually different from FRS 19. Under IAS 12, deferred tax is recognised on the basis of taxable temporary difference (subject to certain exceptions). Temporary differences include all timing differences and many permanent differences. Under FRS 19, deferred tax is recognised on the basis of timing differences (subject to certain exceptions).

- Under IAS 12, deferred tax is always recognised on revaluation gains. Under FRS 19, deferred tax on revaluation gains is only recognised (i) if there is a binding agreement to sell the revalued asset and the gain expected to arise on sale has been recognised; or (ii) where an asset is continuously revalued to fair value with changes in fair value being recognised in the profit and loss account.

- IAS 12 prohibits the discounting of deferred tax. FRS 19 permits, but does not require, discounting of deferred tax.

- IAS 12 requires a reconciliation of the total (current and deferred) tax charge to the standard tax charge. FRS 19 requires the reconciliation to be carried out for the current tax charge.

IFRS	IAS 14, Segment reporting	
UK	SSAP 25, Segmental reporting	3

- The scope of IAS 14 and SSAP 25 differs. IAS 14 applies to entities whose equity or debt securities are publicly traded or in the process of being so. SSAP 25 applies to public companies, banking and insurance companies and groups and certain other large entities. In addition, Schedule 4 of the Companies Act 1985 also contains certain segmental reporting requirements that apply to all companies reporting under UK GAAP.

- The Act and SSAP 25 each contain an exemption from the disclosure requirements where disclosure would be seriously prejudicial to the entity's interests. There is no such exemption in IAS 14.

- The disclosure requirements of IAS 14 are more extensive than in SSAP 25.

- IAS 14 provides that one basis of segmentation is primary and the other is secondary. Extensive disclosure is required for primary segments, with considerably less information required to be disclosed for secondary segments. This differs from SSAP 25 which does not make such a distinction.

- IAS 14 is based on management's approach to organising the business. An entity's internal organisational and management structure and its system of internal financial reporting to the board of directors and the chief executive officer should normally be the basis for determining which reporting format is primary and which is secondary. There are exceptions: if the entity's risks and rates of return are strongly affected by both products/ services and geography; and if the internal reporting is not based on products/services or on geography. The approach in IAS 14 differs from the risk/returns approach of SSAP 25, although in practice the results may be similar.

- In November 2006, the IASB issued IFRS 8, 'Operating segments', which replaces IAS 14 and aligns segment reporting with the requirements of the US standard SFAS 131, 'Disclosures about segments of an enterprise and related information'. The new standard uses a 'management approach' under which segment information is presented on the same basis as that used for internal reporting purposes. IFRS 8 is effective for periods beginning on or after 1 January 2009.

IFRS	IAS 16, Property, plant and equipment	
UK	FRS 15, Tangible fixed assets	3

- IAS 16 excludes from its scope property, plant and equipment classified as held for sale in accordance with IFRS 5, biological assets related to agricultural activity (covered by IAS 41), the recognition and measurement of exploration and evaluation assets (covered by IFRS 6) and mineral rights and mineral reserves. FRS 15 does not exclude these types of asset from its scope. However, both IAS 16 and FRS 15 exclude investment properties (covered by IAS 40 and SSAP 19 respectively).

- IAS 16 capitalises subsequent expenditure on an asset using the same criteria as the initial spend, that is, when it is probable the future economic benefits associated with the item will flow to the entity and the cost of the item can be measured reliably. If part of an asset is replaced, then the part it replaces is derecognised, regardless of whether it has been depreciated separately or not. FRS 15, on the other hand, requires capitalisation of subsequent expenditure only when the expenditure improves the condition of the asset beyond its previously assessed standard of performance, which generally would have been reflected in the asset's depreciation.

- IAS 16 states that if fixed assets are acquired in exchange for a non-monetary asset, the cost of the acquired asset is measured at fair value unless (a) the exchange transaction lacks commercial substance or (b) the fair value of neither the asset received nor the asset given up is reliably measurable. A transaction has commercial substance if the future cash flows are expected to change significantly as a result of the transaction. Fair value is taken as the fair value of the asset given up, unless the fair value of the asset received is more reliably measurable. This will be a new requirement for UK companies as FRS 15 does not contain equivalent rules.

- Where a company adopts a policy of valuations, there is a key difference in principle between IAS 16 and FRS 15. IAS 16 requires revaluations to be at fair value. It states that fair value is usually 'determined from market-based evidence' (for land and buildings) or 'market value' (for plant and equipment), which is generally taken to mean open market value. FRS 15 uses the 'value to the business' model and requires revaluations to 'current value', which is defined as being the lower of replacement cost and recoverable amount. As a consequence, FRS 15 is more prescriptive in requiring non-specialised properties to be valued at existing use value (EUV), specialised properties to be valued at depreciated replacement cost and properties surplus to requirements at open market value.

- IAS 16 adopts a simpler approach to recognising revaluation losses than FRS 15:

  - Revaluation losses that are due to a clear consumption of economic benefits are charged to the profit and loss account under FRS 15, whereas under IAS 16, if there is a previous revaluation surplus on that asset, the revaluation loss is first charged against the surplus to the extent of that surplus, with the balance of the loss then being charged to the profit and loss account.

  - Where there is no clear consumption of economic benefits IAS 16 requires the same treatment, that is any loss is first taken against a previous revaluation surplus on the same asset, with the balance being charged to profit and loss account. Under FRS 15 the loss is taken to the STRGL (and to revaluation reserve) to the extent that there is a previous revaluation surplus on the same asset, that is until the carrying value of the asset reaches depreciated historical cost. Any further revaluation loss represented by a difference between depreciated historical cost and recoverable amount is taken to the profit and loss account, but further losses represented by a difference between recoverable amount and the revalued amount are taken to the STRGL and reserves.

- IAS 16 requires residual values to be based on prices current at the balance sheet date, whereas under FRS 15 residual values are based on prices prevailing at the date of acquisition (or revaluation) of an asset and do not take account of price changes. Whilst this difference has little effect on the depreciation of assets carried at current values, it could make a significant difference to depreciation charges in respect of assets carried at historical cost.

- There are no requirements under IAS 16 to carry out impairment reviews at the end of each reporting period where no depreciation charge is made on the grounds that it would be immaterial or where the estimated useful life of the tangible fixed asset exceeds 50 years (although impairment reviews may be required under IAS 36 if there is a trigger event).

IFRS and UK GAAP – A comparison

- FRS 15 contains specific rules on the circumstances in which renewals accounting for infrastructure assets is permitted. IAS 16 does not include any reference to renewals accounting and, therefore, does not allow any departure from the principle that the depreciation expense is determined by reference to an asset's depreciable amount.

- Under IAS 16 comparatives are required for all disclosures, including the table reconciling the carrying amount of each class of property, plant and equipment.

IFRS	IAS 17, Leases	
UK	SSAP 21, Accounting for leases and hire purchase contracts	2

- The broad approach of the international and the UK standard is similar. Both IAS 17 and SSAP 21 require leases to be classed as finance leases or operating leases. The definition of a finance lease is the same in both standards. However, IAS 17 does not provide a quantitative test of whether a lease is a finance lease (the '90% test'), instead it provides additional guidance on when a lease should be classified as finance lease.

- IAS 17 requires that a lease of land and buildings should be split at inception of the lease into a separate lease of land and a lease of buildings. Unless title is expected to pass to the lessee at the end of the lease term, leases of land should normally be treated as operating leases. The buildings element would be classified as an operating or finance lease as appropriate. This means that leases of buildings are more likely to be classified as finance leases under IAS 17 than under SSAP 21 where the land and buildings are considered together.

- Income recognition by lessors for finance leases is different under the two standards. SSAP 21 requires the use of the net cash investment method whilst IAS 17 requires the net investment method to be used. This can give rise to materially different income recognition profiles, particularly where the tax effects of a lease are significant.

- IFRIC 4 sets out criteria for determining whether arrangements that do not take the legal form of a lease (for example, outsourcing arrangements and take-or-pay contracts) should, nonetheless, be accounted for in accordance with IAS 17. There is no direct equivalent in UK GAAP, but the principles of FRS 5 would generally apply to transactions of this type.

- IAS 17 requires a number of detailed disclosures that are not required by SSAP 21.

IFRS	IAS 18, Revenue	
UK	FRS 5 Application Note G, Revenue recognition SSAP 9 (for long-term contracts)	1

- In November 2003, the ASB issued 'Amendment to FRS 5, 'Reporting the substance of transactions': Revenue recognition'. This is intended as an interim step to provide guidance in the UK until a new standard is developed internationally. It takes the form of an additional application note to FRS 5 (Application note G). This sets out the basic principles of revenue recognition that should be applied in all situations and specifically addresses five key areas (long-term contracts, separation and linking of contracts, bill and hold arrangements, sales with right of return and presentation of turnover by principals and agents).

- In addition, FRS 5 deals with some specific types of transaction, including consignment stocks and sale and repurchase agreements and SSAP 9 deals with income from long-term contracts. Several UITF Abstracts also deal with issues relating to revenue recognition and the related matter of cost recognition. These include UITF 24, 'Accounting for start-up costs', UITF 26, 'Barter transactions for advertising', UITF 28, 'Operating lease incentives', UITF 34, 'Pre-contract costs', and UITF 36, 'Contracts for sales of capacity'.

- IAS 18 is generally consistent with the principles set out in the ASB's Statement of principles for financial reporting and, prior to the issue of Application Note G, has been used widely, together with US GAAP, by UK companies for guidance on revenue recognition. Application Note G is considered to have moved UK accounting closer to IAS 18. However, the detailed illustrative guidance in IAS 18 for specific situations could lead to differences with UK GAAP in certain industries.

IFRS	IAS 19, Employee benefits	
UK	FRS 17, Retirement benefits	3

- FRS 17 and IAS 19 are similar in their rules regarding measurement and disclosure of retirement benefits, but there are some differences in the recognition of actuarial gains and losses and the presentation of items in the financial statements.

- Both standards require that defined benefit scheme assets and liabilities are valued at each balance sheet date to produce an asset or liability for recognition on the balance sheet. All of the items recognised in the profit and loss account under FRS 17 are treated in a similar way under IAS 19. However, for actuarial gains and losses that are recognised immediately in the STRGL under FRS 17, there is a choice of policy under IAS 19. These can be recognised in the income statement, usually over a period representing the expected average remaining working lives of employees participating in the scheme (with any deferred actuarial gains and losses carried on the balance sheet as part of the net pension asset or liability). Alternatively, entities have an option to recognise actuarial gains and losses in full as they arise, outside profit or loss, in a 'statement of recognised income and expense' (similar to the treatment under FRS 17).

- Additionally, whereas FRS 17 requires that pension assets and liabilities are shown net of any related deferred tax, this presentation is not permissible under IAS 12.

- There are exemptions from defined benefit accounting for certain multi-employer and group pension plans. IAS 19 has specific rules for group pension plans (that is, plans involving entities under common control), which, unlike FRS 17, differ from those for multi-employer plans. One significant difference from FRS 17 is that, under IAS 19, if defined contribution accounting is used by group entities, the plan has to be accounted for as a defined benefit plan in the sponsoring employer's individual financial statements.

- The accounting for defined contribution schemes is the same under FRS 17 and IAS 19.

- IAS 19 goes further than FRS 17 to consider accounting for and disclosure of other employee benefits such as wages and salaries, bonuses and termination benefits.

- In December 2006, the ASB issued an amendment to FRS 17, replacing the disclosures required by FRS 17 with those of IAS 19. This achieves convergence between FRS 17 and IAS 19 for pensions disclosures. As a further alignment with IAS 19, the ASB has also amended FRS 17 so that for quoted securities the current bid price (rather than the mid-market value) is taken as fair value. The amendment is effective for periods beginning on or after 6 April 2007.

- In addition, the ASB has published a reporting statement, 'Retirement benefits – Disclosures', which recommends additional disclosures and is intended to be best practice for entities with defined benefit pension schemes (whether they report under UK GAAP or IFRS). The disclosures complement those set out in the amended FRS 17 and in IAS 19.

IFRS	IAS 20, Accounting for government grants and disclosure of government assistance	
UK	SSAP 4, Accounting for government grants	1

- The requirements of IAS 20 are similar to those of SSAP 4. One difference in practice is that under IAS 20, grants that relate to recognised assets are presented in the balance sheet either as deferred income, or by deducting the grant from the cost of the asset. Although deduction from the cost of a fixed asset is possible in principle under SSAP 4, it is not permitted by company law for companies reporting under UK GAAP.

IFRS	IAS 21, The effects of changes in foreign exchange rates	
UK	SSAP 20, Foreign currency translation	2
UK	FRS 23 (IAS 21), The effects of changes in foreign exchange rates	1

SSAP 20

- IAS 21's definition of functional currency is similar to SSAP 20's 'local currency', however, applying IAS 21's detailed guidance on how to determine the functional currency of subsidiaries may lead to the selection of a functional currency that may be different from the local currency determined under UK GAAP. IAS 21 requires (like SSAP 20) that entities should measure their results in their functional currency. However, IAS 21 permits entities to present their financial statements in any currency, not necessarily their functional currency, and calls this the 'presentation' currency.

- On initial recognition, both IAS 21 and SSAP 20 require transactions denominated in a foreign currency to be translated at the exchange rate in operation on the date of the transaction. However, SSAP 20 permits the use of the exchange rate specified in a related or matching forward contract. IAS 21 does not permit this. Monetary assets and liabilities denominated in a foreign currency are retranslated at the closing (period-end) rate.

- IAS 21 requires the income and expense items of foreign entities, with a different functional currency to the group's presentation currency, to be translated at the transaction rate and suggests that the average rate may be a good approximation of that rate. IAS 21 does not permit the choice, allowed under SSAP 20, of using the closing rate for the profit and loss account when applying the closing rate/net investment method of translation.

- IAS 21 contains specific rules requiring goodwill and fair value adjustments arising on the acquisition of a foreign operation to be treated as assets and liabilities of the foreign operation and translated at the closing rate. SSAP 20 does not specifically address this point, although current practice since publication of FRS 11 has increasingly been to regard goodwill as a currency asset in line with the requirements contained in IAS 21.

- IAS 21 requires exchange differences on a monetary item forming part of a reporting entity's net investment in a foreign operation to be recognised in a separate component of equity in the reporting entity's consolidated financial statements. However, in the reporting entity's separate financial statements the differences should be recognised in profit or loss. SSAP 20 requires such exchange differences to be taken to reserves in the reporting entity's consolidated financial statements and, where recognised, in its separate financial statements.

- Under IAS 21, net exchange differences classified as equity must be separately tracked and the cumulative amounts disclosed. On disposal of a foreign entity, the appropriate amount of cumulative translation difference relating to the entity is included in the gain or loss on sale in the income statement. SSAP 20 does not permit such 'recycling' of exchange gains and losses.

- IAS 21 does not contain the requirements of SSAP 20 relating to the treatment of hedges of net investments in foreign operations. These matters are covered by IAS 39.

- Under IAS 21, the financial statements of an entity whose functional currency is the currency of a hyper-inflationary economy must be restated under IAS 29 prior to translation into a different presentation currency. IAS 29 requires such an entity's results to be restated in terms of the measuring unit current at the balance sheet date. The alternative method of using a relatively stable currency as the functional currency of the relevant hyperinflationary economy, specified in UITF 9, is not permitted under IFRS.

- IAS 21 has more extensive disclosure requirements than SSAP 20.

FRS 23

- In December 2004, the ASB issued FRS 23 (IAS 21), 'The effects of changes in foreign exchange rates', which is almost identical to IAS 21. FRS 23's effective date is determined by reference to the application of FRS 26, 'Financial instruments: Measurement'.

IFRS	IAS 23, Borrowing costs	
UK	FRS 15, Tangible fixed assets (part)	2

- A policy of capitalisation is allowed under both IAS 23 and FRS 15 for borrowing costs that are directly attributable to the acquisition, construction or production of a qualifying asset. A qualifying asset is an asset that necessarily takes a substantial period of time to get ready for its intended use or sale.

- Where specific borrowings are taken out to finance an asset, there are differences in the determination of the interest that can be capitalised. Under IAS 23, the amount of interest eligible for capitalisation is the actual costs incurred on the borrowings less any interest earned on the temporary reinvestment of funds not used. Under FRS 15, the amount of interest eligible for capitalisation is limited to costs incurred on borrowings in respect of expenditures to date.

- In May 2006, the IASB published an exposure draft proposing to require an entity to capitalise borrowing costs directly attributable to the acquisition, construction or production of a qualifying asset as part of the cost of that asset. The option of immediately expensing those borrowing costs would be removed.

IFRS	IAS 24, Related party disclosures	
UK	FRS 8, Related party disclosures	2

- IAS 24 contains similar requirements and definitions to FRS 8. However, IAS 24 does not include most of the exemptions available under FRS 8.

- IAS 24 does not exempt subsidiaries from disclosing related party transactions. Under FRS 8, there is no requirement to disclose transactions with other group entities (or other related party investees) in the financial statements of 90 per cent (or more) owned subsidiaries, provided the parent's consolidated financial statements in which those subsidiaries are included are publicly available.

- Also, IAS 24 requires disclosure of related party transactions in the separate financial statements of parent entities. Under FRS 8, there is an exemption when the parent's own financial statements are presented with its consolidated financial statements.

- IAS 24 requires the disclosure of key management compensation in aggregate, split into various categories. All directors are regarded as key management, but the definition of key management is not confined to directors. Senior employees may also be regarded as key management for related party disclosure purposes if they have authority and responsibility for planning, directing and controlling the entity's activities. FRS 8 excludes management compensation from its scope. The structure of the disclosures required by IAS 24 differs from that required for directors' remuneration by the Companies Act 1985, so even where the key management of a company consists solely of its directors, separate analyses of their remuneration is usually required to satisfy each requirement.

- IAS 24 does not include the exemption in FRS 8 whereby the related party disclosure rules do not apply if this conflicts with the reporting entity's duties of confidentiality arising by the operation of the law.

- There is no specific requirement in IAS 24 to disclose the name of the related party (other than the controlling and ultimate parties). However, this disclosure may be necessary in order to meet the requirement to disclose the information necessary for an understanding of the potential effect of the related party relationship on the financial statements.

- The specific guidance in FRS 8 on determining whether a related party transaction is material for disclosure purposes and particularly the specification that a related party transaction is material if regarded as material for individual related parties is not included in IAS 24. IAS 24 gives no guidance on the materiality of related party transactions requiring disclosure, but general guidance on materiality in respect of disclosures is included in IAS 1.

IFRS	IAS 27, Consolidated and separate financial statements SIC 12, Consolidation – special purpose entities	
UK	FRS 2, Accounting for subsidiary undertakings FRS 5, Reporting the substance of transactions (quasi-subsidiaries)	2

- The scope of IAS 27 and FRS 2 is similar, except that IAS 27 includes guidance on the treatment of investments in subsidiaries in the parent's separate financial statements, whereas FRS 2 does not.

- IAS 27 does not specify that the parent of wholly-owned or partially-owned subsidiaries must be located in a particular country for the exemption from the requirement to produce consolidated financial statements to apply. Instead, the ultimate or any intermediate parent must produce consolidated IFRS financial statements available for public use. In the past, FRS 2 required the immediate parent to be established under the law of an EC Member State. However, for accounting periods beginning on or after 1 January 2005, the exemption is extended to intermediate parent undertakings that are majority-owned subsidiaries of parents that are not governed by the law of an European Economic Area (EEA) State. This is subject to various conditions, including the foreign parent preparing consolidated financial statements in a manner equivalent to the Seventh Directive.

- IAS 27's definition of a subsidiary is simply *"an entity, including an unincorporated entity such as a partnership, that is controlled by another entity (known as the parent)"*. Control is defined as the *"power to govern the financial and operating policies of an entity so as to obtain benefits from its activities"*. The circumstances where there is control are similar to most of those contained within FRS 2.

- IAS 27 states that the existence and effect of potential voting rights that are currently exercisable (or convertible) should be considered when assessing whether an entity controls another entity. This is a subtle difference from the UK position where options are taken into account in determining whether a party has a majority of the voting rights only when the option has been exercised. However, in practice other factors, such as dominant influence, may well make the decision to consolidate the same under both sets of accounting standards.

- FRS 2 requires a subsidiary to be excluded from consolidation where severe long-term restrictions substantially hinder the exercise of the parent undertaking's rights over the assets or management of the subsidiary undertaking. IAS 27 does not have such an exclusion exemption. However, severe restrictions would be considered in determining whether control exists. Control must be lost for exclusion to occur.

- The method of consolidation of subsidiaries is broadly the same under IFRS as it is under UK GAAP. Also, both IAS 27 and FRS 2 specify that consolidated financial statements should be prepared using uniform accounting policies for like transactions and other events in similar circumstances.

- Under both UK GAAP and IFRS, the reporting periods of the reporting entity and its subsidiaries should be consistent. Where this is not possible, UK GAAP allows consolidation of the subsidiary's reported results where the subsidiary's period end is no more then three months before the parent's reporting year end. IAS 27 is more flexible and allows consolidation of non-coterminous reported financial statements where the subsidiary's period end is within three months of the period end of the parent (that is, subsidiary financial statements for a period ending after the group's period end may be consolidated).

- SIC 12, 'Consolidation – Special purpose entities', deals with the accounting for a special purpose entity (SPE). Similar to UK GAAP, SIC 12 requires SPEs to be consolidated where the substance of the relationship is that of control.

- The calculation of the gain or loss on disposal of a subsidiary differs. Under IAS 27, it excludes goodwill previously written off to equity. Under FRS 2, goodwill previously written off to reserves is included in the calculation of the gain or loss on disposal.

- In June 2005, the IASB published proposed amendments to IAS 27, which would mean that transactions with minority shareholders would be treated as if they were transactions with owners (the 'economic entity' model). In July 2005, the ASB published proposed amendments to FRS 2 based on the IASB's proposals.

IFRS	IAS 28, Investments in associates	
UK	FRS 9, Associates and joint ventures (part)	2

- Under IAS 28, the definition of associate is similar to that in FRS 9, although FRS 9's definition is more restrictive as it requires that the investor must actually exercise significant influence for an associate relationship to exist. Under IAS 28, an investor has to have significant influence, which is defined as the power to participate in the financial and operating policy decisions of the investee, regardless of whether that power is actually exercised. Consequently, some associates under IAS 28 would not be classified as such under FRS 9.

- Both IAS 28 and FRS 9 use the equity method of accounting for associates. The investor presents its share of the associate's profits or losses in its income statement. IAS 28 requires the investor's share of the profit or loss of associates to be separately disclosed, but does not specify where in the income statement this should be presented. This is dealt with in IAS 1, which presents the share of the associate's profits or losses (net of tax and minority interests) after the line item for finance costs, but before the line item for tax expense. FRS 9 is more detailed and does require the investor's share of the associate's operating profit, exceptional items, interest and tax to be presented separately.

- The requirements under IAS 28 to equity account associates include those investors that do not have subsidiaries, but do have interests in associates. The only exception to this requirement is for those investors that are exempt from the requirement to prepare consolidated financial statements or those that would be exempt under similar conditions had they interests in subsidiaries. This is different to the treatment under FRS 9, as such interests are dealt with by additional disclosure rather than inclusion. Under FRS 9, an investor that is not required to produce consolidated financial statements because it has no subsidiaries, treats interests in associates as investments and carries them at cost or valuation. FRS 9 requires additional disclosures of the relevant equity accounted amounts for these associate interests. Such disclosures are not required for those associates not included because the investor was exempt from the requirement to prepare consolidated financial statements (or would be if the investor had subsidiaries).

- FRS 9 exempts investment funds (for example, venture capitalists) from the requirement to equity account those investments over which they have significant influence or joint control. IAS 28 excludes from its scope investments in associates held by venture capital organisations, mutual funds, unit trusts and similar entities including investment-linked insurance funds that upon initial recognition are designated as at fair value through profit or loss or are classified as held for trading and accounted for in accordance with IAS 39.

- FRS 9 requires extensive additional disclosures in aggregate or individually where certain measurement thresholds are exceeded. IAS 28 requires summarised aggregated financial information disclosures for all associates.

IFRS	IAS 29, Financial reporting in hyperinflationary economies	
UK	UITF 9, Accounting for operations in hyper-inflationary economies	3
UK	FRS 24 (IAS 29), Financial reporting in hyperinflationary economies	1

UITF 9

- IAS 29 deals with the situation where the reporting entity itself reports in the currency of a hyper-inflationary economy. Prior to the issue of FRS 24 (see below), this was not specifically dealt with in UK GAAP. Instead, UITF 9 deals with the translation of foreign entities included in consolidated financial statements.

- UITF 9 permits a choice of policy for translating the results of a subsidiary in a hyper-inflationary economy – either adjusting the local currency financial statements to reflect current price levels prior to translation or using a relatively stable currency as the measurement currency of the foreign operation. Under IAS 21, the results of an entity whose functional currency is the currency of a hyper-inflationary economy must be restated under IAS 29 prior to translation into a different presentation currency. IAS 29 requires such an entity's results to be restated in terms of the measuring unit current at the balance sheet date.

- Where the reporting entity itself reports in the currency of a hyper-inflationary economy, IAS 29 requires it to prepare financial statements based on the measuring unit current at the balance sheet date (that is, adjusting the financial statements to reflect current price levels). Comparative amounts for prior periods are also restated into the measuring unit at the current balance sheet date. Any gain or loss on the net monetary position arising from the restatement of amounts into the measuring unit current at the balance sheet date must be included in net income and separately disclosed.

FRS 24

- In December 2004, the ASB issued FRS 24 (IAS 29), 'Financial reporting in hyper-inflationary economies', which is almost identical to IAS 29. FRS 24's effective date is determined by reference to the application of FRS 26, 'Financial instruments: Measurement'.

IFRS	IAS 31, Interests in joint ventures	
UK	FRS 9, Associates and joint ventures (part)	3

- IAS 31 identifies three types of joint ventures, namely jointly controlled 'entities', jointly controlled operations and jointly controlled assets. Under FRS 9, only jointly controlled 'entities' are classified as joint ventures and the definition is more restrictive than IAS 31. Under IAS 31, 'entities' can be corporations, partnerships or other entities. This is similar to FRS 9, but such undertakings are only treated as joint ventures under FRS 9 if they carry on their own trade or business. Jointly controlled operations or assets fall within the FRS 9 category of 'joint arrangements that are not entities'.

- For jointly controlled entities, IAS 31 requires use of either proportionate consolidation or the equity method. FRS 9 does not permit proportionate consolidation and requires use of the 'gross equity' method for joint ventures (that is, use of the equity method, but with separate presentation of the investor's share of gross assets and liabilities and turnover on the face of the balance sheet and income statement).

- The requirements under IAS 31 to either proportionately consolidate or equity account interests in jointly controlled entities include those venturers that do not have subsidiaries, but do have interests in jointly controlled entities. The only exception to this requirement is for those venturers that are exempt from the requirement to prepare consolidated financial statements or those that would be exempt under similar conditions had they interests in subsidiaries. This is different to FRS 9 as such interests are dealt with by additional disclosure rather than inclusion. Under FRS 9, a venturer that is not required to produce consolidated financial statements because it has no subsidiaries treats interests in joint ventures as investments and carries them at cost or valuation. Additional disclosures are required of the relevant gross equity accounted amounts for these joint venture interests, although this does not apply when the joint venture is not included because the venturer was exempt from the requirement to prepare consolidated financial statements (or would be if the venturer had subsidiaries).

- FRS 9 exempts investment funds (for example, venture capitalists) from the requirement to gross equity account those investments over which they have joint control. IAS 31 excludes from its scope investments in jointly controlled entities held by venture capital organisations, mutual funds, unit trusts and similar entities including investment-linked insurance funds that upon initial recognition are designated as at fair value through profit or loss or are classified as held for trading and accounted for in accordance with IAS 39.

- IAS 31 does not include the same detailed disclosure requirements of FRS 9, in particular, it does not include the extensive additional disclosures required in aggregate or individually where certain measurement thresholds are exceeded. IAS 31 does require additional aggregate disclosures when the line-by-line reporting format for proportionate consolidation or the equity method is used for reporting interests in jointly controlled entities.

IFRS	IAS 32, Financial instruments: Presentation	
UK	FRS 25 (IAS 32), Financial instruments: Presentation	1

- The presentation requirements in FRS 25 are effective for all companies reporting under UK GAAP for accounting periods beginning on or after 1 January 2005. FRS 25 derives from IAS 32 and is almost identical to that standard. FRS 25 also includes certain paragraphs of IAS 1, 'Presentation of financial statements'.

IFRS	IAS 33, Earnings per share	
UK	FRS 22 (IAS 33), Earnings per share	1

- FRS 22 applies to listed companies and those in the process of listing and is effective for accounting periods beginning on or after 1 January 2005. It derives from IAS 33 and is almost identical to that standard. However, FRS 22 includes additional guidance in an appendix on the calculation of earnings per share for business combinations.

IFRS	IAS 34, Interim financial reporting	
UK	ASB Statement – Interim reporting	1

- There is no requirement under IFRS to publish an interim financial report. However, entities that are required by local regulators or voluntarily elect to publish an interim financial report in accordance with IFRS, must apply IAS 34. In the UK, listed companies are required by the Listing Rules to publish half-yearly interim reports. The Listing Rules set out minimum requirements for interim reports and, under UK GAAP, are supplemented by the ASB's statement of best practice.

- IAS 34 defines the minimum content of an interim report, including disclosures together with the recognition and measurement principles to be applied. The requirements are broadly consistent with the UK requirements.

- One difference is that, under IAS 34, comparatives for the balance sheet are required to be disclosed as at the end of the previous full financial year, whereas in the UK, the Listing Rules require balance sheet comparatives for the corresponding interim date in the prior year. The Listing Rules do not require disclosure for the previous full financial year, but it is recommended by the ASB's statement and, in practice, this disclosure is given by UK companies that publish interim reports.

- Furthermore, under IAS 34, quarterly interim reports must contain figures (other than for the balance sheet) for the cumulative period to date and for the corresponding period of the preceding year. This is not specified under UK GAAP.

- IAS 34 requires detailed disclosures, in accordance with the requirements of IFRS 3, 'Business combinations', in respect of business combinations during the period. The ASB's interim statement refers only to narrative commentary in respect of major acquisitions in the period.

IFRS	IAS 36, Impairment of assets	
UK	FRS 11, Impairment of fixed assets and goodwill	2

- The basic approach in IAS 36 is the same as that in FRS 11 – impairment is measured by comparing the carrying value of fixed assets and goodwill with the higher of fair value less costs to sell (equivalent to net selling price) and value in use. Value in use is calculated by discounting the cash flows that are expected to be generated from the assets.

- However, there are some differences between IAS 36 and FRS 11 arising from the UK view of intangible assets as being of a similar nature to goodwill, whereas under IFRS, intangible assets are treated as akin to tangible fixed assets. The main implications of this arise in:

- The allocation of impairment losses, which under IAS 36 are allocated first to goodwill and then pro-rata to intangible assets and other tangible fixed assets. Under FRS 11, losses are allocated first to goodwill, then to intangible assets and then to other tangible fixed assets.

- Under IAS 36, reversals of impairment of goodwill are prohibited. Reversals of impairments on intangible assets are permitted where there are indicators that the impairment no longer exists or is reduced. FRS 11 permits reversals of impairments of goodwill and intangible assets in restricted circumstances.

- Goodwill is not amortised under IFRS. Instead, IAS 36 requires an annual impairment review, which should take place at the same time each year (not necessarily the year end, although if there is a trigger event subsequent to an impairment test being performed on goodwill, then the impairment test must be updated). UK GAAP requires a review of goodwill at the end of the first full year after acquisition, but then only requires such reviews when there has been a trigger event or where goodwill is amortised over more than 20 years (or carried indefinitely without being amortised).

- Where acquired entities are merged with existing operations, FRS 11 requires calculation of the internally generated goodwill of the pre-existing operation to facilitate a more accurate assessment of whether acquired goodwill has been subsequently impaired. There is no similar requirement in IAS 36.

- Both standards require that in determining value in use, future cash flows should be estimated for the asset in its current condition and should not include estimated cash flows from future restructuring to which the entity is not yet committed or future expenditure that will improve or enhance the asset. However, FRS 11 includes an exception for newly-acquired income generating units and permits these future cash flows to be taken into account if they were anticipated at the time of performing the impairment review in the first full year after acquisition and were consistent with plans and budgets at that time.

- The accuracy of previous value in use calculations over the last five years have to be monitored under FRS 11 ('look-back test'), with any impairment that should have been recognised being required to be charged when actual cash flows are substituted. IAS 36 requires management to assess the reasonableness of the assumptions in its current cash flow projections by examining the causes of differences between past cash flow projections and actual cash flows, but there is no requirement to recognise losses that would have arisen in the past (but which have since reversed).

- FRS 11 requires impairments of revalued assets that are clearly caused by the consumption of economic benefits to be recognised in the profit and loss account, whereas IAS 36 requires such impairments to be recognised in the profit and loss account only to the extent that the loss exceeds the balance on the revaluation reserve relating to the specific asset.

- IAS 36 requires extensive disclosure of impairments by segment and, where material, by cash-generating unit. In addition there is extensive narrative disclosure required on the impairment testing process and, in certain circumstances, disclosure of the key assumptions made in impairment tests and sensitivity analysis.

IFRS	IAS 37, Provisions, contingent liabilities and contingent assets	
UK	FRS 12, Provisions, contingent liabilities and contingent assets	1

- IAS 37 and FRS 12 were developed at the same time and there are no significant differences between the two. FRS 12 deals with the circumstances in which an obligation recognised as a provision results in the recognition of an asset. IAS 37 does not deal with this in the standard, but there is an illustrative example that is consistent with the FRS 12 guidance. Also, FRS 12 includes more guidance than IAS 37 on the discount rate to be used in determining the present value of a provision.

- IAS 37 is being reconsidered as part of the IFRS/US convergence project. It is proposed that IAS 37 is re-titled 'Non-financial liabilities' and that it would require entities to recognise all obligations that satisfy the IASB framework's definition of a liability, unless they cannot be measured reliably. Uncertainty about the amount or timing of the obligation would no longer affect whether or not a liability should be recognised, but would be reflected in the obligation's measurement. There are also proposed amendments to accounting for restructuring provisions and termination benefits (in IAS 19). In July 2005, the ASB published FRED 39, based on the IASB's proposals.

IFRS	IAS 38, Intangible assets	
UK	FRS 10, Goodwill and intangible assets SSAP 13, Accounting for research and development	3

- A wider range of intangible assets are recognised under IFRS, particularly in respect of business combinations (see IFRS 3).

- Under both IFRS and UK GAAP, an intangible asset is an identifiable non-monetary asset without physical substance. Under IAS 38, an asset is identifiable when it is separable (that is, capable of being sold separate from the entity) or arises from contractual or other legal rights. Under FRS 10, the assets have to be capable of being disposed of separately from the business.

- FRS 10 requires an internally generated intangible to have a readily ascertainable market value before it can be recognised. IAS 38 allows internally generated assets to be recognised provided they meet criteria similar to those contained within SSAP 13 for development costs. Internally generated brands, mastheads, publishing titles, customer lists and similar items cannot be recognised, as they cannot be distinguished from the development of the business as a whole.

- IAS 38 does not contain a rebuttable presumption that the useful economic life of an intangible asset is 20 years or less, whereas FRS 10 does, although both standards state that an intangible asset can have an indefinite life and if this is the case they need not be amortised.

- Both IFRS and UK GAAP require annual impairment reviews for intangible assets with an indefinite life. The requirements differ for intangible assets with a finite life. IAS 38 only requires an impairment review if there is an indication of impairment, whereas FRS 10 additionally requires an annual impairment review where the 20-year useful life presumption is rebutted. IAS 38 also requires an annual impairment review for an intangible asset that is not yet ready for use.

- Under IAS 38, research costs must be written off as incurred, whereas development costs should be capitalised where particular criteria are met. This contrasts with SSAP 13 where an entity may choose to capitalise development costs.

IFRS	IAS 39, Financial instruments: Recognition and measurement	
UK	FRS 26 (IAS 39), Financial instruments: Recognition and measurement	2
UK	FRS 4, Capital instruments FRS 5, Reporting the substance of transactions (derecognition)	3

- IAS 39 covers the recognition, measurement and derecognition of financial instruments, in addition to rules on hedge accounting. Prior to the publication of FRS 26, there was no UK standard that comprehensively addressed accounting for financial instruments. FRS 5 covers recognition and derecognition, but it specifically scopes out derivatives.

- FRS 26 derives from IAS 39, but the initial version of the standard did not include the recognition and derecognition material in IAS 39 and its scope is narrower than IAS 39. For listed entities, the original version of FRS 26 applies for accounting periods beginning on or after 1 January 2005. For entities using the fair value accounting rules set out in the Companies Act 1985, FRS 26 applies for accounting periods beginning on or after 1 January 2006. For entities not using FRS 26, an amended version of FRS 4 applies.

- An amendment to FRS 26 was published in April 2006, implementing IAS 39's recognition and derecognition material. The derecognition requirements of FRS 5, 'Reporting the substance of transactions', are superseded for transactions that fall within the amended IAS 39's scope, but FRS 5 continues to apply to transactions in non-financial assets and liabilities. The amendment is effective for accounting periods beginning on or after 1 January 2007.

- The definition of a financial instrument under IAS 39 (and FRS 26) is wide and includes cash, debt and equity investments, loans, trade receivables and payables, certain provisions, derivatives (including embedded derivatives). There is no exemption for short-term debtors and creditors. See also 'What is a financial instrument?'.

- IAS 39 (and FRS 26) is a partial rather than a full fair value model. Financial assets and liabilities are measured at fair value or amortised cost depending on which defined category they fall into under the standard. All derivative financial instruments (including embedded derivatives) are required to be recognised in the balance sheet at fair value. Changes in the fair value of derivatives that are not hedging instruments are recognised in the income statement. Hedge accounting is more complicated.

- In order to qualify for hedge accounting, formal documentation is required and the entity must be able to measure and track the effectiveness of the hedging instrument at the start and on an ongoing basis. IAS 39 (and FRS 26) includes rules for fair value hedges, cash flow hedges and net investment hedges.

- For more details see the executive summary of IAS 32 and IAS 39 in chapter 6 of the Manual of Accounting – IFRS for the UK.

IFRS	IAS 40, Investment property	
UK	SSAP 19, Accounting for investment properties	3

- There are significant differences between IAS 40 and SSAP 19 in terms of the measurement bases that may be used and the recognition of gains and losses on revaluation.

- Under IAS 40 an entity can choose, for all investment property (with some specified exceptions), between the fair value model and depreciated cost. This differs from the treatment required by SSAP 19, which requires investment properties to be carried at open market value and does not permit such property to be carried at depreciated historical cost.

- Under IAS 40, a property interest held by a lessee under an operating lease may be accounted for as an investment property if the property would otherwise meet the definition of an investment property, the lease is accounted for as if it were a finance lease and the fair value model is adopted (for all investment properties).

- When the fair value model is applied under IAS 40, the carrying amount is not depreciated. Gains or losses arising from changes in the asset's fair value are recognised in the income statement. Again, this differs from SSAP 19 where a revaluation gain or loss is recognised in the STRGL, unless it is a permanent deficit (or its reversal) that should be recognised in the profit and loss account.

- When there is a change in use of the investment property, IAS 40 provides detailed guidance for subsequent classification. Investment property to be developed for sale is reclassified as inventory and investment property to be owner-occupied is reclassified as property, plant and equipment. There is no guidance in SSAP 19 on this issue although properties would be similarly reclassified, but there are some differences in the accounting for transfer values.

- The disclosure requirements of IAS 40 are more extensive than the requirements of SSAP 19.

IFRS	IAS 41, Agriculture	
UK	No corresponding UK standard	3

- IAS 41 deals with accounting for agricultural activity. This is defined as the managed biological transformation of biological assets (living animals and plants) for sale, into agricultural produce (harvested product of biological assets) or into additional biological assets. There is currently no equivalent UK standard, although SSAP 9 applies to stocks (see above).

- Under IAS 41, all biological assets should be measured at fair value less estimated point-of-sale costs, with the change in the carrying amount reported as part of profit or loss from operating activities. Agricultural produce harvested from an entity's biological assets should be measured at fair value less estimated point-of-sale costs at the point of harvest; thereafter IAS 2 or another applicable standard applies.

- IAS 41 does not establish any new principles for land related to agricultural activity. Instead, an entity follows IAS 16, IAS 17 or IAS 40 depending on which standard is appropriate in the circumstances.

IFRS	IFRS 2, Share-based payment	
UK	UITF 17, Employee share schemes UITF 38, Accounting for ESOP trusts	3
UK	FRS 20 (IFRS 2), Share-based payment	1

- In February 2004, the IASB issued IFRS 2, which deals with share-based payments (including equity-settled transactions and cash-settled transactions where the amount paid is based on the value of the entity's equity instruments). In April 2004, the ASB issued a standard (FRS 20) that is identical to IFRS 2, with the exception of a deferred implementation date for unlisted entities. Therefore, there will be no difference in the future accounting for share-based payments under UK GAAP and IFRS. However, the accounting for employee share schemes under IFRS 2/FRS 20 will differ significantly from the previous treatment in the UK under UITF 17.

- The scope of IFRS 2 is wider than UITF 17 as it relates to all share-based payment transactions, not just those made to employees, and also has no exemption for SAYE schemes.

- IFRS 2 requires that for equity-settled transactions with employees (for example, share option awards), the fair value of the employee services received should be measured by reference to the fair value of the equity instrument (for example, the share option) at the grant date. UITF 17 requires that the charge to the profit and loss account should, as a minimum, be based on the difference between the fair value of the shares at the date of grant and the exercise price (that is, an 'intrinsic value' basis).

- Under IFRS 2, the charge is spread over the 'vesting period', which differs to the requirement in UITF 17 to spread the charge over the 'performance period'. No distinction is drawn in IFRS 2 between vesting periods during which employees have to satisfy specific performance conditions and vesting periods during which there are no particular requirements other than to remain in the entity's employ. Hence, a vesting period in the context of IFRS 2 is different from a performance period referred to in UITF 17.

- IFRS 2 provides additional guidance on the treatment where terms and conditions are modified, including cancellations and settlements.

- Accounting for ESOP trusts is governed in the UK by UITF 38 (which superseded UITF 13). UITF 38 requires the assets and liabilities of an employee share ownership plan (ESOP) trust to be recognised in the sponsoring company's financial statements where the sponsoring company has de facto control of those assets and liabilities. Own shares held through an ESOP trust should be presented as a deduction in arriving at the sponsoring company's shareholders' funds (rather than the previous UITF 13 treatment as an asset). Any gains or losses on those own shares are also reflected through shareholders' funds. Under IFRS, an entity that controls an employee benefit trust (or similar entity) is required by SIC 12 to consolidate that trust (which differs to the UK GAAP requirement for the sponsoring company to aggregate the trust into its own financial statements) and, in doing so, apply the requirements of IAS 32 to the entity's own shares held by the trust (that is, present them as a deduction from equity).

IFRS	IFRS 3 , Business combinations	
UK	FRS 6, Acquisitions and mergers FRS 7, Fair values in acquisition accounting FRS 10, Goodwill and intangible assets	3

- Under IFRS 3, merger accounting is prohibited and business combinations are required to be accounted for as acquisitions using the purchase method. Under UK GAAP, merger accounting for business combinations is required in limited circumstances if specified criteria are met. (Merger accounting means that the consideration for the combination and the net assets acquired are not recorded at fair values and, consequently, no goodwill arises.)

- IFRS 3 applies to all business combinations, except (i) the formation of joint ventures, (ii) combinations involving entities under common control, (iii) combinations involving two or more mutual entities and (iv) business combinations brought about by contract alone (for example, dual listed companies). FRS 6 does not have scope exclusions.

- For acquisition accounting, under both IFRS 3 and UK GAAP, from the date of acquisition an acquirer should incorporate into the income statement the results of operations of the acquiree and recognise in the balance sheet the identifiable assets and liabilities (measured at fair values) of the acquiree and any goodwill arising on the acquisition. However, there are some significant differences between IFRS and UK GAAP as follows.

- IFRS 3 requires that all the acquiree's intangible assets at the acquisition date should be recognised separately in the consolidated financial statements if they meet the definition of an intangible asset in IAS 38 and if their fair value can be measured reliably. Under IAS 38, there is a rebuttable presumption that the intangible asset's fair value can be measured reliably if it has a finite useful life. UK GAAP is not as stringent as IFRS with regard to identifying intangibles and does not rule out the possibility of many intangible assets being subsumed within goodwill.

- Where the acquisition takes place in stages, under IFRS 3, each exchange transaction is treated separately for the purpose of determining the fair values of the identifiable assets and liabilities acquired and for determining the amount of any goodwill on that transaction. Under UK GAAP, the Companies Act 1985 differs as it requires that identifiable assets and liabilities acquired are measured at their fair values at the date the investee becomes a subsidiary. However, FRS 2 notes that, in some circumstances, it may be appropriate to use a true and fair override of the Act's requirements in order to use fair values at the dates of earlier purchases, which would be consistent with IFRS 3.

- Under both IFRS 3 and FRS 7, the identifiable assets and liabilities of an acquired business are those that existed at the date of acquisition measured at their fair values at that date. Both standards permit fair values to be initially determined provisionally, but the hindsight periods in which adjustments to fair values/goodwill can be made differ. Under IFRS 3, adjustments to the provisional fair values should be made *within twelve months of the acquisition date*, with a corresponding adjustment to goodwill. Under FRS 7, adjustments should be made in the financial statements for the first full financial year following the acquisition, which can be a longer period than under IFRS.

- Under IFRS 3, adjustments to provisional fair values should be recognised as if the initial accounting had been completed at the acquisition date, that is, comparatives should be restated. Under UK GAAP, the adjustments to provisional fair values are accounted for in the period that the adjustments are made.

- Under both IFRS and UK GAAP, goodwill arising on an acquisition is treated as an asset. IFRS 3 prohibits amortisation of goodwill and, instead, subjects it to an annual impairment review. Under FRS 10, there is a rebuttable presumption that the useful life of goodwill does not exceed 20 years, but it permits an indefinite useful life (with annual impairment reviews).

- IFRS 3 does not use the term 'negative goodwill' and, instead, terms it as 'excess of acquirer's interest in the net fair value of acquiree's identifiable assets' and requires it to be taken to profit or loss in the year of acquisition. FRS 10 requires that negative goodwill, up to the aggregate fair value of the non-monetary assets acquired should be recognised in the income statement to match the depreciation of those assets. The balance, if any, is recognised in the income statement over the period likely to benefit.

- In June 2005, the IASB published proposed amendments to IFRS 3, which would mean recognising the full fair value of the acquired business, including any minority interest in goodwill; and fair valuing contingent consideration at the acquisition date, with any subsequent changes recognised in profit or loss. Transactions with minority shareholders would be treated as if they were transactions with owners. In July 2005, the ASB published FRED 36 based on the IASB's proposals.

IFRS	IFRS 4, Insurance contracts	
UK	FRS 27, Life assurance	3

- IFRS 4 applies to all insurance contracts issued by an insurer. An 'insurer' is any entity that issues an insurance contract. Under UK GAAP, insurance contracts are scoped out of most general accounting standards such as FRS 12 and FRS 5 Application Note G. Accounting for insurance contracts by insurance companies is dealt with by Schedule 9A of the Companies Act 1985, the Association of British Insurers (ABI) SORP 'Accounting for insurance business' and, for accounting periods ending on or after 23 December 2005, by FRS 27.

- IFRS 4 gives detailed guidance on what constitutes an insurance contract (principally contracts with significant insurance risk). Under UK GAAP, sections that define the scope of IFRS 4, IAS 32 and IAS 39 – including the definition of 'insurance contracts' – are included in FRS 26 and will, therefore, apply to entities complying with that standard.

- Any contract that meets the IFRS 4 definition will be accounted for as an insurance contract and be subject to the requirements of IFRS 4, under which an entity may continue to use its existing policies for recognition and measurement (subject to the ASB's Memorandum of Understanding with the ABI and major insurers and bancassurers, under which the companies will voluntarily comply with the requirements of FRS 27 from 2005).

- Contracts that do not meet the criteria of an insurance contract under IFRS 4 will generally be regarded as a financial instrument. Hence they will fall within the scope of IAS 32 and IAS 39 and will be required to be recognised and measured in accordance with those standards.

- IFRS 4 and IAS 1 do not address the specific presentation of the primary financial statements for insurers. Whereas, for UK companies Schedule 9A of the Companies Act specifies the presentation of the profit and loss account and the balance sheet of insurance companies and groups.

IFRS	IFRS 5, Non-current assets held for sale and discontinued operations	
UK	FRS 3, Reporting financial performance (part)	3

- IFRS 5 sets out requirements for the classification, measurement and presentation of non-current assets held for sale. There is no equivalent UK standard.

- IFRS 5 introduces the concept of a 'disposal group'. Assets classified as held for sale and the assets in a disposal group that is classified as held for sale are presented separately from other assets in the balance sheet. The liabilities of a disposal group classified as held for sale should be presented separately from other liabilities. There is no equivalent UK rule.

- An asset held for sale, or included within a disposal group that is held for sale, is not depreciated under IFRS 5. This differs to UK GAAP where depreciation would continue until the asset was actually disposed of.

- Under IFRS 5, subsidiaries acquired exclusively with a view to resale that meet the conditions to be classified as held for sale are consolidated, but their results are presented within the single line item for discontinued operations. They are presented in the balance sheet as two separate items (that is, assets, including goodwill, and liabilities) measured at fair value less costs to sell. Under UK GAAP, these subsidiaries are exempt from consolidation and are included in the balance sheet as a single asset at fair value based on net proceeds.

- The definitions of discontinued operations differ. Under IFRS 5, a discontinued operation is a separate major line of business or geographical area of operations or is part of a single plan to dispose of a major line of business or geographical area of operations or is a subsidiary acquired exclusively with a view to resale. FRS 3 requires the discontinued operation to have a material effect on the nature and focus of the reporting entity's operations.

- Under IFRS 5, an operation is classified as discontinued at the date the operation meets the criteria to be classified as held for sale or when the entity has disposed of the operation. 'Held for sale' means that the asset (or disposal group) must be available for immediate sale in its present condition and its sale must be highly probable. To be highly probable, management should be committed to a plan to sell and an active programme to locate a buyer and complete the plan should have begun. The sale should be completed within one year of the date of classification as held for resale (except if this is delayed due to circumstances beyond the entity's control). Disposed operations may qualify as discontinued earlier than they would have done under UK GAAP as FRS 3 specifies a three month cut-off period after the period end.

- IFRS 5 requires a single number to be disclosed on the face of the income statement, being the total of (i) the discontinued operations' post-tax profit/loss and (ii) the post-tax gain/loss recognised in the measurement of the fair value less costs to sell or on the disposal of the discontinued operations' assets. A breakdown of this number is required to be given either on the face of the income statement or in the notes. FRS 3 requires disclosure of the split in the pre-tax figures on the face of the income statement.

- IFRS 5 requires disclosure of the net cash flows attributable to operating, investing and financing activities of discontinued operations, whereas under UK GAAP, FRS 1 only encourages disclosure of cash flows from discontinued operations.

IFRS	IFRS 7, Financial instruments: Disclosures	
UK	FRS 29 (IFRS 7), Financial instruments: Disclosures	1
UK	FRS 13, Derivatives and other financial instruments: Disclosures	2

- In August 2005, the IASB issued a new standard on disclosures in respect of financial instruments. This replaces IAS 30 and the disclosure requirements in IAS 32 and locates in one place all disclosures relating to financial instruments. The new requirements incorporate many of IAS 32's disclosures as well as additional qualitative and quantitative disclosures on the risks arising from financial instruments.

- In December 2005, the ASB issues FRS 29, which largely replicates IFRS 7's requirements. It supersedes FRS 13 and FRS 25's disclosure requirements.

- For a comparison of the disclosure requirements in IFRS 7 (FRS 29), IAS 32 (FRS 25) and the Companies Act 1985, see Technical paper – 'Financial instrument disclosures: Comparison of UK GAAP v IFRS v New Companies Act requirements'.

IFRS	IFRS 8, Operating segments	
UK	SSAP 25, Segmental reporting	3

- In November 2006, the IASB issued IFRS 8, 'Operating segments', which replaces IAS 14 and aligns segment reporting with the requirements of the US standard SFAS 131, 'Disclosures about segments of an enterprise and related information'. IFRS 8 is effective for periods beginning on or after 1 January 2009.

- The scope of IFRS 8 and SSAP 25 differs. IFRS 8 applies to entities whose equity or debt securities are publicly traded or in the process of being so. SSAP 25 applies to public companies, banking and insurance companies and groups and certain other large entities. In addition, Schedule 4 of the Companies Act 1985 also contains certain segmental reporting requirements that apply to all companies reporting under UK GAAP.

- The Act and SSAP 25 each contain an exemption from the disclosure requirements where disclosure would be seriously prejudicial to the entity's interests. There is no such exemption in IFRS 8.

- IFRS 8 uses a 'management approach' under which segment information is presented on the same basis as that used for internal reporting purposes. The approach in IFRS 8 differs from the risk/returns approach of SSAP 25.

- This approach in IFRS 8 applies to both the identification of segments and the amounts reported (which may be non-GAAP). An explanation of the basis on which the segment information is prepared and a reconciliation to the amount recognised in the financial statements is required.

- The disclosure requirements of IFRS 8 are more extensive than in SSAP 25.

IFRS	No corresponding IAS	
UK	FRS 5, Reporting the substance of transactions	2

Substance over form

- Although there is no specific international standard dealing with the concept of 'substance over form', this issue is considered by the IASB's Framework and in IAS 8 when selecting accounting policies where there is no specific accounting standard . The Framework considers that for financial statements to meet the objective of reliability, transactions should be reported according to their substance and not necessarily their legal form. The Framework covers just one example of a transaction whose substance is not reflected in its legal form (that being the transfer of legal title to an asset from one party to another where the transferor retains the economic benefits of that asset) although the principles of substance over form are the same. In addition, SIC 12, 'Consolidation – special purpose entities', and SIC 27, 'Evaluating the substance of transactions involving the legal form of a lease', apply the principle of substance over form.

Offsetting assets and liabilities

- Rules for offsetting financial assets and liabilities under international accounting standards can be found in IAS 32. Under IFRS, financial assets and liabilities should be offset where there is a legally enforceable right of set-off and the entity intends to settle the transaction on a net basis or to realise the asset and settle the liability simultaneously.

- Under UK GAAP, FRS 5 was amended by FRS 25. Under FRS 5, assets and liabilities should not be offset. Debit and credit balances should be aggregated into a single net item where, and only where, they do not constitute separate assets and liabilities. For offset of financial assets and financial liabilities, FRS 25 (which is similar to IAS 32) applies.

Service concession agreements

- FRS 5 Application note F, 'Private finance initiative and similar contracts', provides guidance on which party's balance sheet the assets used to fulfil PFI contracts should be included. It also applies to contracts such as capital intensive outsourcing and franchising arrangements. IFRIC 12, 'Service concession agreements', is narrower in scope and applies to contractual arrangements whereby a private sector operator participates in the development, financing, operation and maintenance of infrastructure for public sector services, for example, under PFI contracts.

- IFRIC 12 includes specific accounting rules, depending on whether the entity has a right to a financial asset (where the entity has an unconditional contractual right to receive cash or other financial assets from the grantor) or an intangible asset (where the entity has a right to charge users of the public service). This could result in different accounting, including revenue recognition, than under UK GAAP.

Detailed summaries

IAS 1 and FRS 18 – Presentation of financial statements

IAS 1, Presentation of financial statements	FRS 18, Accounting policies
Effective for accounting periods beginning on or after 1 July 1998.	*Effective for accounting periods accounting periods ending on or after 22 June 2001.*
The revised standard (2003) is effective for annual periods beginning on or after 1 January 2005.	
An amendment to IAS 1 on capital disclosures was published in August 2005 and is effective for annual periods beginning on or after 1 January 2007.	

Related pronouncements

FRS 3, Reporting financial performance (part).

FRS 28, Corresponding amounts

UITF 4, Presentation of long-term debtors in current assets

Schedule 4 to the Companies Act 1985.

Overview

The main components of a set of IFRS financial statements are broadly similar to those required for UK financial statements and include a balance sheet; an income statement; a statement showing either all changes in equity or changes in equity other than those arising from capital transactions with owners and distributions to owners; a cash flow statement; and explanatory notes (including accounting policies).

IAS 1 incorporates to some extent the UK concept that performance should be measured more broadly than the 'profit' shown in the income statement. However, under IAS 1 the equivalent statement to FRS 3's STRGL can be presented either as a 'traditional' equity reconciliation in columnar form showing all the components of equity (including a sub-total for total income and expense for the period), or as a separate statement of performance in its own right (a statement of recognised income and expense – SORIE) (as required under UK GAAP), together with a note of other transactions with owners. (The SORIE is required by IAS 19, 'Employee benefits', where an entity chooses a policy of recognising actuarial gains and losses in equity.)

Unlike UK GAAP, IAS 1 does not prescribe the strict order or format in which items are to be presented in the financial statements. It simply provides a list of items that are so different in nature or function that they deserve separate presentation on the face of the balance sheet and in the income statement. However, the list is very similar to the format line items specified in the EC 4th and 7th Directives and in the UK Companies Act 1985.

IAS 1 does not require disclosure of operating profit. Under IAS 1, entities may strike a sub-total at operating profit, whereas under FRS 3 this is required.

FRS 3 identifies three categories of exceptional item ('super-exceptional'), which must be shown after operating profit even though they often operating items. Under IAS 1, the total of the post-tax profit or loss of discontinued operations and the post-tax gain or loss recognised on the measurement to 'fair value less costs to sell' or on the disposal of the discontinued operation is shown after tax. Other exceptional items, which would be classed as super-exceptional under FRS 3, must be dealt with in the appropriate operating line items.

IAS 1 requires entities to present current and non-current assets and current and non-current liabilities as separate classifications on the face of the balance sheet, except when a liquidity presentation provides reliable and more relevant information. UK GAAP has specific rules on classification of assets and liabilities.

IAS 1 requires disclosure of the judgements that management has made in the process of applying accounting policies that have the most significant effect on the amounts recognised in the financial statements (for example, management's judgement in determining whether financial assets are held-to maturity investments).

IAS 1 requires disclosure of information regarding key assumptions about the future and other key sources of estimation uncertainty at the balance sheet date that have a significant risk of causing a material adjustment to the carrying amounts of assets and liabilities within the next financial year. FRS 18 requires a description of those estimation techniques adopted that are significant. For this purpose, an estimation technique is significant only if the range of reasonable monetary amounts is so large that the use of a different amount from within that range could materially affect the view shown by the entity's financial statements.

Convergence

The IASB is working with the FASB on a project on comprehensive income. The ASB is considering its plans for convergence with IFRS.

First-time adoption of IFRS

IFRS 1 requires that, to comply with IAS 1, an entity's first IFRS financial statements should include at least one year of comparative information under IFRS.

Summary of main points

Scope

IAS 1 applies to all financial statements that are prepared under international financial reporting standards (IFRS). It applies equally to all entities whether or not they prepare consolidated financial statements or separate financial statements, as defined in IAS 27. [IAS 1 paras 2, 3].	FRS 18 and FRS 3 apply to all financial statements that are intended to give a true and fair view (although entities applying the FRSSE are exempt). Schedule 4 and 4A of the Companies Act 1985 apply to individual and consolidated financial statements respectively and apply to all companies, except those that are applying Schedule 8 or 8A (small companies) or Schedule 9 (banks) or Schedule 9A (insurance companies).

Components of financial statements

A complete set of financial statements includes the following components:

- A balance sheet.

- An income statement.

- A statement of changes in equity showing either:

  - All changes in equity, or
  - Changes in equity other than those arising from transactions with equity holders acting in their capacity as equity holders (called a 'statement of recognised income and expense').

- A cash flow statement.

Notes, comprising a summary of significant accounting policies and explanatory notes.

[IAS 1 para 8].

A set of financial statements includes the following components:

- A balance sheet. [CA85 4 Sch].

- A profit and loss account. [CA85 4 Sch, FRS 3].

- A statement of total recognised gains and losses (STRGL). [FRS 3 para 27].

- A note of the historical cost profit or loss for the period. [FRS 3 para 26].

- A cash flow statement (although certain entities are exempt). [FRS 1 para 5].

- Notes to the balance sheet and profit and loss account. [CA85 4 Sch].

- Notes detailing significant accounting policies and estimation techniques. [FRS 18 para 55].

Overall considerations

Fair presentation

Financial statements must 'present fairly' the financial position, financial performance and cash flows of an entity. [IAS 1 para 13]. A 'fair presentation' is equivalent to a 'true and fair view'. [Framework para 46].

The balance sheet should give a true and fair view of the state of affairs as at the end of the financial year and the profit and loss account should give a true and fair view of the profit or loss for the financial year. [CA85 Sec 226A(2), 227A(2)].

Application of IFRS (defined as including IASs, IFRIC and SIC interpretations) is presumed to result in a fair presentation. [IAS 1 para 13].

An entity should adopt accounting policies that enable its financial statements to give a true and fair view. Accounting policies should be consistent with accounting standards, UITF Abstracts and company legislation. [FRS 18 para 14].

An entity whose financial statements comply with IFRS should make an explicit and unreserved statement of such compliance in the notes. Financial statements should be described as complying with IFRS only where they comply with all of the requirements of IFRS. [IAS 1 para 14].

Financial statements should disclose whether they have been prepared in accordance with applicable accounting standards. Particulars of any material departure from those standards should be disclosed and explained. [CA85 4 Sch 36A, FRS 18 para 62].

A 'true and fair override' of IFRS is required in extremely rare cases where compliance with IFRS would conflict with the objective of financial statements set out in the IASB's Framework. IAS 1 sets out disclosure requirements in such circumstances. [IAS 1 paras 17 to 20].

A 'true and fair override' of the law is required when compliance with the law would be inconsistent with the requirement for the financial statements to give a true and fair view. [CA85 Sec 226A(5), 227A(5)]. A 'true and fair override' of accounting standards or UITF Abstracts is required in the exceptional cases where compliance would conflict with the requirement for the financial statements to give a true and fair view. [FRS 18 para 62]. Sections 226A, 227A and para 62 of FRS 18 set out disclosure requirements where the true and fair override is used.

Other considerations

Financial statements should be prepared on a going concern basis, unless management either intends to liquidate the entity or to cease trading, or has no realistic alternative but to do so. [IAS 1 para 23].

Similar. [FRS 18 para 21].

An entity should prepare its financial statements, except for cash flow information, under the accrual basis of accounting. [IAS 1 para 25].

Similar. [FRS 18 para 26].

Entities must retain the same presentation and classification of items from one period to the next unless there is a significant change in the nature of operations or there is a review of the financial statements, either of which indicates that another presentation or classification would be more appropriate or a change in presentation is required by IFRS. [IAS 1 para 27].

The directors should adopt the same format in preparing the financial statements for subsequent years, unless in their opinion there are special reasons for a change. [CA85 4 Sch 2(1)].

Each material class of similar items should be presented separately. Immaterial amounts can be aggregated with a mounts of classes of other items. [IAS 1 para 29].

Items to which Arabic numbers have been assigned in any of the formats may be combined if their individual amounts are not material or if the combination facilitates the assessment of the company's affairs (with separate disclosure in the notes). [CA85 4 Sch 3(4)].

Offsetting of assets and liabilities, or of income and expenses, is not permitted unless required by IFRS. [IAS 1 para 32].

Offsetting of assets and liabilities, or of income and expenditure, is not permitted. [CA85 4 Sch 5, FRS 5 para 29].

Comparatives are required for all amounts reported in the financial statements. Comparative narrative and descriptive information must be included when it is relevant to an understanding of the current period financial statements. [IAS 1 para 36].

Corresponding amounts must be shown for all items in the balance sheet and profit and loss account, even when no such item exists for the current period. [CA85 4 Sch 4].

When the presentation or classification of items is amended, the comparative amounts should be reclassified, unless the reclassification is impracticable (that is, cannot be done after *"making every reasonable effort to do so"*). Additional disclosures are required when such a reclassification of comparatives takes place. Similarly, additional disclosures are required when comparatives are not restated following a change in presentation. [IAS 1 paras 11, 38-41].

Under the Companies Act 1985, where the amount for the previous year is not comparable with the amount to be shown in respect to the current year, the previous year's amount may be adjusted. Particulars of the non-comparability and of any adjustment must be disclosed. [CA85 4 Sch 4(2)]. The rules for restating comparatives are dealt with in FRS 28. Unless an accounting standard or a UITF Abstract requires or permits otherwise, comparatives should be adjusted to be comparable with the current period. Particulars of the adjustment and the reasons for it should be disclosed in a note to the financial statements. [FRS 28 para 9].

Financial statements must be clearly identified and distinguished from other information in the same document. The entity must display prominently the name of the reporting entity (including any change in the name during the period), whether the financial statements are for the individual entity or a group of entities, the balance sheet date or period of the relevant component, the presentation currency and the level of rounding used (for example, thousands or millions of the presentation currency). [IAS 1 paras 44, 46].

Equivalent rules do not exist specifically in UK GAAP, but are adopted by convention. All documents supplied to the Registrar of Companies, including financial statements, must state the registered number of the company to which they relate. [CA85 Sec 706].

Financial statements are required annually. Where a financial period is not one year (or 52 weeks) the entity must disclose the reason for using a period other than one year and the fact that comparatives for the income statement, changes in equity, cash flows and related notes are not entirely comparable. [IAS 1 para 49].

The directors of a company must prepare individual financial statements and, where the company is a parent, group financial statements for each financial year of their company. [CA85 Sec 226, 227]. A company may shorten or extend its accounting period, subject to certain conditions. [CA85 Sec 225].

Face of the balance sheet

Current/non-current distinction

Current and non-current assets, and current and non-current liabilities, must be shown as separate classifications on the face of the balance sheet, except when a liquidity presentation provides information that is reliable and more relevant. [IAS 1 para 51]. A liquidity presentation is likely to be more appropriate in entities that do not have a clearly identifiable operating cycle (for example, financial institutions).

Schedule 4 prescribes the order and format of the balance sheet. Fixed assets, current assets, creditors due within one year, creditors due after more than one year and provisions are all separately disclosed. Non-current debtors are included within current assets, but may be separately disclosed on the face of the balance sheet. [UITF 4]. Banks and insurance companies present their financial statements in accordance with Schedules 9 and 9A.

An asset that is expected to be realised, or is held for sale or consumption in the normal course of the company's operating cycle is a current asset even though it may not be realised within 12 months of the balance sheet date. [IAS 1 paras 57 to 59]. Similarly, a liability that will be settled in the normal course of the entity's operating cycle is a current liability, regardless of the settlement date. [IAS 1 paras 60 to 62].

A fixed asset is one intended for use on a continuing basis in the company's activities. Current assets are those not intended for such use. [CA85 Sec 262].

The standard gives additional guidance on the classification of liabilities that are refinanced or rescheduled after the balance sheet date, but before the financial statements are authorised for issue. [IAS 1 paras 63, 64]. Additional guidance is also given in respect of liabilities subject to a borrowing covenant that has been breached. [IAS 1 paras 65, 66].

FRS 21's (and previously SSAP 17's) rules applied to post year end refinancing would require the same treatment. In addition, material from IAS 1 relating to post year end refinancing has been included in FRS 25. [FRS 25 paras 50A to 50E].

Balance sheet line items

IAS 1 specifies the minimum line items that should be included on the face of the balance sheet. [IAS 1 paras 68, 68A].

Schedule 4 prescribes the line items to be presented.

Additional line items, headings and sub-totals should be presented when relevant to understanding the entity's financial position. [IAS 1 para 69].

An item may be shown in greater detail than the prescribed formats require. [CA85 4 Sch 3(1)].

The standard does not prescribe the order and format of the balance sheet line items. [IAS 1 para 71].

Schedule 4 prescribes the order and format of the balance sheet line items. Companies may choose either format 1 or format 2. The arrangement, headings, and the sub-headings of items assigned an Arabic number should be adapted where the special nature of the company's business requires such adaptation. [CA85 4 Sch 3(3)].

IAS 1 states that the use of different measurement bases for different assets suggests that the nature or function of those assets is different and that they should, therefore, be presented as separate line items (for example, tangible fixed assets carried at valuation should be disclosed on the face of the balance sheet separately from those carried at depreciated cost). [IAS 1 para 73].

No equivalent rule.

Notes to the balance sheet

Entities must disclose further sub-classifications of the line items in a manner appropriate to the entity's operations. [IAS 1 para 74].

Sub-classifications are prescribed by Schedule 4.

IAS 1 requires detailed disclosures for each class of share capital including a reconciliation of the number of shares at the beginning and end of the period, details of rights, preferences and restrictions attaching to each class of shares and details of shares under option and sales contracts. [IAS 1 para 76(a)].

Similar. [CA85 4 Sch 38 to 41].

The notes must disclose the nature and purpose of each reserve within equity. [IAS 1 para 76(b)].	Schedule 4 requires separate disclosure of reserves, including share premium account, revaluation reserve, capital redemption reserve and other reserves. [CA85 4 Sch formats 1, 2].

Face of the income statement

IAS 1 specifies the minimum line items that should be included on the face of the income statement. [IAS 1 paras 81, 82].	Schedule 4 prescribes the order and format of the profit and loss account line items. FRS 3 requires additional line items (such as, operating profit) to be disclosed.
Additional line items, headings and sub-totals should be presented when relevant to understanding the entity's financial performance. [IAS 1 para 83].	An item may be shown in greater detail than the prescribed formats require. [CA85 4 Sch 3(1)].
The total of the post-tax profit or loss of discontinued operations and the post-tax gain or loss recognised on the measurement to 'fair value less costs to sell' or on the disposal of the discontinued operation is shown after tax. [IAS 1 para 81].	Under FRS 3, the pre-tax profit or loss on disposal of an operation is shown as a post-operating profit exceptional item (analysed between continuing and discontinued operations). [FRS 3 para 20].
Items should not be presented as extraordinary, either on the face of the income statement or in the notes. [IAS 1 para 85].	FRS 3 defines extraordinary items such that no item will ever be extraordinary.
Entities should present an analysis of expenses using either the 'nature of expenses' method or the 'cost of sales' method. Entities are encouraged to present this analysis on the face of the income statement, but it may be disclosed in the notes. [IAS 1 paras 88, 89].	The 'nature of expenses' method is similar to format 2 under Schedule 4 to the Companies Act 1985. The 'cost of sales' method is similar to format 1 under Schedule 4 to the Companies Act 1985).

Notes to the income statement

Where items of income and expense are material, their nature and amount should be disclosed separately (equivalent to FRS 3 'exceptional items'). Entities are not precluded from making this disclosure on the face of the income statement. [IAS 1 para 86].	Similar, except that FRS 3 identifies three categories of exceptional item ('super-exceptional') that must be shown after operating profit (even though they are often operating items). Under IAS 1, the total of the post-tax profit or loss of discontinued operations and the post-tax gain or loss recognised on the measurement to 'fair value less costs to sell' or on the disposal of the discontinued operation is shown after tax. Other exceptional items, that would be classed as super-exceptional under FRS 3, must be dealt with in the appropriate operating line items.
Where an entity elects to use the 'cost of sales' method of analysing expenses, the entity must disclose depreciation and amortisation expense and employee benefits expense. [IAS 1 para 93].	The charge for depreciation must be disclosed. [CA85 4 Sch format 14, FRS 15 para 100(c)]. Staff costs must be separately disclosed. [CA85 Sec 231A]. Pension costs must be separately disclosed. [FRS 17 paras 75(b), 82-85].
An entity must disclose the amount of dividends recognised during the period and the related amount per share. This disclosure may be given on the face of the income statement or statement of changes in equity or in the notes. [IAS 1 para 95].	Aggregate dividends for each class of share are disclosable. [FRS 4 para 59 or FRS 25 para 63(f)]. Schedule 4 of the Companies Act 1985 also requires disclosure in respect of dividends paid, payable and proposed.

Statement of changes in equity

An entity is required to present a statement showing either all changes in equity (including a sub-total for total income and expense for the period) or a 'statement of recognised income and expense', which shows changes in equity other than those arising from capital transactions with owners and distributions to owners. [IAS 1 paras 96, 97]. (The latter is required by IAS 19, 'Employee benefits', where an entity chooses a policy of recognising actuarial gains and losses in equity.)

FRS 3 requires the presentation of a statement of total recognised gains and losses. [FRS 3 para 27]. This is equivalent to a statement of changes in equity that excludes transactions with owners and distributions to owners.

If the statement does not show changes in equity arising from capital transactions with owners and distributions to owners, these should be shown in the notes. [IAS 1 para 97].

Schedule 4 requires disclosure of movements in share capital and reserves. [CA85 4 Sch 38, 39, 46].

Notes to the financial statements

The notes to the financial statements must disclose the following:

- The basis of preparation and significant accounting policies, including the measurement basis adopted in preparing the financial statements. [IAS 1 paras 103(a),108].

  FRS 18 requires disclosure of significant accounting policies and estimation techniques. Where financial statements are not prepared on a going concern basis, entities must disclose that fact. [FRS 18 paras 55, 61].

- Information required by other IFRS or interpretations. [IAS 1 para 103(b)].

  As set out in accounting standards and UITF Abstracts.

- Additional information that is relevant to an understanding of the components of the financial statements. [IAS 1 para 103(c)]

  Additional information must be disclosed where necessary for financial statements to give a true and fair view. [CA85 Sec 226A(4), 227A(4)].

- The judgements (apart from estimations – see next bullet point) that management has made in the process of applying the accounting policies and that have the most significant effect on the amounts recognised in the financial statements (for example, in determining whether financial assets are held-to maturity investments). [IAS 1 para 113].

  No equivalent requirement.

- Information regarding key assumptions about the future and other key sources of estimation uncertainty at the balance sheet date that have a significant risk of causing a material adjustment to the carrying amounts of assets and liabilities within the next financial year. [IAS 1 para 116].

  Similar. FRS 18 requires a description of those estimation techniques adopted that are significant (that is, where the range of reasonable monetary amounts is so large that use of a different amount from within that range could materially affect the view shown by the entity's financial statements). [FRS 18 paras 55(b), 57].

- The amount of dividends proposed or declared after the balance sheet date and the related amount per share. [IAS 1 para 125(a)].

  Aggregate dividends for each class of share are disclosable. [FRS 4 para 59 or FRS 25 para 63(f)]. Schedule 4 of the Companies Act 1985 also requires disclosure in respect of dividends paid, payable and proposed.

- The amount of any cumulative preference dividends not recognised. [IAS 1 para 125(b)].

  Similar. [CA85 4 Sch 49].

• Information that enables users of an entity's financial statements to evaluate the entity's objectives, policies and processes for managing capital (applicable for annual periods beginning on or after 1 January 2007).	For those companies electing to prepare an OFR, disclosures on capital structure are recommended by the ASB's Reporting Statement, 'The Operating and Financial Review'.
• The domicile and legal form of the entity, its country of incorporation and address of its registered office (or principal place of business, if different). [IAS 1 para 126(a)].	No equivalent requirement. All documents supplied to the Registrar of Companies, including financial statements, must state the registered number of the company to which they relate. [CA85 Sec 706].
• A description of the entity's operations and its principal activities. [IAS 1 para 126(b)].	Disclosable in the directors' report. [CA85 7 Sch 6].
• The name of the parent and ultimate parent of the group. [IAS 1 para 126(c)].	Similar. The ultimate parent is disclosable. [CA85 5 Sch 12, 31]. The controlling party and ultimate controlling party are also disclosable. [FRS 8 para 5].

IAS 2 and SSAP 9 – Inventories

IAS 2, Inventories	SSAP 9, Stocks and long-term contracts
Effective for accounting periods beginning on or after 1 January 2005.	*Effective for accounting periods beginning on or after 1 July 1988.*

Related pronouncements

–	–

Overview

In this summary, references to IAS 2 relate to the revised standard issued in December 2003. Both IAS 2 and SSAP 9 require that inventories should be measured at the lower of cost and net realisable value. Cost comprises all costs of purchase, costs of conversion and other costs in bringing the inventories to their present location and condition.

IAS 2 requires that an entity must use the same cost formula for all inventories having a similar nature and use to the entity. This is not specifically stated in SSAP 9, although the principle of consistency under FRS 18 should lead to a similar treatment.

Under IAS 2, where there are deferred payment terms for the purchase of inventories, this is regarded as a financing arrangement and the standard requires the difference between the price that would have been paid for 'normal' credit terms and the actual amount paid to be recognised as an interest expense over the period of the financing. SSAP 9 does not deal with this.

Convergence

In May 2002, the ASB issued FRED 28 proposing that the revised IAS 2 should replace SSAP 9's rules on stocks (and that IAS 11 should replace SSAP 9's rules on long-term contracts). However, a new UK standard has not yet been issued and this now forms part of the wider debate on convergence with IFRS.

First-time adoption of IFRS

There are no specific rules in IFRS 1 in respect of IAS 2 and so the general rule of retrospective application will apply.

Summary of main points

Scope

IAS 2 does not apply to:

• Work in progress arising under construction contracts (see IAS 11). [IAS 2 para 2(a)].	The scope of SSAP 9 is wider and also covers long-term contracts. These are dealt with separately in the IAS 11 comparisons summary.
• Financial instruments. [IAS 2 para 2(b)].	Financial instruments not mentioned.
• Biological assets related to agricultural activity and agricultural produce at the point of harvest (see IAS 41). [IAS 2 para 2(c)].	No similar exclusion from scope.

IAS 2 does not apply to the measurement of inventories held by:

• Producers of agricultural and forest products, agricultural produce after harvest, minerals and mineral products where they are measured at net realisable value (with changes taken to the income statement) in accordance with industry practice. [IAS 2 para 3(a)].	No similar exclusion from scope.

IFRS and UK GAAP – A comparison

• Commodity broker-traders who measure their inventories at fair value less costs to sell (with changes taken to the income statement). [IAS 2 para 3(b)].	No similar exclusion from scope.
Inventories are assets:	Wider definition of 'stocks' in SSAP 9. Stocks include goods purchased for resale, consumable stores, raw materials, work-in-progress, long-term contract balances and finished goods. [SSAP 9 para 16].
• Held for sale in the ordinary course of business.	
• In the process of production for such sale.	
• In the form of materials or supplies to be consumed in the production process or in the rendering of services.	
[IAS 2 para 6].	

Measurement

Inventories should be measured at the lower of cost and net realisable value. [IAS 2 para 9].	Similar. [SSAP 9 para 26].
Inventories are usually written down to net realisable value on an item by item basis. In some circumstances, however, it may be appropriate to group similar or related items. [IAS 2 para 29].	Same. [SSAP 9 para 2].

Cost

Cost comprises all costs of purchase, conversion and other costs incurred in bringing the inventories to their present location and condition. [IAS 2 para 10].	Same. [SSAP 9 para 17].
Costs of purchase comprise purchase price, import duties and other taxes, transport, handling and other directly attributable costs less trade discounts, rebates and similar items. [IAS 2 para 11].	Same. [SSAP 9 para 18].
Costs of conversion include costs directly related to the units of production (such as direct labour). They also include a systematic allocation of fixed and variable production overheads. [IAS 2 para 12].	Same. [SSAP 9 para 19].
The allocation of fixed production overheads to the costs of conversion is based on the normal capacity of the production facilities. [IAS 2 para 13].	Similar [SSAP 9 para 20].
In periods of abnormally high production, the amount of fixed overhead allocated to each unit of production is decreased so that inventories are not measured above cost. [IAS 2 para 13].	No specific mention in SSAP 9, but similar principle would apply so that stock is not overstated.
General administrative overheads are excluded from the cost of inventories. [IAS 2 para 16].	Similar. [SSAP 9 App 1, para 5].
No guidance included.	An appendix to SSAP 9 includes guidance on the allocation of overheads. [SSAP 9 App 1, paras 1-10].
In 'limited circumstances', borrowing costs are included in the cost of inventories, as set out in IAS 23. [IAS 2 para 17].	Similar. The Act permits interest to be included in cost if it relates to capital borrowed to finance the production of the asset insofar as it arises in the period of production. [CA85 4 Sch 26].

Where inventories are purchased on deferred payment terms, the difference between the price that would have been paid for 'normal' credit terms and the actual amount paid should be recognised as an interest expense over the period of the financing. [IAS 2 para 18].	Not dealt with in SSAP 9.

Net realisable value

Net realisable value is the estimated selling price less the estimated costs of completion and the estimated selling costs. [IAS 2 para 6].	Similar. [SSAP 9 para 21].
Estimates of net realisable value take account of price fluctuations relating to events after the end of the period to the extent that such events confirm conditions existing at the end of the period. [IAS 2 para 30].	Similar. [SSAP 9 App 1, para 19].
Estimates of net realisable value should take into consideration the purpose for which the inventories are held (that is, specific contracts or general sales). [IAS 2 paras 30, 31].	Similar is implied by paragraph 19 in Appendix 1 to SSAP 9.

Techniques for cost measurement

The standard cost method or the retail method, may be used if the results approximate to cost. [IAS 2 para 21].	Similar. [SSAP 9 para 4].
IAS 2 includes guidance on the gross margins to be used in applying the retail method. [IAS 2 para 22].	No specific guidance included.

Cost formulas

Individual costs should be assigned to items that are not interchangeable and goods produced for specific projects. [IAS 2 para 23].	Similar. Cost (or net realisable value) applies to separate items of stock or to groups of similar items. [SSAP 9 para 26].
The cost of inventories, other than those above, should be assigned by using the first-in, first-out (FIFO) or weighted average cost formulas. Methods such as LIFO are not appropriate. [IAS 2 para 25].	Similar. Common costing methods include FIFO and weighted average cost. Methods such as base stock and LIFO are not appropriate. [SSAP 9 App 1, para 12].
An entity should use the same cost formula for all inventories having similar nature and use to the entity. [IAS 2 para 25].	Management must exercise judgement to ensure that the method chosen to allocate costs to stocks provides the fairest possible approximation to cost. [SSAP 9 para 4 and SSAP 9 App 1, para 12]. Use of the same cost formula for all similar stocks is not specified, but consistency is a fundamental principle.

Recognition as an expense

When inventories are sold, the carrying amount of those inventories should be recognised as an expense in the period in which the related revenue is recognised. [IAS 2 para 34].	Similar.

The amount of any write-down of inventories to net realisable value (and any reversals of previous write-downs) should be recognised as an expense (or a reduction of the expense) in the period the write-down (or reversal) occurs. [IAS 2 para 34].	Similar.

Disclosure

The financial statements should disclose:

• The accounting policies adopted in measuring inventories, including the cost formula used. [IAS 2 para 36(a)].	Similar. [SSAP 9 para 32]. Also, FRS 18 requires disclosure of material accounting policies and significant estimation techniques. [FRS 18 para 55].
• The total carrying amount of inventories and the carrying amount in classifications appropriate to the entity. [IAS 2 para 36(b)].	Similar. Stocks are classified as prescribed by the Act's Schedule 4 balance sheet formats. The categories are raw materials and consumables; work in progress; finished goods and goods for resale; and payments on account. (that is, payments made for the purchase of stock). [SSAP 9 para 27].
• The carrying amount of inventories carried at fair value less costs to sell (for example, inventories held by commodity broker-dealers) [IAS 2 para 36(c)].	The Act requires disclosure of the difference (where material) between the replacement cost (or most recent actual purchase price) and the carrying amount of stocks. [CA85 4 Sch 27].
• The amount of inventories recognised as an expense during the period (that is, cost of sales). [IAS 2 para 36(d)].	Not specified in SSAP 9. Disclosure of expense categories is required by the Act's Schedule 4 profit and loss account formats. Under format 1, expenses are classified by function (for example, cost of sales). Under format 2, expenses are classified by type (for example, raw materials and consumables).
• The amount of any write-down or reversal of a previous write-down of inventories to net realisable value, with explanation for reversals. [IAS 2 paras 36(e), (f) and (g)].	No specific requirement.
• The carrying amount of inventories pledged as security for liabilities. [IAS 2 para 36(h)].	The Act requires disclosure of any charges on assets. [CA85 4 Sch 48, 50].
Not specified.	Where differing bases have been adopted for different types of stocks, the amount for each type must be disclosed. [SSAP 9 para 14].

IAS 7 and FRS 1 – Cash flow statements

IAS 7, Cash flow statements	FRS 1, Cash flow statements
Effective for accounting periods beginning on or after 1 January 1994.	*Effective for accounting periods ending on or after 23 March 1997.*

Related pronouncements

–	–

Overview

In this summary, references to IAS 7 include consequential amendments in subsequent standards. There are some major differences between a cash flow statement prepared under IAS 7 and one prepared under FRS 1. The cash flows reported under IAS 7 relate to movements in cash and cash equivalents (defined as short-term highly liquid investments that are readily convertible into known amounts of cash and subject to insignificant risk of changes in value). FRS 1 requires the movement of cash (defined as cash in hand and deposits repayable on demand, less overdrafts) to be reported in the cash flow statement. Under FRS 1, there is no concept of 'cash equivalents', but cash flows relating to IAS 7 'cash equivalents' would be included in 'management of liquid resources'.

IAS 7 requires cash flows to be reported under three sections: operating, investing and financing, whereas FRS 1 requires cash flows to be reported in far greater detail under nine standard headings.

IAS 7 does not require a reconciliation of movements in cash flows to the movement in net debt.

Under FRS 1, foreign currency exchange differences on cash balances are not reported on the face of the cash flow statement as they are non-cash items. However, IAS 7, requires foreign currency exchange differences on cash and cash equivalents to be reported on the face of the cash flow statement in order to reconcile the opening and closing cash and cash equivalent balances.

IAS 7 has none of the exemptions that allow many entities not to prepare cash flow statements under FRS 1.

Convergence

The IASB is intending to reconsider IAS 7 as part of its work on the presentation of financial statements. The ASB is considering its plans for convergence with IFRS.

First-time adoption of IFRS

There are no specific rules in IFRS 1 in respect of IAS 7 and so the general rule of retrospective application will apply.

Summary of main points

Scope

Applies to all entities. [IAS 7 para 1].	Some entities are exempt including small entities and subsidiary undertakings where 90 per cent or more of the voting rights are controlled within the group, provided that the subsidiary is included in publicly available consolidated financial statements. [FRS 1 para 5].

Preparation

The cash flow statement should include all the reporting entity's inflows and outflows of cash and cash equivalents for the period. [IAS 7 para 10, para 6].	The cash flow statement should include all the reporting entity's inflows and outflows of cash for the period. [FRS 1 para 6].

Cash comprises cash on hand and demand deposits. [IAS 7 para 6].

Similar. Cash is defined as cash in hand and deposits repayable on demand (that is, without notice and without penalty or if a period of notice is required it must not exceed 24 hours) with any qualifying financial institution, less overdrafts repayable on demand. [FRS 1 para 2].

Cash equivalents are short-term, highly liquid investments that are readily convertible to known amounts of cash and which are subject to an insignificant risk of changes in value. [IAS 7 para 7].

–

No concept of 'cash equivalents', but cash flows relating to IAS 7 'cash equivalents' are reported under the heading 'Management of liquid resources'.

Liquid resources are current asset investments that are readily disposable (that is, disposable by the reporting entity without curtailing or disrupting its business; and either readily convertible into known amounts of cash at or close to carrying amount, or traded in an active market). [FRS 1 para 2].

Format

Cash flows should be classified under the following standard headings. [IAS 7 para 10]:

Cash flows should be classified under the following standard headings. [FRS 1 para 7]:

- Operating activities.
  (Includes principal revenue-producing activities and other activities that are not investing or financing.) [IAS 7 para 6].

- Investing activities.
  (Includes acquisition and disposal of long-term assets and other investments not included in cash equivalents.) [IAS 7 para 6].

- Financing activities.
  (Includes activities that result in changes in the size and composition of the contributed equity and borrowings.) [IAS 7 para 6]

- Operating activities.
- Dividends from joint ventures and associates.
- Returns on investments and servicing of finance.
- Taxation.
- Capital expenditure and financial investments.
- Acquisitions and disposals.

- Equity dividends paid.
- Management of liquid resources.
- Financing.

Individual categories of cash inflows and outflows must be shown under the appropriate headings on the face of the primary cash flow statement. [IAS 7 para 21].

Individual categories can be shown in the notes and so the primary cash flow statement can include only the cash flows relating to the standard headings shown above. [FRS 1 para 8].

Classification

No separate heading.

Dividends received from joint ventures and associates should be included as separate items between operating activities and returns on investment and servicing of finance. [FRS 1 para 12A].

Interest paid or interest and dividends received may be classified as operating, investing or financing activities. [IAS 7 para 31].

Separate heading 'Returns on investments and servicing of finance' includes receipts from investments and payments to providers of finance, non-equity shareholders and minority interests. [FRS 1 para 13].

Dividends paid may be classified as operating or financing cash flows. [IAS 7 para 34].

Separate heading for equity dividends paid. [FRS 1 para 7].

Tax cash flows should be included under operating activities, unless they can be specifically identified with a financing or investing activity in which case they should be reported under those headings as appropriate [IAS 7 para 35] with disclosure of total tax paid [IAS 7 para 36].

'Taxation' includes cash flows to or from taxation authorities in respect of the reporting entity's revenue and capital profits. [FRS 1 para 16].

IAS 7 does not deal with exceptional cash flows.

Exceptional items are classified under the relevant headings according to their nature. [FRS 1 para 37]. Also disclose exceptional cash flows where no exceptional item is reported in the profit and loss account. [FRS 1 para 38].

Gross or net cash flows

Report gross inflows and outflows [IAS 7 para 18, para 21], except for:

Report gross inflows and outflows [FRS 1 para 8], except for:

Cash flows from operating activities can be reported net under the indirect method. [IAS 7 para 18(b)].

Same. [FRS 1 para 7].

Cash receipts and payments on behalf of customers when the cash flows reflect the activities of the customer rather than the entity. [IAS 7 para 22(a)].

No equivalent provision.

Cash receipts and payments may be reported net for items for which the turnover is quick, the amounts are large and the maturities are short. [IAS 7 para 22(b)].

Similar. Cash inflows and outflows may be reported net for items with short maturities and high turnover occurring from rollover or reissue; or a single financing transaction. [FRS 1 para 9].

Foreign currency

Exchange differences on cash and cash equivalents are reported on the face of primary cash flow statement in order to reconcile opening and closing cash and cash equivalent balances. [IAS 7 para 28]

Exchange differences on cash are non-cash items and are not reported on the face of the primary cash flow statement.

The reporting entity's own foreign currency cash flows should be translated at the exchange rate at the dates of the cash flows (or a weighted average exchange rate for the period). [IAS 7 paras 25, 27].

Similar treatment.

The cash flows of a foreign subsidiary should be translated at the exchange rate at the dates of the cash flows (or a weighted average exchange rate for the period). [IAS 7 paras 26, 27].

The cash flows of a foreign subsidiary should be translated on the basis used for translating the results in the consolidated profit and loss account (that is average or closing rate). The actual rate at the date of the transaction can be used for intra-group transactions. [FRS 1 para 41].

Acquisitions and disposals

Cash paid or received as purchase or sale consideration is reported in the cash flow statement net of cash and cash equivalents acquired or disposed of (under investing activities). [IAS 7 para 42].

Cash paid or received as purchase or sale consideration is disclosed separately from cash balances acquired or disposed of (under acquisition and disposals). [FRS 1 paras 23, 24].

Disclose summary of the effects of acquisitions and disposals of subsidiary undertakings (and other businesses) indicating how much of the consideration comprised cash and cash equivalents. [IAS 7 para 40].

Disclose summary of the effects of acquisitions and disposals of subsidiary undertakings (and other businesses) indicating how much of the consideration comprised cash. [FRS 1 para 45].

Disclose net cash flows attributable to operating, investing and financing activities of discontinued operations. [IFRS 5 para 33(c)].	Disclose the effects of acquisitions and disposals on amounts reported under each of the standard headings. [FRS 1 para 45].

Other notes to the cash flow statements

Reconciliation of profit or loss to net cash flow reported on the face of the cash flow statement or in the notes. [IAS 7 para 20].	Reconciliation of net operating profit to net cash flow reported as a separate statement. [FRS 1 para 12].
No equivalent requirement.	Reconciliation to net debt. [FRS 1 para 33].
Components of cash and cash equivalents and reconciliation to amounts presented in the balance sheet. [IAS 7 para 45].	Analysis of changes in net debt and reconciliation to amounts presented in the balance sheet. [FRS 1 para 33].
Non cash transactions. [IAS 7 para 43].	Non cash transactions. [FRS 1 para 46].
Restricted cash balances – disclose, together with a commentary, significant cash and cash equivalent balances held by the entity that are not available for use by the group. [IAS 7 para 48].	Restriction on remittability – identify amounts and explain circumstances that prevent the transfer of cash from one part of the group to another. [FRS 1 para 47].
IFRS 5 requires separate disclosure of the cash flow activity of discontinued operations for the period. [IFRS 5 para 33(c)].	Disclosure of cash flows from discontinued operations is encouraged. [FRS 1 para 56].

Disclosure encouraged under IFRS

Reporting of gross operating cash flows. [IAS 7 para 19].	Reporting of gross operating cash flows encouraged. [FRS 1 para 7].
Unused borrowing facilities. [IAS 7 para 50(a)].	-
Aggregate amounts of each of the operating, investing and financing cash flows related to interests in joint ventures reported using proportional consolidation. [IAS 7 para 50(b)].	No equivalent disclosure as proportional consolidation is not permitted under UK GAAP.
Operating capacity – separate disclosure of cash flows representing increases in operating capacity from those required to maintain operating capacity. [IAS 7 para 50(c)].	The OFR should discuss investment expenditure. [RS para 50].
Segmental cash flows – operating, investing and financing cash flows for each reported industry and geographical segments. [IAS 7 para 50(d)].	Cash flow classifications may be subdivided to provide segmental information [FRS 1 para 8]. Also, where segmental cash flows are significantly out of line with segmental revenues or profits, this should be indicated and explained in the OFR. [RS para 72].

IAS 8 and FRS 3/FRS 18 – Changes in accounting policies and errors

IAS 8, Accounting policies, changes in accounting estimates and errors	FRS 3, Reporting financial performance (part) FRS 18, Accounting policies (part)
The revised standard (2003) was effective for annual periods beginning on or after 1 January 2005.	*FRS 3 was effective for accounting periods ending on or after 22 June 1993.*
	FRS 18 was effective for accounting periods ending on or after 22 June 2001.

Related pronouncements

–	–

Overview

In this summary, references to IAS 8 relate to the revised standard and consequential amendments in subsequent standards. The scope of FRS 3 and FRS 18 is wider than that of IAS 8 and only the equivalent parts are dealt with in this summary.

In IAS 8, there is no distinction between fundamental errors and other material errors and all are required to be corrected by retrospective restatement. This differs to FRS 3, which is more restrictive in respect of errors and only restates prior period figures for the correction of fundamental errors.

IAS 8 requires retrospective application of changes in accounting policies and retrospective restatement to correct all material prior period errors and gives guidance on how this should be applied. In particular, IAS 8 does not permit the use of hindsight when applying a new accounting policy or when correcting prior period errors. FRS 3 does not include guidance on the use of hindsight, but otherwise has similar provisions

IAS 8 sets out a hierarchy of guidance to which management refers and whose applicability it considers when selecting accounting policies. Management is required to use its judgement in applying accounting policies that result in information that is relevant, reliable, reflects economic reality and is neutral, prudent and complete. FRS 18 requires that an entity should select the accounting policies that are judged by the entity to be most appropriate to its particular circumstances for the purpose of giving a true and fair view.

IAS 8 and FRS 18 use different terminology for when accounting policies can be changed voluntarily. IAS 8 only permits a change in policy if it results in the financial statements providing reliable and more relevant information about the effects of transactions, other events or conditions on the entity's financial position, financial performance or cash flows. FRS 18 requires that an entity's accounting policies should be reviewed regularly to ensure that they remain the most appropriate to its particular circumstances for the purpose of giving a true and fair view.

IFRS includes more detailed disclosure requirements for changes in accounting policy and correction of errors. In particular, under IAS 8, the nature of a future change in an accounting policy when an entity has yet to implement a new standard that has been issued, but not yet come into effect is required to be disclosed, together with details of its impact (where known or reasonably estimable).

Changes to accounting estimates are accounted for prospectively under both IFRS and UK GAAP. IAS 8 requires disclosure of the nature and amount of a change in an estimate that has an effect in the current period or is expected to have an effect in future periods, except for the disclosure of the effect on future periods when it is impracticable to estimate that effect. FRS 18 requires a description of the change and, where practicable, disclosure of the effect on the results for the current period if material.

Convergence

The ASB is considering its plans for convergence with IFRS.

First-time adoption of IFRS

IAS 8 does not deal with changes in accounting policies that occur when an entity first adopts IFRSs. Therefore, IAS 8's requirements for disclosures about changes in accounting policies do not apply in an entity's first IFRS financial statements.

<hr>

Summary of main points

Scope

IAS 8 sets out the requirements for selecting and applying accounting policies, accounting for changes in accounting policies, changes in accounting estimates and corrections of prior period errors. [IAS 8 para 3].

The scope of FRS 3 and FRS 18 is wider than that of IAS 8 and also covers matters dealt with in IAS 1, 'Presentation of financial statements' (see separate summary).

<hr>

Selecting accounting policies

Accounting policies are defined as "*the specific principles, bases, conventions, rules and practices applied by an entity in preparing and presenting financial statements". [IAS 8 para 5].*

Similar, but FRS 18 expands and states that policies are for recognising, selecting measurement bases for, and presenting assets, liabilities, gains, losses and changes to shareholders' funds. [FRS 18 para 4].

Accounting policies are determined by applying any applicable standard or interpretation and considering any relevant implementation guidance issued by the IASB for the standard or interpretation. [IAS 8 para 7].

An entity should adopt accounting policies that enable its financial statements to give a true and fair view. Those accounting policies should be consistent with the requirements of accounting standards, UITF abstracts and companies legislation. [FRS 18 para 14].

In the absence of a standard or an interpretation that specifically applies to a transaction, other event or condition, management should use its judgement in applying accounting policies that result in information that is relevant, reliable, reflects economic reality and is neutral, prudent and complete. IAS 8 sets out a hierarchy of guidance to which management refers and whose applicability it considers when selecting accounting policies. [IAS 8 para 10].

The appropriateness of accounting policies is judged in terms of relevance, reliability, comparability and understandability. FRS 18 also allows consideration of the cost vs benefit of the information provided under an accounting policy. [FRS 18 paras 30, 31]. UK GAAP does not specify a hierarchy of guidance.

In making the above judgement, management should refer to, and consider the applicability of, the following sources in descending order:

Where it is necessary to choose between accounting policies, an entity should select those policies judged most appropriate to its particular circumstances for the purpose of giving a true and fair view. [FRS 18 para 17].

- the requirements and guidance in standards and interpretations dealing with similar and related issues; and

- the definitions, recognition criteria and measurement concepts for assets, liabilities, income and expenses in the Framework.

[IAS 8 para 11].

In making the above judgement, management may also consider the most recent pronouncements of other standard-setting bodies that use a similar conceptual framework to develop accounting standards. [IAS 8 para 12].

UK GAAP does not specify a similar hierarchy of guidance.

Accounting policies should be applied consistently for similar transactions, other events and conditions, unless a standard or an interpretation specifically requires or permits categorisation of items for which different policies may be appropriate. [IAS 8 para 13].

Similar. [FRS 18 para 39].

IAS 8 includes a definition of 'material' and states that the accounting policies in IFRSs need not be applied when the effect of applying them is immaterial. [IAS 8 para 8]. This complements the statement in IAS 1 that disclosures required by IFRSs need not be made if the information is immaterial.

A similar definition of materiality is included in the Statement of Principles. [SoP paras 3.28 to 3.32]. The ASB's Foreword to Accounting standards states that accounting standards need not be applied to immaterial items. [Foreword para 13].

Disclosure requirements for accounting policies are set out in IAS 1, 'Presentation of financial statements'.

Disclosure requirements for accounting policies are set out in paragraph 55 of FRS 18.

Changes in accounting policies

An entity should change an accounting policy only if the change:

FRS 18 is similar, although it uses different terminology, referring to policies that are the most appropriate to an entity's particular circumstances for the purpose of giving a true and fair view. [FRS 18 para 45].

- is required by a standard or an interpretation; or

- results in the financial statements providing reliable and more relevant information about the effects of transactions, other events or conditions on the entity's financial position, financial performance or cash flows.

[IAS 8 para 14].

Changes in accounting policy should be applied retrospectively (unless a standard or interpretation includes transitional provisions). Retrospective application means that the entity should adjust the opening balance of each affected component of equity for the earliest prior period presented and the other comparative amounts disclosed for each prior period presented as if the new accounting policy had always been applied. [IAS 8 paras 19(b), 22].

FRS 3 similarly requires retrospective application for changes in accounting policy. [FRS 3 para 29].

There is an exemption from retrospective application, to the extent that it is impracticable to determine either the period-specific effects or the cumulative effect of the change. When it is impracticable to determine the cumulative effect, the entity changes the comparative information as if the new accounting policy had been applied prospectively from the earliest date practicable. [IAS 8 paras 23 to 25].

FRS 3 does not include an exemption from retrospective application for changes in accounting policy where this is impracticable.

The standard includes a definition of 'impracticable' and guidance on its interpretation. [IAS 8 paras 5, 50-53]. This clarifies that retrospectively applying a new accounting policy requires distinguishing information that provides evidence of circumstances that existed on the date as at which the transaction, other event or condition occurred and would have been available when the financial statements for that prior period were authorised for issue. In other words, IAS 8 does not permit the use of hindsight when applying a new accounting policy.

FRS 3 does not include guidance on the use of hindsight.

The application of an accounting policy for transactions, other events or conditions that differ in substance from those previously occurring or that did not occur previously or were immaterial is not considered to be a change in accounting policy. [IAS 8 para 16].

This is not specified in FRS 18, although it is inferred.

IAS 8 specifies that the initial application of a policy to revalue assets in accordance with IAS 16, 'Property, plant and equipment', is a change in an accounting policy to be dealt with as a revaluation in accordance with IAS 16, rather than by retrospective application. [IAS 8 para 17].

Not dealt with in FRS 3, but such a change would normally be dealt with by re to retrospective application under UK GAAP.

Disclosures for changes in accounting policy

IAS 8 sets out disclosure requirements for situations where a change in policy has an effect on the current period or any prior period, or would have such an effect except that it is impracticable to determine the amount of the adjustment, or might have an effect on future periods. [IAS 8 paras 28, 29].

FRS 18 and FRS 3 set out disclosure requirements for changes in accounting policy (see below).

This disclosure includes:

Disclosure includes:

- the nature of the change in accounting policy;

- the title of the standard or interpretation and, when applicable, that the change is made in accordance with its transitional provisions (with a description, including those that might have an effect on future periods) (for non-voluntary changes);

- the reasons the new policy provides reliable and more relevant information (for voluntary changes);

- for the current period and each prior period presented, to the extent practicable, the amount of the adjustment for each line item affected and if IAS 33 applies, for basic and diluted earnings per share;

- the amount of the adjustment relating to the periods before those presented, to the extent practicable; and

- if retrospective application is impracticable for any period, the circumstances that led to this and a description of how and from when the change in accounting policy has been applied.

[IAS 8 paras 28, 29].

- details of any changes to accounting policies;

- an explanation of why each new accounting policy is more appropriate;

- where practicable, the effect of a prior period adjustment on the results for the preceding period; and

- where practicable, an indication of the effect of a change in accounting policy on the results for the current period;

Where it is not practicable to make the disclosures on the effect of the prior period, that fact, together with the reasons, should be stated.

[FRS 18 para 55; FRS 3 para 29].

The nature of a future change in an accounting policy when an entity has yet to implement a new standard that has been issued, but not yet come into effect is required to be disclosed, together with an estimate of its impact (or if the impact is not known or reasonably estimable, a statement to that effect). [IAS 8 para 30].

No similar requirement.

Changes in accounting estimates

The effect of a change in an accounting estimate should be recognised prospectively (that is, from the date of change) as follows:

- by including it in profit or loss in:

  - the period of the change, if the change affects that period only; or

  - the period of the change and future periods, if the change affects both; or

- to the extent that a change in an accounting estimate gives rise to changes in assets and liabilities, or relates to an item of equity, adjusting the carrying amount of the related asset, liability or equity item in the period of the change.

[IAS 8 paras 36, 37].

No description is included in FRS 18 of the treatment required for a change in estimation technique, but the standard states that it should not be treated as prior period adjustment. [FRS 18 para 54].

When it is difficult to distinguish a change in an accounting policy from a change in an accounting estimate, the change is treated as a change in an accounting estimate. [IAS 8 para 35].

No similar concession.

An entity should disclose the nature and amount of a change in an accounting estimate that has an effect in the current period or is expected to have an effect in future periods (unless the latter is impracticable, in which case that fact should be disclosed). [IAS 8 paras 39, 40].

Similar, although there is no reference to future periods. [FRS 18 para 55].

Errors

Material prior period errors should be corrected retrospectively in the first set of financial statements authorised for issue after their discovery by restating the comparative amounts for the prior period(s) presented in which the error occurred or if the error occurred before the earliest prior period presented, restating the opening balances of assets, liabilities and equity for the earliest prior period presented. [IAS 8 para 42].

FRS 3 restricts prior period adjustments to the correction of fundamental errors (that is, those errors that, exceptionally, are of such significance that they destroy the true and fair view). [FRS 3 para 29, 60].

There is an exemption from retrospective restatement, to the extent that it is impracticable to determine either the period-specific effects or the cumulative effect of the error. When it is impracticable to determine the amount of an error for all prior periods, the comparative information is restated prospectively from the earliest date practicable. [IAS 8 paras 43 to 45].

FRS 3 does not include an exemption from retrospective application for corrections of fundamental errors where this is impracticable.

The standard includes a definition of 'impracticable' and guidance on its interpretation. [IAS 8 paras 5, 50-53]. Similar to the treatment of changes in accounting policies, IAS 8 does not permit the use of hindsight when correcting prior period errors.

FRS 3 does not include guidance on the use of hindsight.

IAS 8 sets out disclosure requirements for material prior period errors as follows:

- the nature of the prior period error;

- for each prior period presented, to the extent practicable, the amount of the correction for each line item affected; and if IAS 33 applies, for basic and diluted earnings per share.

- the amount of the correction at the beginning of the earliest prior period presented; and

- if retrospective application is impracticable for any period, the circumstances that led to this and a description of how and from when the error has been corrected.

[IAS 8 para 49].

Where practicable, the effect of a prior period adjustment on the results for the preceding period should be disclosed. Where it is not practicable to make this disclosure, that fact, together with the reason, should be stated. [FRS 3 para 29].

IAS 10 and FRS 21 – Events after the balance sheet date

IAS 10, Events after the balance sheet date	FRS 21 (IAS 10), Events after the balance sheet date
The revised standard (2003) is effective for annual periods beginning on or after 1 January 2005.	*Effective for accounting periods beginning on or after 1 January 2005.*

Related pronouncements

IAS 1, Presentation of financial statements, (for going concern).	FRS 18, Accounting policies, (for going concern).

Overview

In this summary, references to IAS 10 relate to the revised standard issued in December 2003. Under both standards, assets and liabilities should be adjusted for subsequent events providing further evidence of conditions that existed at the balance sheet date, but not for events that are indicative of conditions that arose subsequent to the balance sheet date.

Convergence

FRS 21 is identical to IAS 10 and was issued by the ASB as part of its programme of convergence with IFRS.

First-time adoption of IFRS

The first-time adoption rules in IFRS 1 include specific rules on estimates that override certain of the requirements of IAS 10. IFRS 1 requires that estimates made on transition to IFRS (and at the end of any comparative periods) are consistent with those of an entity's previous GAAP, even if post-balance sheet information would have led to an adjustment of an amount, unless there was an error in the previous estimate.

Summary of main points

Definitions

Events after the balance sheet date are those events, favourable and unfavourable, that occur between the balance sheet date and the date when the financial statements are authorised for issue. [IAS 10 para 3].	Same. [FRS 21 para 3].
An adjusting event is one that provides evidence of conditions that existed at the balance sheet date. [IAS 10 para 3].	Same. [FRS 21 para 3].
A non-adjusting event is one that is indicative of conditions that arose after the balance sheet date. [IAS 10 para 3].	Same. [FRS 21 para 3].
Examples of adjusting post balance sheet events are provided in paragraph 9 of IAS 10.	Same. [FRS 21 para 9].
Examples of non-adjusting post balance sheet events are provided in paragraph 11 and paragraph 22 of IAS 10.	Same. [FRS 21 paras 11, 22].

Post balance sheet events

An entity should adjust the amounts recognised in its financial statements to reflect adjusting events after the balance sheet date. [IAS 10 para 8].	Same. [FRS 21 para 8].
An entity should not adjust the amounts recognised in its financial statements to reflect non-adjusting events after the balance sheet date. [IAS 10 para 10].	Same. [FRS 21 para 10].

IFRS and UK GAAP – A comparison

Dividends

Dividends declared to holders of equity instruments after the balance sheet date should not be recognised as a liability at the balance sheet date. [IAS 10 para 12]. 'Declared' means that the dividends are appropriately authorised and no longer at the entity's discretion. Disclosure of dividends proposed or declared after the balance sheet date is required by IAS 1. [IAS 1 para 125(a)]	Same. [FRS 21 para 312]. Disclosure of dividends proposed or declared after the balance sheet date is required. [CA 85 4Sch 35A].
Dividends receivable should be recognised when the shareholder's right to receive payment is established. [IAS 18 para 30].	Same. Dividends receivable should be recognised as assets when and only when the shareholder has a right to receive payment. [FRS 5 para 2].

Going concern

An entity should not prepare its financial statements on a going concern basis if management determines after the balance sheet date either that it intends to liquidate the entity or to cease trading, or that it has no realistic alternative but to do so. [IAS 10 para 14].	Same. [FRS 21 para 14].
This applies where the going concern assumption is not appropriate to the entity as a whole (which is consistent with IAS 1 para 23). Therefore, it does not apply where the going concern assumption is not appropriate for just part of the entity.	Same. [FRS18 para 21].

Disclosure

Disclosure of the date the financial statements were authorised for issue. [IAS 10 para 17].	Same. [FRS 21 para 17].
Disclosure of who authorised the issue of the financial statements and if shareholders or other parties have the power to amend the statements after issue, disclosure of that fact. [IAS 10 para 17].	Same. [FRS 21 para 17]. In addition, a company's annual financial statements shall be approved by the board of directors and signed on behalf of the board by a director of the company. [CA 85 s233(1)]. The balance sheet should state the name of the person who signed the balance sheet on behalf of the board. [CA 85 s233(3)].
If an entity receives information after the balance sheet date about conditions that existed at the balance sheet date, the entity should update disclosures that relate to these conditions, in the light of the new information. [IAS 10 para 19].	Same. [FRS 21 para 19].
IAS 10 states that if non-adjusting events after the balance sheet date are material, non-disclosure could influence the economic decisions of users taken on the basis of the financial statements. Therefore, an entity should disclose the following for each material category of non-adjusting event after the balance sheet date:	Same. [FRS 21 para 21].

- The nature of the event

- An estimate of its financial effect or a statement that such an estimate cannot be made.

[IAS 10 para 21].

When the financial statements are not prepared on a going concern basis, that fact should be disclosed, together with the basis on which the financial statements are prepared and the reason why the entity is not regarded as a going concern. [IAS 1 para 23].	Same. [FRS 18 para 61(c)].
When management is aware, in making its assessment of going concern, of material uncertainties related to events or conditions that may cast significant doubt upon the entity's ability to continue as a going concern, those uncertainties should be disclosed. [IAS 1 para 23].	Same. [FRS 18 para 61(a)].

IAS 11 and SSAP 9 – Construction contracts

IAS 11, Construction contracts	SSAP 9, Stocks and long-term contracts
Effective for accounting periods beginning on or after 1 January 1995.	*Effective for accounting periods beginning on or after 1 July 1988.*

Related pronouncements

IAS 18, Revenue.	FRS 5 Application note G, Revenue recognition.
	UITF 34, Pre-contract costs.

Overview

IAS 11 applies to construction contracts and contracts for services directly related to the construction of an asset. This is more specific in scope than SSAP 9, which also includes contracts for the provision of services. However, contracts for services are covered by IAS 18, 'Revenue', which refers back to the principles in IAS 11.

IAS 11 requires contracts to be combined when part of a package, or segregated when each contract is part of a separate proposal and revenues and costs can be clearly identified. UK GAAP has similar rules and requires that contractual arrangements should be accounted for as two or more separate transactions only where the commercial substance is that the individual components operate independently of each other and reliable fair values can be attributed to the individual components.

Both IAS 11 and SSAP 9 use the 'percentage of completion' method to recognise revenue and expenses. Under IAS 11, the stage of completion may be assessed based on, for example, costs incurred for work performed to date, surveys of work performed or completion of the physical proportion of the contract work. UK GAAP allows similar methods, but specifically only permits revenue to be derived from the proportion of costs incurred where these provide evidence of the entity's performance and, hence, the extent to which it has obtained the right to consideration.

IAS 11 applies the 'percentage of completion' method if the outcome of the contract can be estimated reliably. SSAP 9 places more emphasis on prudence and recognises 'prudently calculated attributable profit' if the outcome of the contract can be assessed with reasonable certainty. Where the above outcome criteria are not met, both IAS 11 and SSAP 9 use the 'zero profit method', under which revenue is recognised only to the extent that costs are incurred that are expected to be recovered. The accounting treatment for loss-making contracts is consistent under IAS 11 and SSAP 9.

The presentation in the balance sheet differs. Under IAS 11, an asset is shown for the gross amount due from customers for contract work. Under SSAP 9, the asset (net of payments on account) is split between debtors ('amounts recoverable on contracts') and stocks ('long-term contract balances').

Convergence

In May 2002 the ASB issued FRED 28, which proposed that IAS 11 should replace the SSAP 9 rules on long-term contracts (and that IAS 2 should replace SSAP 9's rules on stocks). FRED 28 also included limited text from IAS 18 to ensure that accounting for revenue from long-term service contracts continues to be addressed in UK GAAP. However, a new UK standard has not yet been issued and this now forms part of the wider debate on convergence with IFRS.

First-time adoption of IFRS

There are no specific rules in IFRS 1 in respect of IAS 11 and so the general rule of retrospective application will apply.

Summary of main points

Scope

Applies to accounting for construction contracts in the financial statements of contractors. [IAS 11 para 1]. This includes contracts for the rendering of services that are directly related to the construction of the asset. [IAS 11 para 5].

Scope is wider than IAS 11 and applies to both construction contracts and contracts for services. [SSAP 9 para 22].

Applies to short-term as well as long-term contracts, when the date at which the contract activity is entered into and the date when the activity is completed fall in different accounting periods. [IAS 11 Objective].

Similar. The contract period normally exceeds one year, but some contracts with a shorter duration should be accounted for as long-term contracts if they are sufficiently material to the period's activity that not to record turnover and attributable profit would lead to a distortion of the period's turnover and results. [SSAP 9 para 22].

SSAP 9 also covers stocks. These are dealt with separately in the IAS 2 comparisons summary.

Definition

A construction contract is one for the construction of an asset or a combination of assets that are closely interrelated in terms of their design, technology and function or their ultimate purpose or use. [IAS 11 para 3].

Similar. It applies to contracts for the design, manufacture or construction of a single substantial asset or the provision of service (or a combination of assets or services which together constitute a single project). [SSAP 9 para 22].

Combining and segmenting contracts

Each contract is usually assessed separately. However, in certain circumstances, the IAS is applied to the separately identifiable components of a single contract or to a group of contracts together in order to reflect the substance. [IAS 11 para 7].

Similar. Long-term contracts should be assessed on a contract by contract basis. [SSAP 9 para 28]. However, a contract should be accounted for as separate components where the substance is that the individual components operate independently of each other. [FRS 5 App G para G25].

When a contract covers a number of assets, each asset should be treated as a separate contract when it has been subject to separate proposals and negotiation and the costs and revenues of each asset can be identified. [IAS 11 para 8].

Where prices are determined and invoiced according to separate parts of the contract, costs are usually matched against performance on the separable parts of the contract, treating each part as a separate contract. [SSAP 9 App 1 para 22].

A group of contracts should be treated as a single contract when it is negotiated as a single package and the contracts are in effect one contract with a single profit margin. [IAS 11 para 9].

Similar. Where two or more contracts do not operate independently of each other, they should be accounted for together to reflect the entity's performance of its obligations as a whole in obtaining the right to consideration. [FRS 5 App G paras G26, G32].

Recognition

Contract costs

Contract costs should comprise:

- costs that relate directly to the specific contract;

- attributable costs that can be allocated to the contract; and

- costs that are chargeable to the customer under the terms of the contract.

[IAS 11 para 16].

Similar. [SSAP 9 paras 17 to 20].

Costs that cannot be attributed to contract activity include general administration costs, selling costs and non-reimbursable research and development costs. [IAS 11 para 20].

Similar. [SSAP 9 App 1 para 5].

Pre-contract costs

Pre-contract costs are capitalised once it is probable that the contract will be obtained. Costs incurred in securing a contract that are recognised as expenses when they are incurred cannot be reinstated as part of the cost of an asset in a subsequent period. [IAS 11 para 21].

UITF 34 is stricter in that it only permits pre-contract costs to be recognised as an asset when it is virtually certain that a contract will be obtained. [UITF 34 para 15].

Revenue and profit recognition

Total contract revenue should comprise the initial revenue agreed in the contract; and variations, claims and incentive payments, to the extent that it is probable that they will result in revenue and they can be reliably measured. [IAS 11 para 11].

SSAP 9 does not provide a definition of turnover in view of the different methods of ascertaining it. However, it requires disclosure of the means by which turnover is ascertained. [SSAP 9 App 1 para 23].

Where the outcome of a contract can be estimated reliably, contract revenue and costs should be recognised by reference to the stage of completion of the contract activity. [IAS 11 para 22].

Turnover is recognised when, and to the extent that, the entity obtains the right to consideration. This should be derived from an assessment of the fair value of the goods or services provided to the reporting date as a proportion of the total fair value of the contract. [FRS 5 App G para G18]. When the outcome can be assessed with reasonable certainty, the prudently calculated attributable profit should be recognised as the difference between the reported turnover and related costs for that contract. [SSAP 9 para 29].

Attributable profit is that part of the total estimated profit on the contract after allowing for remedial, maintenance and irrecoverable costs, that fairly reflects the profit attributable to that part of the work performed at the accounting date. [SSAP 9 para 23].

The recognition of revenue and expenses by reference to the stage of completion of a contract is often referred to as the percentage of completion method. [IAS 11 para 25].

Same.

The stage of completion may be assessed according to, for example, costs incurred for work performed to date, surveys of work performed or completion of the physical proportion of the contract work. [IAS 11 para 30].

UK GAAP allows similar methods, but specifically only permits turnover to be derived from the proportion of costs incurred where these provide evidence of the entity's performance and, hence, the extent to which it has obtained the right to consideration. [FRS 5 App G para G21].

Turnover (and the related debtor, being a contractual right to cash) should be discounted to fair value, with the unwinding of the discount credited to finance income. [IAS 39 paras 43, 46, AG79].

Similar. Where payment is received in arrears and the time value of money is material, the amount recognised as turnover should be discounted to its fair value, with the unwinding of the discount credited to finance income. [FRS 5 App G para G8].

Contract costs that relate to future activity are recognised as an asset provided it is probable that they will be recovered. Such costs are often classified as contract work-in-progress. [IAS 11 para 27].

Same.

When the outcome cannot be estimated reliably, revenue can only be recognised to the extent of contract costs incurred that it is probable will be recoverable. Contract costs should be recognised as an expense in the period in which they are incurred (that is, no profit is recognised). [IAS 11 para 32].

Where the outcome of long-term contracts cannot be assessed with reasonable certainty, no profit should be recognised in the profit and loss account, although if no loss is expected it may be appropriate to show as turnover a proportion of the total contract value using a zero estimate of profit. [SSAP 9 para 10].

Expected losses

When it is probable that total contract costs will exceed total contract revenue, the expected loss should be recognised as an expense immediately. [IAS 11 para 36].

Foreseeable losses should be recognised in full immediately. [SSAP 9 para 11].

The expected loss is determined irrespective of whether or not work has commenced on the contract; or the stage of completion of contract activity, or the amount of profits expected to arise on other contracts. [IAS 11 para 37].

Similar. [SSAP 9 para 24].

Disclosure

An entity should disclose:

- Amount of contract revenue recognised in the period. [IAS 11 para 39(a)].

  No similar requirement. Contract revenue is included in reported turnover.

- Methods used to determine contract revenue. [IAS 11 para 39(b)].

  Similar. The method of ascertaining turnover should be disclosed. [SSAP 9 para 32].

- Methods used to determine the stage of completion. [IAS 11 para 39(c)].

  Similar. The method of ascertaining attributable profit should be disclosed. [SSAP 9 para 32].

- For contracts in progress at the balance sheet date:

  - Aggregate of costs and recognised profits (less losses) to date. [IAS 11 para 40(a)].

    No similar requirement.

  - Amount of advances received. [IAS 11 para 40(b)].

    The balance of payments on account (in excess of amounts (i) matched with turnover; and (ii) offset against long-term contract balances) should be classified as payments on account and separately disclosed within creditors. [SSAP 9 para 30(b)].

  - Amount of retentions. [IAS 11 para 40(c)].

    No similar requirement.

- Gross amount due from customers for contract work (shown as an asset). [IAS 11 para 42(a)].

  The excess of foreseeable losses over costs incurred (after transfers to cost of sales) should be included within provisions or creditors as appropriate. [SSAP 9 para 30(d)].

Contingent assets and contingent liabilities (such as warranty costs, claims, penalties or possible losses) should be disclosed in accordance with IAS 37. [IAS 11 para 45].

Similar disclosure required by FRS 12.

IAS 12 and FRS 19 – Income taxes

IAS 12, Income taxes	FRS 19, Deferred taxation
Effective for accounting periods beginning on or after 1 January 1998.	*Effective for accounting periods ending on or after 23 January 2002.*

Related pronouncements

SIC 21, Income taxes – Recovery of revalued non-depreciable assets	FRS 16, Current tax (*Effective for accounting periods ending on or after 23 March 2000.*)
SIC 25, Income taxes – Changes in the tax status of an enterprise or its shareholders	FRS 3, Reporting financial performance

Overview

In this summary, references to IAS 12 include consequential amendments in subsequent standards. IAS 12 is similar to FRS 16 in respect of current taxes, except that IAS 12 requires current tax to be presented separately on the face of the balance sheet (there is no such requirement in FRS 16). In addition, IAS 12 requires current tax to be charged directly to equity if it relates to items that are also charged or credited directly to equity. FRS 16 requires all current tax to be included in the statements of performance (that is, profit and loss account or STRGL).

In respect of deferred tax, IAS 12 is conceptually different from FRS 19. Instead of accounting for timing differences (the basis used in FRS 19), it uses a balance sheet concept of temporary differences – differences between the carrying amount of an asset or liability and its tax base (the amount attributed to it for tax purposes). Temporary differences include not only timing differences, but other differences between the accounting and tax bases of assets and liabilities that are not timing differences, for example, revaluation of assets for which no equivalent adjustment is made for tax purposes.

IAS 12 prohibits the discounting of deferred tax. FRS 19 permits, but does not require, discounting deferred tax.

IAS 12 requires a reconciliation of the total (current and deferred) tax charge to the tax charge that would result from applying the standard rate of tax to the profit on ordinary activities before tax. FRS 19 requires the reconciliation to be carried out for the current tax charge.

The summary below deals with the comparison of IFRS and UK GAAP for deferred taxation.

Convergence

IAS 12, SIC 21 and SIC 25 are being reviewed as part of the IFRS/US convergence project and an exposure draft is expected to be published in 2007. In the UK, the ASB is considering its plans for convergence with IFRS.

First-time adoption of IFRS

There are no specific rules in IFRS 1 in respect of IAS 12 and so the general rule of retrospective application will apply. Any deferred tax impacts from accounting policy changes made on transition to IFRS should be accounted for as part of the adjustments made on transition, against retained earnings or, if appropriate, another category of equity. Also, any adjustments to deferred tax as a result of adjustments to amounts recorded on past business combinations should be made on transition against retained earnings, unless IFRS 1 specifies otherwise.

Summary of main points

Recognition of deferred tax assets and liabilities

General principles

Full provision.	Full provision using 'incremental liability' approach.
Deferred tax should be recognised on the basis of taxable *temporary* difference (subject to certain exceptions). [IAS 12 para 15].	Deferred tax should be recognised on the basis of *timing differences* (subject to certain exceptions). [FRS 19 para 7].

Temporary difference is defined as the difference between the carrying value of an asset or liability and its tax base. [IAS 12 para 5].

Timing difference is defined as the difference between accounting profit and taxable profit that arises from the inclusion of gains and losses in tax assessments in periods different from those in which they are recognised in the financial statements. Timing differences originate in one period and are capable of reversal in one or more subsequent periods. [FRS 19 para 2].

Temporary differences include all timing differences and many permanent differences.

Deferred tax should not be recognised on permanent differences. [FRS 19 para 7(b)].

Revaluation of non-monetary assets

Deferred tax should always be recognised on the difference between the revalued amount of the asset and its tax base using the tax rates that reflect the expected manner of recovery of the asset. [IAS 12 paras 20, 51].

Deferred tax should be provided *only* if:

a) the asset is revalued to fair value in each period with changes in fair values reported in the profit and loss account; or

b) the company has entered into a binding agreement to sell the revalued asset, has recognised the gain or loss on sale and does not expect to obtain rollover relief.

[FRS 19 paras 12, 14, 15].

Sale of assets where rollover relief has been or might be claimed

Deferred tax should always be recognised.

Deferred tax should not be recognised. [FRS 19 para 15].

Business combinations

Deferred tax should always be provided on the difference between the fair value and tax base of identifiable assets and liabilities acquired in a business combination. [IAS 12 para 19].

Deferred tax should be provided only where it would be recognised if the fair value adjustments were timing differences arising in the acquired entity's financial statements. [FRS 7 para 74].

IAS 12 does not permit a deferred tax provision in respect of the initial recognition of acquired goodwill or its subsequent reduction if impaired. [IAS 12 paras 21, 21A].

Comparable.

However, deferred tax liabilities for taxable temporary differences relating to goodwill that arise after initial recognition (for example, where the goodwill is tax deductible annually) are recognised. [IAS 12 para 21B].

Comparable.

If the acquirer is able to utilise its own unused tax losses against the acquired entity's future taxable profit, it should recognise a deferred tax asset, but this is not part of the accounting for the business combination and does not affect goodwill. [IAS 12 para 67].

Comparable. Deferred tax should not be recognised as part of the fair value exercise (hence goodwill should not be adjusted) because the tax asset is not the asset of the acquired entity. [FRS 7 para 75].

Unremitted earnings of subsidiaries, associates and joint ventures (JVs)

Deferred tax should be provided on the unremitted earnings of subsidiaries, branches, associates and JVs except to the extent that both of the following conditions are satisfied:

Deferred tax should be provided only to the extent that:

a) the parent/investor is able to control the timing of the remittance of the earnings; and

b) it is probable that remittance will not take place in the foreseeable future.

[IAS 12 para 39].

a) dividends from a subsidiary, associate or JV have been accrued as receivable at the balance sheet; or

b) a binding agreement to distribute the past earnings in future has been made.

[FRS 19 para 21].

Foreign currency items

If an entity's taxable profit or tax loss (and, hence, the tax base of its non-monetary assets and liabilities) is determined in a different currency to its functional currency, changes in the exchange rate give rise to temporary differences that result in a recognised deferred tax liability or asset. [IAS 12 para 41].

Deferred tax should not be provided, as there is no timing difference.

Profits and losses arising on intra-group transactions that are eliminated on consolidation

Deferred tax should be provided on the difference between the reduced carrying amount of say, inventory in the balance sheet and the higher tax base (the amount paid by the receiving company) at the *receiving* company's tax rate.

Deferred tax should be provided on the timing difference at the *supplying* company's tax rate.

Share-based payment

Equity-settled

A deductible temporary difference may arise on the difference between the tax base of the employee services received to date (being the future tax deduction, where there is one) and the carrying amount of nil in the balance sheet, resulting in a deferred tax asset (subject to IAS 12's recognition criteria). Where the future tax deduction depends on the share price at the date of exercise, the tax base of the employee services received is remeasured at the end of each period, with a resulting adjustment to the deferred tax asset.

If the amount of the tax deduction (or estimated future tax deduction) exceeds the amount of the related cumulative remuneration expense, the excess of the associated current or deferred tax should be recognised directly in equity. [IAS 12 para 68C].

A timing difference arises on the difference between the share-based payment charge in the profit and loss account and the related deduction for tax purposes where that will be received in the future, resulting in a deferred tax asset (subject to FRS 19's recognition criteria). However, if the tax deduction that will be obtained (based on the share price at the date of exercise) exceeds the award's fair value at date of grant, the excess is regarded as a permanent difference and is accounted for when it crystallises, that is, when the share options are exercised.

All tax relating to the deduction is recognised in the profit and loss account. [FRS 16 para 5; FRS 19 para 34].

Cash-settled

A deductible temporary difference may arise if the liability's carrying amount exceeds the liability's tax base (being the carrying amount less any amounts that will be deductible for tax purposes in the future), resulting in a deferred tax asset (subject to IAS 12's recognition criteria).

The tax effects of cash-settled share-based payments are recognised in the income statement.

A timing difference arises on the difference between the share-based payment charge (remeasured to fair value) in the profit and loss account and the related deduction for tax purposes where that will be received in the future, resulting in a deferred tax asset (subject to FRS 19's recognition criteria).

The tax effects of cash-settled share-based payments are recognised in the profit and loss account.

Deferred tax assets

A deferred tax asset should be recognised for deductible temporary differences, unused tax losses and unused tax credits to the extent that it is probable that the deferred tax asset will be recovered. [IAS 12 paras 24, 34].

A deferred tax asset should be recognised on timing differences and tax losses to the extent that it is regarded as more likely than not that the deferred tax asset will be recovered. [FRS 19 para 23].

IAS 12 does not specify a time period in which tax losses should be recovered. Therefore, where tax losses are recoverable under the relevant tax rules, there should be no arbitrary cut-off in the time horizon over which an assessment of recoverability is made. Only if it is not probable that taxable profit will be available is a deferred tax asset not recognised. Otherwise, a deferred tax asset is recognised to the extent it is considered probable there will be future taxable profits.

FRS 19 has similar general requirements to IAS 12 for recognising deferred tax assets for losses. However, FRS 19 has specific guidance to the effect that, if it is expected that it will take some time for tax losses to be relieved, the recoverability of the resulting deferred tax asset is likely to be relatively uncertain. In such circumstances, it may not be appropriate to recognise the deferred tax asset. [FRS 19 para 32].

Measurement

Deferred tax should be measured using tax rates that have been enacted or substantively enacted at the balance sheet date. [IAS 12 para 47].

Comparable. [FRS 19 para 37].

IAS 12 defines 'substantively enacted' as the announcement of the tax rate by the government. [IAS 12 para 48].

FRS 19 defines 'substantively enacted' as the inclusion of the rate in either a Bill approved by the House of Commons or a Parliamentary resolution having statutory effect. [FRS 19 para 40].

The measurement of deferred tax liabilities and assets should reflect the tax consequences that would follow from the manner in which the entity expects, at the balance sheet date, to recover or settle the carrying amount of its assets and liabilities. [IAS 12 para 51].

Not applicable as FRS 19 is based on timing differences, rather than the carrying amounts of assets and liabilities (temporary differences).

Discounting

IAS 12 prohibits discounting of deferred tax. [IAS 12 para 53].

FRS 19 permits, but does not require, discounting of deferred tax. FRS 19 provides detailed guidance on the discounting of deferred tax. [FRS 19 para 42].

Presentation

Deferred tax should be included in profit or loss for the period, except to the extent that the tax arises from a transaction or event that is recognised (in the same or different accounting period) directly in equity, or from a business combination. Deferred tax should be recognised in equity if the tax relates to items that are recognised in equity. [IAS 12 paras 58, 61].

Deferred tax should be recognised in the profit and loss account for the period, except to the extent that it is attributable to a gain or loss that is or has been recognised directly in the STRGL, in which case, the deferred tax attributable to that gain or loss should also be recognised directly in that statement. [FRS 19 paras 34, 35].

Deferred tax assets and deferred tax liabilities should be presented as separate line items in the balance sheet. Deferred tax assets/ (liabilities) should not be classified as current assets/ (liabilities). [IAS 1 paras 68, 70].

FRS 19 requires separate presentation on the face of the balance sheet if the amounts are so material that failure to do so could cause readers to misinterpret the financial statements. [FRS 19 paras 55, 58].

	FRS 19 requires separate presentation on the face of the balance sheet if the amounts are so material that failure to do so could cause readers to misinterpret the financial statements. [FRS 19 paras 55, 58].
Deferred tax assets and liabilities should be offset if, and only if they:	Comparable except that there is no requirement to express an intention to settle on a net basis or simultaneously where different taxable entities are involved. [FRS 19 para 56].
a) relate to taxes levied by the same tax authority; and	
b) arise in the same taxable entity or different taxable entities that intend to recover the tax assets or settle the tax liabilities on a net basis or simultaneously. [IAS 12 para 74].	

Disclosures

Disclosures required by IAS 12 are similar overall to FRS 19. The main differences are:

Disclosure of the aggregate amount of temporary differences associated with investments in subsidiaries, branches, associates and JVs for which deferred tax liabilities have not been recognised. [IAS 12 para 81(f)].	Not required.
Disclosure of the tax expense (on gains/losses on discontinuance and profit/loss for the period) relating to discontinued operations. [IAS 12 para 81(h)].	Not required.
Not required as discounting is not permitted.	Disclosures about the effect of discounting. [FRS 19 paras 60(a)(ii), 61(b)].
Not required as the deferred tax would be recognised.	The circumstances in which deferred tax relating to revaluation and rolled over gains (and other deferred tax unprovided for) would become payable and an indication of the amounts that are expected to become payable in the foreseeable future. [FRS 19 para 64(b), (c)].
A reconciliation of the total (current and deferred) tax charge or credit to the tax charge or credit that would result from applying the standard rate of tax to the profit on ordinary activities before tax. Either the monetary amounts or the rates (as a percentage of profit on ordinary activities before tax) may be reconciled. [IAS 12 para 81(c)].	A reconciliation of the current tax charge or credit on ordinary activities to the current tax charge or credit that would result from applying the standard rate of tax to the profit on ordinary activities before tax. Either the monetary amounts or the rates (as a percentage of profit on ordinary activities before tax) may be reconciled. [FRS 19 para 64(a)].

IAS 14 and SSAP 25 – Segment reporting

IAS 14, Segment reporting	SSAP 25, Segmental reporting
Effective for accounting periods beginning on or after 1 July 1998.	*Effective for accounting periods beginning on or after 1 July 1990.*
Note: IAS 14 is superseded by IFRS 8 for periods beginning on or after 1 January 2009.	

Related pronouncements

–	IFRS 8, Operating segments, effective for accounting periods beginning on or after 1 January 2009.

Overview

In this summary, references to IAS 14 include consequential amendments in subsequent standards. The scope of IAS 14 and SSAP 25 differs. IAS 14 applies to entities whose equity or debt securities are publicly traded or in the process of being so. SSAP 25 applies to public companies, banking and insurance companies and groups and certain other large entities. In addition, the UK Companies Act 1985 also contains certain segmental reporting requirements that apply to all companies.

The Act and SSAP 25 each contain an exemption from the disclosure requirements where disclosure would be seriously prejudicial to the entity's interests. There is no such exemption in IAS 14.

The disclosure requirements of IAS 14 are more extensive than in SSAP 25.

IAS 14 provides that one basis of segmentation is primary and the other is secondary. Extensive disclosure is required for primary segments, with considerably less information required to be disclosed for secondary segments. This differs from SSAP 25 which does not make such a distinction.

IAS 14 is based on management's approach to organising the business. An entity's internal organisational and management structure and its system of internal financial reporting to the board of directors and the chief executive officer should normally be the basis for determining which reporting format is primary and which is secondary. There are exceptions: if the entity's risks and rates of return are strongly affected by both products/services and geography; and if the internal reporting is not based on products/services or on geography. This management-based approach differs from the risk/returns approach of SSAP 25, although in practice the results may be similar.

IAS 14 is superseded by IFRS 8, 'Operating segments', for periods beginning on or after 1 January 2009.

Convergence

In November 2006, the IASB issued IFRS 8, 'Operating segments', which replaces IAS 14 and aligns segment reporting with the requirements of the US standard SFAS 131, 'Disclosures about segments of an enterprise and related information'. The new standard uses a 'management approach' under which segment information is presented on the same basis as that used for internal reporting purposes. IFRS 8 is effective for periods beginning on or after 1 January 2009. The ASB is considering its plans for convergence with IFRS.

First-time adoption of IFRS

There are no specific rules in IFRS 1 in respect of IAS 14 and so the general rule of retrospective application will apply.

Summary of main points

Scope

Applies to public entities – those that have equity or debt securities that are publicly traded or those that are in the process of issuing equity or debt in public securities markets. [IAS 14 para 3].	Applies to public companies, banking and insurance companies/groups and large private companies. [SSAP 25 para 41].

Other entities are encouraged to voluntarily disclose segment information when complying with IAS. [IAS 14 paras 4, 5].	Similar. [SSAP 25 para 42].
If a subsidiary is a publicly traded entity it must comply with IAS 14 in its own financial report. [IAS 14 para 6].	Similar. Also a large private company, which is not a banking or insurance company, is exempt from SSAP 25 if its parent provides segmental information. [SSAP 25 para 41].
No seriously prejudicial exemption under IAS 14.	Seriously prejudicial exemption available. [SSAP 25 para 43].

Types of segments

Business segment is based on consideration of the following factors:	Similar. [SSAP 25 para 12].

- Nature of the products or services.

- Nature of the production processes.

- Type or class of customer for the products or services.

- Methods used to distribute the products or provide the services.

- If applicable, the nature of the regulatory environment, for example, banking, insurance, or public utilities.

[IAS 14 para 9].

Geographical segment is based on consideration of the following factors:	Similar to IAS 14, except that SSAP 25 states that although proximity of operations may indicate similar economic trends and risks this will not necessarily be the case. [SSAP 25 paras 15, 16].

- Similarity of economic and political conditions.

- Relationships between operations in different geographical areas.

- Proximity of operations

- Special risks associated with operations in a particular area

- Exchange control regulations

- Underlying currency risks

[IAS 14 para 9].

Geographical segments are based on either (a) the location of an entity's production or service facilities and other assets; or (b) the location of its markets and customers. [IAS 14 para 13].	Disclosures for turnover are required on both an 'origin' basis and a 'destination' basis (see below).

Identification of reportable segments

The dominant source and nature of an entity's risks and returns should govern whether its primary segment will be business segments or geographical segments. [IAS 14 para 26]. The basis for determining the primary segment should be derived from the entity's risks and returns, its internal organisational and management structure and its system of internal financial reporting. [IAS 14 para 27].

Disclosure is based on classes of business and classes of geographical areas, with no distinction between a primary and secondary reporting segment. In identifying reportable segments management should have regard to the needs of the users of financial statements with respect to information on operations with differing returns on investment, degrees of risk, rates of growth and different potentials for future development. Note that there is no reference in SSAP 25 to internal financial reporting. [SSAP 25 para 8].

Reportable segments

A segment should be identified as reportable if a majority of its revenue is earned from sales to external customers and:

- its revenue from sales to external customers (external revenue) and from transactions with other segments (internal revenue) is ten per cent or more of the total revenue, external and internal, of all segments; or

- its segment result, whether profit or loss, is ten per cent or more of the combined result of all segments in profit or the combined result of all segments in loss, whichever is the greater in absolute amount; or

- its assets are ten per cent or more of the total assets of all segments.

[IAS 14 para 35].

Similar to IAS 14, except that the requirement to contribute to ten per cent of 'total' revenue is based on third party revenue only and the assets test is replaced by ten per cent of 'net' assets. [SSAP 25 para 9].

If less than 75 per cent of external revenue is attributable to reportable segments, additional segments should be identified – even if they do not meet the thresholds above. [IAS 14 para 37].

No equivalent requirement in SSAP 25.

IAS 14 encourages the voluntary reporting of vertically integrated activities as separate segments. [IAS 14 para 40].

No equivalent note in SSAP 25.

Accounting policies

Segment information should be prepared under accounting policies which are consistent with those of the financial statements of the entity. [IAS 14 para 44].

No specific mention in SSAP 25, but the same would apply.

Changes in accounting policies for segmental reporting that have a material effect on segmental information should be disclosed. The disclosure required includes:

Similar. [SSAP 25 para 39].

- Description of the nature of the change.
- Reasons for the change.

- The fact that comparative information has been restated or that it is impracticable to do so.
- The financial effect of the change, if it is reasonably determinable.

[IAS 14 para 76].

Disclosure

For the primary reporting format the following should be disclosed for each reportable segment:	For each business and geographical segment the following should be disclosed:
Segment revenue separating out sales to external customers and sales to other segments. [IAS 14 para 51].	Similar to IAS 14. Disclosure should be given based on turnover by origin and by destination (or a statement that turnover by destination is not materially different from turnover by origin). [SSAP 25 para 34].
Segment result, presenting the result from continuing operations separately from the result from discontinued operations. [IAS 14 para 52].	SSAP 25 requires disclosure of the segment result. FRS 3 requires that where an acquisition, sale or termination has a material impact on a major business segment, the impact should be disclosed. [SSAP 25 para 34; FRS 3 para 53].
Total carrying amount of segment assets. [IAS 14 para 55].	Not required by SSAP 25. An analysis of net assets is required to be disclosed. [SSAP 25 para 24].
Segment liabilities. [IAS 14 para 56].	Not required by SSAP 25.
Capital expenditure (on an accruals basis – not a cash basis). [IAS 14 para 57].	Not required by SSAP 25.
Depreciation and amortisation of segment assets included in segment result (not required if cash flow disclosures for segments, as encouraged by IAS 7, are given). [IAS 14 paras 58, 63].	Not required by SSAP 25.
Other significant non-cash expenses (not required if cash flow disclosures for segments, as encouraged by IAS 7, are given). [IAS 14 paras 61, 63].	Not required by SSAP 25.
For each reportable segment, the share of result and net assets of investments accounted for under the equity method, if substantially all of those equity accounted entities' operations are within that reportable segment. [IAS 14 paras 64 to 66].	Similar to IAS 14, except that SSAP 25 specifies that information is to be given for significant associated undertakings (20 per cent of total result or 20 per cent of total net assets). [SSAP 25 para 36].
Entities are encouraged (but not required) to disclose the nature and amount of exceptional items of segment revenue and expense. [IAS 14 para 59].	Not required per SSAP 25, but FRS 3 states that the effect of exceptional items on segment results should be disclosed where material. [FRS 3 para 53].
For secondary reporting segments, the segment revenue, total carrying amount of segment assets and capital expenditure should be disclosed. [IAS 14 paras 69 to 72].	Not applicable to SSAP 25.
A reconciliation to the figures in the financial statements should be provided (and in the case of segment result, for both continuing and discontinued operations). [IAS 14 para 67].	Similar to IAS 14, but SSAP 25 does not refer to continuing and discontinued operations. [SSAP 25 para 37].

If a segment is not reportable because it earns a majority of its revenue from sales to other segments, but if its revenue from sales to external customers is ten per cent or more of total entity external revenue, the entity should disclose that fact and the amounts of revenue from (a) sales to external customers and (b) internal sales to other segments. [IAS 14 para 74].

This would be a reportable segment under SSAP 25. [SSAP 25 para 9].

In measuring and reporting segment revenue from transactions with other segments, inter-segment transfers should be measured on the basis that the entity actually uses to price those transfers. Disclosure is required of the basis of pricing inter-segment transfers. [IAS 14 para 75].

No equivalent requirement in SSAP 25.

An indication of the types of products/services in each reported business segment and the composition of geographical segments should be given. [IAS 14 para 81].

Similar to IAS 14. [SSAP 25 para 34].

IAS 16 and FRS 15 – Property, plant and equipment

IAS 16, Property, plant and equipment	FRS 15, Tangible fixed assets
Effective for accounting periods beginning on or after 1 July 1999.	*Effective for accounting periods ending on or after 23 March 2000.*
The revised standard (2003) is effective for annual periods beginning on or after 1 January 2005.	

Related pronouncements

IFRIC 1, Changes in existing decommissioning, restoration and similar liabilities.	UITF 5, Transfers from current assets to fixed assets
	UITF 23, Application of transitional rules in FRS 15.
	UITF 24, Accounting for start up costs
	UITF 29, Website development costs. (for IAS see IAS 38 comparison)

Overview

In this summary, references to IAS 16 relate to the revised standard and consequential amendments in subsequent standards. IAS 16 excludes from its scope property, plant and equipment classified as held for sale in accordance with IFRS 5, biological assets related to agricultural activity (covered by IAS 41), the recognition and measurement of exploration and evaluation assets (covered by IFRS 6) and mineral rights and mineral reserves. FRS 15 does not exclude these types of asset from its scope. However, both IAS 16 and FRS 15 exclude investment properties (covered by IAS 40 and SSAP 19 respectively). Borrowing costs are dealt with in IAS 23 (see separate summary).

IAS 16 capitalises subsequent expenditure on an asset using the same criteria as the initial spend, that is, when it is probable the future economic benefits associated with the item will flow to the entity and the cost of the item can be measured reliably. If part of an asset is replaced, then the part it replaces is derecognised, regardless of whether it has been depreciated separately or not. FRS 15, on the other hand, requires capitalisation of subsequent expenditure only when the expenditure improves the condition of the asset beyond its previously assessed standard of performance, which generally would have been reflected in the asset's depreciation.

IAS 16 states that if fixed assets are acquired in exchange for a non-monetary asset, the cost of the acquired asset is measured at fair value unless (a) the exchange transaction lacks commercial substance or (b) the fair value of neither the asset received nor the asset given up is reliably measurable. A transaction has commercial substance if the future cash flows are expected to change significantly as a result of the transaction. Fair value is taken as the fair value of the asset given up, unless the fair value of the asset received is more reliably measurable. This will be a new requirement for UK companies as FRS 15 does not contain equivalent rules.

Where a company adopts a policy of valuations, there is a key difference in principle between IAS 16 and FRS 15. IAS 16 requires revaluations to be at fair value. It states that fair value is usually 'determined from market-based evidence' (for land and buildings) or 'market value' (for plant and equipment), which is generally taken to mean open market value. FRS 15 uses the 'value to the business' model and requires revaluations to 'current value', which is defined as being the lower of replacement cost and recoverable amount. As a consequence, FRS 15 is more prescriptive in requiring non-specialised properties to be valued at existing use value (EUV), specialised properties to be valued at depreciated replacement cost and properties surplus to requirements at open market value.

IAS 16 adopts a simpler approach to recognising revaluation losses than FRS 15:

- Revaluation losses that are due to a clear consumption of economic benefits are charged to the profit and loss account under FRS 15, whereas under IAS 16, if there is a previous revaluation surplus on that asset, the revaluation loss is first charged against the surplus to the extent of that surplus, with the balance of the loss then being charged to the profit and loss account.

- Where there is no clear consumption of economic benefits IAS 16 requires the same treatment, that is any loss is first taken against a previous revaluation surplus on the same asset, with the balance being charged to profit and loss account. Under FRS 15 the loss is taken to the STRGL (and to revaluation reserve) to the extent that there is a previous revaluation surplus on the same asset, that is until the carrying value of the asset reaches depreciated historical cost. Any further revaluation loss represented by a difference between depreciated historical cost and recoverable amount is taken to the profit and loss account, but further losses represented by a difference between recoverable amount and the revalued amount are taken to the STRGL and reserves.

IAS 16 requires residual values to be based on prices *current* at the balance sheet date, whereas under FRS 15 residual values are based on prices prevailing at the date of acquisition (or revaluation) of an asset and do not take account of price changes. Whilst this difference has little effect on the depreciation of assets carried at current values, it could make a significant difference to depreciation charges in respect of assets carried at historical cost.

There are no requirements under IAS 16 to carry out impairment reviews at the end of each reporting period where no depreciation charge is made on the grounds that it would be immaterial or where the estimated useful life of the tangible fixed asset exceeds 50 years (although impairment reviews may be required under IAS 36 if there is a trigger event).

FRS 15 contains specific rules on the circumstances in which renewals accounting for infrastructure assets is permitted. IAS 16 does not include any reference to renewals accounting and, therefore, does not allow any departure from the principle that the depreciation expense is determined by reference to an asset's depreciable amount.

Under IAS 16 comparatives are required for all disclosures, including the table reconciling the carrying amount of each class of property, plant and equipment.

Convergence

In May 2002, the ASB issued FRED 29 proposing that FRS 15 should be replaced by IAS 16. However, a new UK standard has not yet been issued and this now forms part of the wider debate on convergence to IFRS.

First-time adoption of IFRS

IFRS 1 includes an exemption allowing fair value to be used as deemed cost for any item of property, plant and equipment (PPE) at the date of transition to IFRS. Also, subject to certain criteria, a revaluation made under previous GAAP may also be used as the basis for deemed cost. An entity that uses the exemption is not required to adopt a policy of regular revaluation under IAS 16 in future periods.

Summary of main points

Scope

Applies to all property, plant and equipment (PPE) except:	Wider scope. Applies to all tangible fixed assets except:
• Investment property (IAS 40 applies). [IAS 16 para 5].	Investment properties (SSAP 19 applies). [FRS 15 para 4].
• PPE classified as held for sale in accordance with IFRS 5. [IAS 16 para 3(a)].	Investment properties (SSAP 19 applies). [FRS 15 para 4].
• Biological assets related to agricultural activity (IAS 41 applies) [IAS 16 para 3(b)]. However it does apply to PPE used to develop or maintain those assets.	
• The recognition and measurement of exploration and evaluation assets (IFRS 6 applies). [IAS 16 para 3(c)]. However, it does apply to PPE used to develop or maintain those assets.	

- Mineral rights and mineral reserves such as oil, natural gas and similar non-regenerative resources. [IAS 16 para 3(d)]. However, it does apply to PPE used to develop or maintain those assets.

Assets held by insurance companies and groups are exempt from the requirements for the treatment of revaluation gains and losses, where revaluation changes are taken to profit and loss account. [FRS 15 para 71].

Definitions

PPE is defined as tangible items that (a) are held for use in the production or supply of goods and services, for rental to others, or for administrative purposes; and (b) are expected to be used during more than one period. [IAS 16 para 6].

Definition of tangible fixed assets is similar, although the wording differs slightly, as the definition refers to the asset having physical substance and being used on a continuing basis in the entity's activities. [FRS 15 para 2].

Residual value is defined as the estimated amount that an entity would currently obtain from disposal of the asset, after deducting the estimated costs of disposal, if the asset were already of the age and in the condition expected at the end of its useful life. [IAS 16 para 6].

Residual values are based on prices prevailing at the date of acquisition (or revaluation). [FRS 15 para 2]. Thus whilst IAS 16 takes account of price changes up to the balance sheet date, the FRS 15 definition does not (unless the asset is revalued at the balance sheet date). Neither the IAS 16 nor FRS 15 definitions take into account expected future price changes.

Other definitions are similar to those in IAS 16

Recognition

An item of PPE should be recognised as an asset when it is probable that future economic benefits associated with the asset will flow to the entity and the item's cost can be measured reliably. [IAS 16 para 7].

No specific recognition criteria in FRS 15, but similar to general recognition criteria in FRS 5 (para 20).

An entity applies the above recognition principle to its PPE costs at the time they are incurred (for both initial costs and subsequent expenditure). [IAS 16 para 10].

Initial measurement

Initial measurement should be at cost. [IAS 16 para 15].

Same. [FRS 15 para 6].

Cost comprises:

Similar. [FRS 15 paras 7, 8; FRS 12 para 66].

- purchase price (after deducting trade discounts and rebates);

- any directly attributable costs of bringing the asset to the location and condition necessary for it to be capable of operating in the manner intended by management; and

- the initial estimate of costs of dismantling and removing the item and restoring the site, where the entity incurs an obligation to do so.

[IAS 16 para 16].

No specific definition of directly attributable costs is given, but examples are listed. [IAS 16 para 17].	Directly attributable costs are defined as being:
	• labour costs of own employees arising directly from the acquisition or construction of the specific asset; and
	• incremental costs that would have been avoided only if the asset had not been constructed for acquired.
	A list of examples is also given which is similar to that in IAS 16. [FRS 15 paras 9, 10].
Costs of testing whether the asset is functioning properly are directly attributable costs. However, start-up costs of new facilities, products or services are excluded. [IAS 16 paras 17, 19].	Similar. [FRS 15 paras 14, 16].
Administration and general overhead costs are excluded. [IAS 16 para 19].	Similar. [FRS 15 para 9].
Capitalisation of costs ceases when the asset is in the location and condition necessary for it to be capable of operating in the manner intended by management. [IAS 16 paras 19, 20].	Similar. [FRS 15 para 12].
Initial operating losses are expensed. [IAS 16 para 20].	Similar. [FRS 15 para 16].
If an entity makes similar assets for sale in the normal course of business, the cost of constructing the asset is usually the same as the cost of producing the assets for sale under IAS 2 – that is, it appears to include indirect costs. [IAS 16 para 22].	No mention in FRS 15, but would need to strip out indirect costs of production.
Abnormal costs should be excluded. [IAS 16 para 22].	Similar. [FRS 15 para 11].
No mention of donated assets.	Charities should recognise donated tangible fixed assets at their current value on the date received. [FRS 15 para 17].
Where payment is deferred, cash payments are discounted to the cash price equivalent. [IAS 16 para 23].	No mention of deferred payments, but applying FRS 12 gives a similar effect.

Exchanges of assets

An exchange of assets is recognised at fair value, unless the exchange transaction lacks commercial substance or the fair value of neither the asset received nor the asset given up is reliably measurable. If not measured at fair value for either of the reasons above, the cost is measured at the carrying amount of the asset given up. [IAS 16 paras 24, 25].	No mention of exchanges of assets.

Subsequent costs

Subsequent costs are capitalised when they meet IAS 16's recognition criteria, that is, when it is probable that the future economic benefits will flow to the entity and the costs can be reliably measured. Subsequent costs may include replacement of significant components and costs of regular major inspections. [IAS 16 paras 13, 14].

Similar. Subsequent expenditure is capitalised when:

- it enhances the economic benefits beyond that previously assessed;

- a separately depreciated component of an asset has been replaced or restored; or

- it is a major inspection or overhaul of the asset, that restores the economic benefits of the asset and has already been reflected in depreciation.

[FRS 15 para 36].

All other subsequent expenditure is expensed as incurred. [IAS 16 para 12].

Similar. [FRS 15 para 34].

Measurement subsequent to initial recognition

An entity should choose either the cost model or the revaluation model as its accounting policy and should apply that policy to an entire class of PPE. [IAS 16 para 29].

Similar. Where a policy of revaluation is adopted, it should be applied to individual classes of tangible fixed assets. [FRS 15 para 42].

Cost model

Under the cost model, PPE is carried at cost less accumulated depreciation and accumulated impairment losses. [IAS 16 para 30].

Same, where a policy of historical cost is adopted.

Revaluation model

Under the revaluation model, an entire class of PPE is revalued to fair value. PPE is carried at fair value at the date of revaluation less any subsequent accumulated depreciation and impairment losses. [IAS 16 paras 31, 36].

When a policy of revaluation is adopted, entire classes of assets should be revalued to their current value at the balance sheet date. [FRS 15 paras 43, 61].

No reference to an exception for individual assets in a class of assets where valuations are impossible to obtain.

There is an exception for individual assets in a class where, rarely, it is impossible to obtain a reliable valuation. [FRS 15 para 61].

Fair value of land and buildings is usually determined from market-based evidence. The fair value of plant and equipment is usually market value. [IAS 16 para 32].

Current value is defined as the lower of replacement cost and recoverable amount (the 'value to the business' model). [FRS 15 para 2]. Therefore, for unimpaired assets, current value is:

- Existing use value, plus acquisition costs, for non-specialised properties.

- Open market value less selling costs for properties surplus to requirements.

- Market value for tangible fixed assets other than properties.

Specialised assets are valued using an income based approach or at depreciated replacement cost. [IAS 16 para 33].

- Depreciated replacement cost for specialised properties or other assets where there is no market value.

[FRS 15 paras 53, 59].

Revaluations should be carried out with sufficient regularity so that carrying amount does not differ materially from fair value at the balance sheet date. Where there are significant movements in fair value, annual valuations may be needed. Otherwise a valuation every 3 to 5 years may be sufficient. [IAS 16 paras 31, 34].

Full valuations should be carried out at least every five years, with an interim valuation in year 3 and other years where there is a material change in value. [FRS 15 para 45].

No mention of use of external valuers, although valuations would 'normally' be undertaken by professionally qualified valuers. [IAS 16 para 32].

For properties, a qualified external valuer should be involved in the five yearly full valuation. [FRS 15 para 48].

A revaluation gain is credited directly to equity, unless it reverses a revaluation decrease of the same asset previously recognised as an expense. [IAS 16 para 39].

Similar. Revaluation gains credited to equity should be shown in the STRGL. [FRS 15 para 63].

Revaluation losses are charged directly against any related revaluation surplus on the same asset. Any excess revaluation losses are expensed. [IAS 16 para 40].

Similar in most cases, but revaluation losses caused by a clear consumption of economic benefits should all go to the profit and loss account. Otherwise, losses to the asset's depreciated historical cost are taken to the STRGL and, thereafter, to the profit and loss account, unless it can be demonstrated that the asset's recoverable amount is higher than its revalued amount. [FRS 15 para 65].

The revaluation surplus in equity may be transferred to retained earnings when the asset is derecognised, that is, when the asset is disposed of or retired. Some of the surplus may be transferred as the asset is used by the entity (and depreciation is charged on the revalued asset). [IAS 16 para 41].

Same permitted under the Companies Act 1985.

Depreciation

Same basic principles as in IAS 16, but more requirements in respect of non-depreciation.

The depreciable amount of an asset should be allocated on a systematic basis over its useful life. [IAS 16 para 50].

Same. [FRS 15 para 77].

Each significant part of an item of PPE should be depreciated separately, but those with the same useful lives and depreciation methods may be grouped for depreciation purposes. [IAS 16 paras 43, 45].

Similar. Where an asset comprises two or more major components with substantially different lives, they should be depreciated separately over their individual lives. [FRS 15 para 83].

Repair and maintenance of an asset do not negate the need to depreciate it. [IAS 16 para 52].

Same. [FRS 15 para 86].

No equivalent.

Assets, other than non-depreciable land, should be subject to annual impairment reviews when either no depreciation is charged due to immateriality or the estimated remaining useful economic life exceeds 50 years. [FRS 15 para 89].

The useful life, residual values and depreciation method used should be reviewed at least at each financial year end. Any revisions to these estimates should be taken prospectively. [IAS 16 paras 51, 61].

Similar, except that FRS 15 does not refer to annual review of the depreciation method. [FRS 15 paras 93, 95].

No reference to renewals accounting or infrastructure assets.	Renewals accounting is permitted (under certain circumstances) as a means of estimating the depreciation charge for infrastructure systems or networks. [FRS 15 paras 97, 98].

Derecognition

An asset is eliminated from the balance sheet on disposal or when no future economic benefits are expected from its use or disposal. [IAS 16 para 67].	No explicit reference in FRS 15.
Gains and losses on derecognition of an asset are recognised in profit or loss and are determined as the difference between the net disposal proceeds and the carrying amount. [IAS 16 paras 68, 71].	Similar. [FRS 15 para 72].
Impairments or losses of assets, related claims for or compensation payments from third parties and subsequent replacement of the asset should be accounted for separately as follows: • Impair asset or reflect 'disposal' under IAS 36 and IAS 16 respectively. • Include compensation (monetary or non-monetary) from third parties in profit or loss when it becomes receivable. • Capitalise cost of replacement asset under IAS 16. [IAS 16 para 66].	Similar, except that insurance proceeds are normally treated as proceeds on disposal of the asset. Also, where non-monetary compensation is received, realisation principles would mean that compensation is not reflected in the profit and loss account.

Disclosure

For each class of PPE, disclose:

• Measurement bases used for determining gross carrying amount.	No explicit requirement.
• Depreciation methods used.	Same.
• Useful lives or depreciation rates used.	Same.
• Table reconciling opening and closing positions (including depreciation charge). Comparatives are required.	Similar, except that comparatives are specifically not required by FRS 28.
[IAS 16 para 73].	[FRS 15 para 100].
IAS 16 refers to the requirement in IAS 8 to disclose the nature and effect of changes in estimates. [IAS 16 para 76].	Where material, disclose the financial effect of a change in estimate of useful economic lives or residual values or change in depreciation method. Reasons for a change in depreciation method should also be given. [FRS 15 paras 100, 102].

Disclose:

• The existence and amounts of restrictions on title and assets pledged as security.	No explicit requirements in FRS 15, but there is a similar requirement in CA85.
• Amount of expenditure on assets in the course of construction.	No specific requirement.
• Amount of contractual commitments for the acquisition of PPE.	Capital commitments required by CA85.

- If not disclosed on the face of the income statement, the amount of compensation from third parties for items of PPE that were impaired, lost or given up that is included in profit or loss.

No specific requirement.

[IAS 16 para 74].

For revalued assets, disclose:

For each class of revalued assets, disclose:

- The method and significant assumptions applied in estimating fair value.

- Basis of valuation and whether acquisition costs or selling costs have been included or deducted (and total amounts of such costs for all properties).

- Date of revaluation.

- Same, but also required to disclose amounts of revaluation and date of last full valuation.

- Whether an independent valuer was involved.

- Same, plus the name and qualifications of valuer or valuer's organisation and its nature.

- Carrying amount under the cost model, by class of asset.

- Same.

- Revaluation surplus, including changes in the period and any restrictions on the distribution of the balance to shareholders.

- Similar requirement under CA85, except no requirement to refer to distribution restrictions.

- No requirement.

- A statement that the valuations have not been updated as directors are not aware of any material change in value, where applicable.

- Not relevant.

- Where an asset in a class of assets has not been revalued, explain why and give its carrying amount.

- Extent to which fair values have been determined directly by reference to observable market prices or market transactions and extent to which determined using other valuation techniques.

- No equivalent.

[IAS 16 para 77].

[FRS 15 para 74].

The following disclosures are encouraged (but are not mandatory):

- Carrying amount of temporarily idle PPE.

- Gross carrying amount of fully depreciated PPE still in use.

- Carrying amount of PPE retired from active use and not classified as held for sale in accordance with IFRS 5.

- Fair value of PPE held at depreciated historical cost, when materially different from carrying amount.

Required in directors' report for land, if significant, under Schedule 7 of CA85.

[IAS 16 para 79].

IAS 17 and SSAP 21 – Leases

IAS 17, Leases	SSAP 21, Leases and hire purchase contracts
The revised standard (1997) is effective for accounting periods beginning on or after 1 January 1999.	*Effective for accounting periods beginning on or after 1 July 1987.*
The revised standard (2003) is effective for annual periods beginning on or after 1 January 2005.	

Related pronouncements

SIC 15, Operating leases – Incentives.	FRS 5, Substance of transactions.
SIC 27, Evaluating the substance of transactions in the legal form of a lease.	UITF 28, Operating lease incentives.
	Finance and Leasing Association (FLA) SORP.
IFRIC 4, Determining whether an arrangement contains a lease.	

Overview

In this summary, references to IAS 17 relate to the revised standard issued in December 2003. The broad approach of the international and the UK standard is similar. Both IAS 17 and SSAP 21 require leases to be classed as finance leases or operating leases. The definition of a finance lease is the same in both standards. However, IAS 17 does not provide a quantitative test of whether a lease is a finance lease (the '90% test'), instead it provides additional guidance on when a lease should be classified as a finance lease.

IAS 17 requires that a lease of land and buildings should be split at inception of the lease into a separate lease of land and a lease of buildings. Unless title is expected to pass to the lessee at the end of the lease term, leases of land should normally be treated as operating leases. The buildings element would be classified as an operating or finance lease as appropriate. This means that leases of buildings are more likely to be classified as finance leases under IAS 17 than under SSAP 21 where the land and buildings are considered together.

Income recognition by lessors for finance leases is different under the two standards. SSAP 21 requires the use of the net cash investment method whilst IAS 17 requires the net investment method to be used. This can give rise to materially different income recognition profiles, particularly where the tax effects of a lease are significant.

IFRIC 4 sets out criteria for determining whether arrangements that do not take the legal form of a lease (for example, outsourcing arrangements and take-or-pay contracts) should, nonetheless, be accounted for in accordance with IAS 17. There is no direct equivalent in UK GAAP, but the principles of FRS 5 would generally apply to transactions of this type.

IAS 17 requires a number of detailed disclosures that are not required by SSAP 21.

Convergence

The IASB are currently working on a joint project with the FASB on lease accounting. A discussion paper is expected to be issued in 2008. There are currently no plans to update lease accounting guidance under UK GAAP.

First-time adoption of IFRS

There are no specific rules in IFRS 1 in respect of IAS 17 and so the general rule of retrospective application will apply. This will include splitting leases into land and buildings (see below).

Summary of main points

Determining whether an arrangement contains a lease

IFRIC 4 sets out criteria for determining whether arrangements that do not take the legal form of a lease (for example, outsourcing arrangements and take-or-pay contracts) should, nonetheless, be accounted for in accordance with IAS 17. It specifies that an arrangement contains a lease if it depends on the use of a specific asset and conveys a right to control the use of that asset.

There is no direct equivalent in UK GAAP, but the principles of FRS 5 would generally apply to transactions of this type.

Evaluating the substance of transactions involving the legal form of a lease

SIC 27 provides guidance on evaluating and accounting for complex transactions that involve the legal form of a lease.

There is no direct equivalent in UK GAAP, but the principles of FRS 5 would generally apply to transactions of this type.

Lease classification

Lease classification is made at the inception of the lease. Amendments to a lease that would result in a different lease classification are regarded as giving rise to a new lease agreement. However, changes in estimates or changes in circumstances, do not give rise to a new classification. [IAS 17 para 13].

SSAP 21 does not deal with lease reclassification. However, SSAP 21 requires that the 90 per cent test (see below) is carried out at the inception of the lease. [SSAP 21 para 15].

The *inception of the lease* is the earlier of the date of the lease agreement and the date of commitment by the parties to the lease's principal provisions. [IAS 17 para 4].

The *inception of a lease* is the earlier of the time the asset is brought into use and the date from which rentals first accrue. [SSAP 21 para 29]. This is closer to the definition of the 'commencement of the lease term' in IAS 17 (see below).

A *finance lease* is a lease that transfers substantially all the risks and rewards incidental to ownership of an asset. Title may or may not eventually be transferred. [IAS 17 para 4].

The definition is the same, but SSAP 21 also states that it should be presumed that a transfer of risks and rewards occurs if at the inception of the lease the present value of the minimum lease payments amounts to substantially all (normally 90 per cent or more) of the fair value of the leased asset. [SSAP 21 para 15]. However, this presumption can be rebutted. [SSAP 21 para 16].

An *operating lease* is a lease other than a finance lease. [IAS 17 para 4].

Same. [SSAP 21 para 17].

IAS 17 provides the following examples of situations which would normally lead to a lease being classified as a finance lease:

- The lease transfers ownership of the asset to the lessee at the end of the lease term.

- The lessee has the option to purchase the asset at a price that is expected to be sufficiently lower than the fair value at the date the option becomes exercisable for it to be reasonably certain, at the inception of the lease, that the option will be exercised.

SSAP 21 does not provide additional guidance on lease classification in the standard. However, there are extensive guidance notes. Also, the similarity of the definitions used in IAS 17 and SSAP 21 means that in practice a lease that is classed as a finance lease under IAS 17 would in most cases be classed as a finance lease under SSAP 21.

- The lease term is for the major part of the economic life of the asset.

- The present value of the minimum lease payments amounts to at least substantially all of the fair value of the leased asset.

- The leased assets are of a specialised nature. [IAS 17 para 10].

Paragraph 11 of IAS 17 gives indicators of situations that could also lead a lease to be classified as a finance lease.

Minimum lease payments are the payments over the lease term that the lessee is required to make (excluding contingent rent, costs for services and taxes to be paid by the lessor) and in the case of the lessee, any amounts guaranteed by him or by a party related to him. In the case of the lessor, it includes any residual value guaranteed by the lessee, a party related to the lessee, or by an independent third party. [IAS 17 para 4].	Similar. [SSAP 21 para 20].
Unless title is expected to pass to the lessee at the end of the lease term, leases of land should be treated as operating leases. [IAS 17 para 14].	Not specified by SSAP 21.
Land and building elements of a lease are required to be considered separately for the purposes of lease classification. The minimum lease payments are allocated (at inception of the lease) between the land and buildings in proportion to the relative fair values of the leasehold interests in the two elements. If the lease payments cannot be allocated reliably between the two elements, the entire lease is treated as a finance lease, unless it is clear that both elements are operating leases. [IAS 17 paras 15, 16].	Under SSAP 21, there is no requirement to split property leases between land and buildings.
Separate measurement of the land and buildings element is not required when the land element is immaterial or when a lessee's interest in both the land and buildings are classified as an investment property in accordance with IAS 40 and the fair value model is adopted. [IAS 17 paras 17, 18].	Not applicable.

Lessees – finance leases

At the commencement of the lease term, lessees should recognise finance leases as assets and liabilities at fair value of the leased asset or, if lower, at the present value of the minimum lease payments (each determined at the inception of the lease). [IAS 17 para 20].	SSAP 21 requires initial recognition of finance leases to be at the present value of the minimum lease payments. [SSAP 21 para 32]. However, where the fair value of the asset is a sufficiently close approximation to the present value of the minimum lease payments, the fair value may be used instead. [SSAP 21 para 33].
The commencement of the lease term is the date from which the lessee is entitled to exercise its right to use the leased asset. [IAS 17 para 4].	SSAP 21 does not distinguish between the inception of the lease term and the commencement of the lease term for classification and accounting purposes.

In calculating the present value of the minimum lease payments the discount factor is the interest rate implicit in the lease (IAS 17 para 4), if this is practicable to determine. If not, the lessee's incremental borrowing rate should be used. [IAS 17 para 20].

Similar. However, if the interest rate implicit in the lease is not determinable, it should be estimated by reference to the rate that a lessee would be expected to pay on a similar lease. [SSAP 21 para 24].

The lessee's initial direct costs are added to the amount recognised as an asset. [IAS 17 para 24].

Not dealt with by SSAP 21.

Minimum lease payments should be apportioned between the finance charge and the reduction of the outstanding liability. The finance charge should be allocated so as to produce a constant periodic rate of interest on the liability for each period. Contingent rents should be charged as expenses in the periods in which they are incurred. [IAS 17 para 25].

Similar, but SSAP 21 does not deal explicitly with contingent rents. However, contingent rentals would normally be excluded from the calculation of the minimum lease payments [SSAP 21 para 35].

Assets held under finance leases should be depreciated over the shorter of the lease term and the asset's useful life. If, however, there is a reasonable certainty that the lessee will obtain ownership, then the asset can be depreciated over its useful economic life. [IAS 17 para 27].

Same. [SSAP 21 para 36].

In addition to the requirements of IAS 32/IFRS 7, the following disclosures are required by IAS 17:

- For each class of asset the net carrying amount at the balance sheet date. [IAS 17 para 31(a)].

SSAP 21 requires disclosure of the gross amounts and accumulated depreciation for each major class of asset. [SSAP 21 para 49]. Alternatively, the net amount of assets held under finance leases included in total fixed assets should be disclosed. [SSAP 21 para 50].

- A reconciliation between the total of future minimum lease payments at the balance sheet date, and their present value. [IAS 17 para 31(b)].

No similar requirement.

- The total of future minimum lease payments at the balance sheet date, and their present value, for each of the following periods; not later than one year; later than one year and not later than five years; and later than five years. [IAS 17 para 31(b)].

SSAP 21 requires disclosure of the net obligations under finance leases analysed between amounts payable in the next year, in the second to fifth years inclusive and thereafter. [SSAP 21 para 52].

- Contingent rents recognised in income for the period. [IAS 17 para 31(c)].

No specific requirement in SSAP 21, however, paragraph 62 of the guidance notes require disclosure of contingent rentals where such disclosure is necessary to give a true and fair view.

- The total of future minimum sublease payments expected to be received under non-cancellable subleases at the balance sheet date. [IAS 17 para 31(d)].

No similar requirement.

- A general description of the lessee's material leasing arrangements, including disclosures for contingent rent, renewals, options and covenants. [IAS 17 para 31(e)].

SSAP 21 requires disclosure of the policies adopted for accounting for finance leases. [SSAP 21 para 57].

Lessees – operating leases

Payments under operating leases should be recognised as an expense on a straight-line basis over the lease term, unless another systematic basis is more representative of the time pattern of the user's benefit. [IAS 17 para 33].

Same. [SSAP 21 para 37].

The following disclosures are required by IAS 17:

- The total of future minimum lease payments under non-cancellable operating leases for each of the following periods: not later than one year; later than one year and not later than five years; and later than five years. [IAS 17 para 35(a)].

SSAP 21 requires disclosure of the payments which the lessee is committed to make during the next year, analysed between those in which the commitment expires within that year, in the second to fifth years inclusive and over five years from the balance sheet date, showing separately the commitments in respect of leases of land and buildings and other operating leases. [SSAP 21 para 56].

- The total of future minimum sublease payments expected to be received under non cancellable subleases at the balance sheet date. [IAS 17 para 35(b)].

No similar requirement.

- Lease and sublease payments recognised as an expense in the period, with separate amounts for minimum lease payments, contingent rents, and sublease payments. [IAS 17 para 35(c)].

Similar, but SSAP 21 requires the amounts charged to be analysed between leases of plant and machinery and other leases. [SSAP 21 para 55].

- A general description of the lessee's significant leasing arrangements, including disclosures for contingent rent, renewals, options and covenants. [IAS 17 para 35(d)].

SSAP 21 requires disclosure of the policies adopted for accounting for operating leases. [SSAP 21 para 57].

Lessors – finance leases

Lessors should recognise assets held under a finance lease in their balance sheets and present them as a receivable at an amount equal to the net investment in the lease. [IAS 17 para 36].

Similar. [SSAP 21 para 38].

Net investment in the lease is the gross investment in the lease discounted at the interest rate implicit in the lease. [IAS 17 para 4].

SSAP 21 defines the net investment in the lease as the gross investment in the lease less gross earnings allocated to future periods. [SSAP 21 para 22].

Gross investment in the lease is the aggregate of the minimum lease payments receivable by the lessor under a finance lease and any unguaranteed residual value accruing to the lessor. [IAS 17 para 4].

Similar. [SSAP 21 para 21].

The recognition of finance income should reflect a constant periodic rate of return on the lessor's net investment in the finance lease. [IAS 17 para 39].

This is an area of major difference between SSAP 21 and IAS 17. SSAP 21 requires that total gross earnings under a finance lease should normally be allocated to accounting periods to give a constant rate of return on the lessor's net cash investment in the lease. [SSAP 21 para 39]. The net cash investment represents the total cash invested after taking into account all of the cash flows associated with the lease. It differs, therefore, from the amount of the net investment in the lease as it takes account of other cash flows, for example, tax.

For finance leases other than those involving manufacturer or dealer lessors, initial direct costs are included in the initial measurement of the finance lease receivable and reduce the amount of income recognised over the lease term. [IAS 17 para 38].	Initial direct costs may be apportioned over the period of the lease on a systematic and rational basis. [SSAP 21 para 44].

In addition to the requirements of IAS 32/IFRS 7, the following disclosures are required by IAS 17:

• A reconciliation between the gross investment in the lease at the balance sheet date, and the present value of minimum lease payments receivable at the balance sheet date. [IAS 17 para 47(a)].	No similar requirement.
• An entity should disclose the gross investment in the lease and the present value of minimum lease payments receivable at the balance sheet date, for each of the following periods: not later than one year; later than one year and not later than five years; and later than five years. [IAS 17 para 47(a)].	SSAP 21 requires disclosure of the net investment in finance leases and hire purchase contracts at the balance sheet date. [SSAP 21 para 58].
• Unearned finance income. [IAS 17 para 47(b)].	No similar requirement.
• The unguaranteed residual values accruing to the benefit of the lessor. [IAS 17 para 47(c)].	No similar requirement.
• The accumulated allowance for uncollectible minimum lease payments receivable. [IAS 17 para 47(d)].	No similar requirement.
• Contingent rents recognised in income. [IAS 17 para 47(e)].	No similar requirement in SSAP 21. However, paragraph 128 of the guidance notes requires disclosure of contingent rentals where such disclosure is necessary to give a true and fair view.
• A general description of the lessor's material leasing arrangements. [IAS 17 para 47(f)].	No similar requirement.

Lessors – operating leases

Assets subject to operating leases should be classified according to their nature. The assets should be depreciated in accordance with IAS 16 or IAS 38. [IAS 17 paras 49, 53].	Assets held for use in operating leases should be recorded as a fixed asset and depreciated over their useful economic life. [SSAP 21 para 42].
Operating lease income should be recognised on a straight-line basis over the lease term, unless another systematic basis is more representative of the time pattern in which use benefit derived from the leased asset is diminished. [IAS 17 para 50].	Same. [SSAP 21 para 43].
Initial direct costs should be added to the leased asset's carrying amount and recognised as an expense over the lease term on the same basis as the lease income. [IAS 17 para 52].	Initial direct costs are apportioned over the period of the lease on a systematic and rational basis. [SSAP 21 para 44].

The following disclosures are required by IAS 17:

• The future minimum lease payments under non-cancellable operating leases in the aggregate and for each of the following periods: not later than one year; later than one year and not later than five years; later than five years. [IAS 17 para 56(a)].	No similar requirement.
• Total contingent rents recognised in income. [IAS 17 para 56(b)].	No specific requirement in SSAP 21. However, paragraph 128 of the guidance notes requires disclosure of contingent rentals where such disclosure is necessary to give a true and fair view.
• A general description of the lessor's leasing arrangements. [IAS 17 para 56(c)].	No similar requirement. However, SSAP 21 requires the policy adopted in accounting for leases to be disclosed. [SSAP 21 para 60]

Manufacturer/dealer lessors

Manufacturer or dealer lessors should not recognise any selling profit on entering into an operating lease. [IAS 17 para 55].	Same. [SSAP 21 para 45].
For finance leases, manufacturer or dealer lessors should recognise any selling profit or loss in income for the period, in accordance with the policy followed by the entity for outright sales. If artificially low rates of interest are quoted, selling profit should be restricted to that which would apply if a market rate of interest were charged. [IAS 17 para 42].	Similar. SSAP 21 requires that the selling profit under a finance lease is restricted to the excess of the fair value of the asset over the manufacturer's or dealer's cost. [SSAP 21 para 45].
Initial direct costs should be recognised by manufacturer or dealer lessors as an expense when the selling profit is recognised. [IAS 17 para 42].	Not specified by SSAP 21.

Sale and leaseback transactions

If a sale and leaseback transaction results in a finance lease, any excess of sales proceeds over the carrying amount should be deferred and amortised over the lease term. [IAS 17 para 59].	Where the transaction is a sale and leaseback, but the substance is that of a financing, no profit should be recognised on entering into the arrangement and no adjustment made to the carrying value of the asset. [SSAP 21 guidance notes para 155; FRS 5 App Note B20].
If a sale and leaseback transaction results in an operating lease and it is clear that the transaction is established at fair value, any profit or loss should be recognised immediately. [IAS 17 para 61].	Same. [SSAP 21 para 47(a)].
For operating leases, if the sale price is below fair value, any profit or loss should be recognised immediately except that, if the loss is compensated by future lease payments at below market price, it should be deferred and amortised in proportion to the lease payments over the period for which the asset is expected to be used. [IAS 17 para 61].	Similar, except that any apparent profit or loss should be deferred and amortised over the remainder of the lease term, or if shorter, the period during which the reduced rentals are chargeable. [SSAP 21 para 47(b)].
For operating leases, if the sale price is above fair value, the excess over fair value should be deferred and amortised over the period for which the asset is expected to be used. [IAS 17 para 61].:	Similar, except that any apparent profit should be deferred and amortised over the shorter of the lease term or the period to the next rent review. [SSAP 21 para 47(c)].

Operating lease incentives

SIC 15 requires that lessors recognise the cost of lease incentives as a reduction of rental income over the lease term, on a straight line basis and that lessees recognise the aggregate benefit of incentives as a reduction in rental expense over the lease term on a straight-line basis, unless another systematic basis is representative of the time pattern over which the benefit of the leased asset is diminished.

The requirements of UITF 28 are similar although UITF 28 requires the incentive to be spread over the shorter of the lease term or a period ending on a date on which the rent is first adjusted to prevailing market rates.

IAS 19 and FRS 17 – Employee benefits

IAS 19, Employee benefits	FRS 17, Retirement benefits
Effective for accounting periods beginning on or after 1 January 1999.	*Progressive disclosures for accounting periods ending on or after 22 June 2001.*
Amendments to change the definition of plan assets and to introduce requirements for reimbursements were effective for accounting periods beginning on or after 1 January 2001.	*Fully effective for accounting periods beginning on or after 1 January 2005.*
Amendments to clarify the interaction of the spreading mechanisms and the asset ceiling were effective for accounting periods ending on or after 31 May 2002.	*Amendments to the measurement of plan assets and to bring in disclosures based on IAS 19 are effective for periods beginning on or after 6 April 2007.*
Amendments in respect of actuarial gains and losses, multi-employer plans, group plans and disclosures are effective for annual periods beginning on or after 1 January 2006.	

Related pronouncements

—	UITF 35, Death-in-service and incapacity benefits.

Related best practice statement

In January 2007, the ASB published a reporting statement, 'Retirement benefits – Disclosures', which recommends additional disclosures and is intended to be best practice for entities with defined benefit pension schemes (whether they report under UK GAAP or IFRS). The disclosures complement those set out in the amended FRS 17 and in IAS 19.

Overview

FRS 17 and IAS 19 are similar in their rules regarding measurement and disclosure of retirement benefits, but there are some differences in the recognition of actuarial gains and losses and the presentation of items in the financial statements.

Both standards require that defined benefit scheme assets and liabilities are valued at each balance sheet date to produce an asset or liability for recognition on the balance sheet. All of the items recognised in the profit and loss account under FRS 17 are treated in a similar way under IAS 19. However, for actuarial gains and losses that are recognised immediately in the STRGL under FRS 17, there is a choice of policy under IAS 19. These can be recognised in the income statement, usually over a period representing the expected average remaining working lives of employees participating in the scheme (with any deferred actuarial gains and losses carried on the balance sheet as part of the net pension asset or liability). Alternatively, entities have an option to recognise actuarial gains and losses in full as they arise, outside profit or loss, in a 'statement of recognised income and expense' (similar to the treatment under FRS 17).

Additionally, whereas FRS 17 requires that pension assets and liabilities are shown net of any related deferred tax, this presentation is not permissible under IAS 12.

There are exemptions from defined benefit accounting for certain multi-employer and group pension plans. IAS 19 has specific rules for group pension plans (that is, plans involving entities under common control), which, unlike FRS 17, differ from those for multi-employer plans. One significant difference from FRS 17 is that, under IAS 19, if defined contribution accounting is used by group entities, the plan has to be accounted for as a defined benefit plan in the sponsoring employer's individual financial statements.

The accounting for defined contribution schemes is the same under FRS 17 and IAS 19.

IAS 19 goes further than FRS 17 to consider accounting for and disclosure of other employee benefits such as wages and salaries, bonuses and termination benefits. These subjects are not considered in this summary.

FRS 17 takes UK accounting for retirement benefits a significant step closer to IAS 19.

In the future, the IASB will be carrying out a more fundamental review of IAS 19 and the ASB will be making a contribution to this.

In July 2005, the ASB issued FRED 39, 'Amendments to FRS 12 Provisions, contingent liabilities and contingent assets and Amendments to FRS 17 Retirement benefits'. This proposes amendments to FRS 17 to extend its scope to cover termination benefits (based on proposed amendments to IAS 19 published by the IASB in June 2005).

Further to this, in December 2006, the ASB issued an amendment to FRS 17, replacing the disclosures required by FRS 17 with disclosures based on IAS 19. This achieves convergence between FRS 17 and IAS 19 for pensions disclosures. As a further alignment with IAS 19, the ASB has also amended FRS 17 so that for quoted securities the current bid price (rather than the mid-market value) is taken as fair value. The amendment is effective for periods beginning on or after 6 April 2007.

First-time adoption of IFRS

Under IFRS 1, an entity can apply the 'corridor approach' prospectively from the date of transition to IFRS (that is, recognise all cumulative actuarial gains and losses at the date of transition and then spread post-transition actuarial gains and losses in accordance with IAS 19). The exemption must be applied to all of an entity's pension plans if it is used.

Summary of main points (defined benefit schemes)

Scope

Applies to all *employee benefits* (except those to which IFRS 2, 'Share-based payment' applies) that an employer is committed to providing, whether the commitment is statutory, contractual or implicit in the employer's actions. It includes wages, salaries, benefits, bonuses, paid leave, retirement benefits and termination benefits. [IAS 19 paras 1, 3, 4].

Where an employer participates in a multi-employer defined benefit scheme, it should account for the scheme as defined benefit, unless insufficient information is available, in which case the scheme should be treated as defined contribution with additional disclosure. [IAS 19 para 30].

Where there is a contractual agreement between a multi-employer plan and its participants that determines how the surplus in the plan will be distributed (or the deficit funded), a participating entity should recognise the asset or liability that arises from the contractual agreement and the resulting income or expense. [IAS 19 para 32A].

Schemes between entities under common control are not multi-employer plans. Instead, specific rules apply. If there is a contractual agreement or stated policy for charging the net defined benefit cost for a group plan as a whole to the individual group entities, those group entities should recognise the cost so charged. Otherwise, the net defined benefit cost should be recognised in the financial statements of the group

Applies to all *retirement benefits* that an employer is committed to providing, whether the commitment is statutory, contractual or implicit in the employer's actions. [FRS 17 para 4].

Where an employer participates in a multi-employer defined benefit scheme, it should account for the scheme as defined benefit unless:

- contributions relate to only the current period; or

- it cannot identify its share of scheme assets on a consistent and reasonable basis.

In these cases, the scheme should be treated as defined contribution with additional disclosure. [FRS 17 para 9].

Group schemes are a type of multi-employer scheme from the perspective of the individual entities in the group. An entity can treat its participation in a group defined benefit plan as if it were a defined contribution plan in certain circumstances. [FRS 17 para 12].

entity that is legally the sponsoring employer for the plan. In these circumstances, the other group entities would account for the plan as if it were a defined contribution plan. [IAS 19 paras 34, 34A].

Recognition of assets and liabilities

A surplus/deficit in a defined benefit pension scheme, plus/less any actuarial losses/gains not yet recognised in the profit and loss account, less any past service cost not yet recognised, is recognised as an asset/liability on the balance sheet. [IAS 19 para 54].

A surplus/deficit in a defined benefit pension scheme is recognised as an asset/liability on the balance sheet.

If the balance is an asset, the amount recognised should be limited to the sum of:

- any unrecognised actuarial losses and past service costs; and

- the present value of any amount that may be recovered either through reduced contributions or refunds from the scheme.

[IAS 19 para 58].

If the balance is an asset, the amount recognised should be limited to the amount that may be recovered either through reduced contributions or through refunds that have been agreed by the balance sheet date. [FRS 17 paras 37, 42].

Where it is virtually certain that another party (for example, the members) will help fund a defined benefit obligation, the fair value of the amount to be reimbursed should be recognised as a separate asset. [IAS 19 para 104A].

Where members' contributions are increased to help fund a deficit, the present value of the required additional contributions should be deducted from the liability recognised in the balance sheet. [FRS 17 para 40].

Measurement of assets and liabilities

Scheme assets should be measured at fair value. [IAS 19 paras 54, 102]. In the case of quoted and unitised securities this means bid price.

Scheme assets should be measured at fair value. [FRS 17 para 14] In the case of quoted and unitised securities this means mid-market price. For accounting periods beginning on or after 6 April 2007, FRS 17 has been amended such that for quoted securities, the bid price is taken as the fair value.

Scheme assets are assets held by a long-term employee benefit fund and qualifying insurance policies. In each case, the assets/proceeds:

Scheme assets are not defined.

- can be used only to pay or fund employee benefits;

- are not available to the employer's own creditors, even in bankruptcy;

- cannot be returned/paid to the employer, unless:

    - all benefit obligations are already covered by other assets/proceeds; or

    - they reimburse the employer for benefits already paid.

[IAS 19 para 7].

Scheme assets exclude unpaid contributions due from the reporting entity to the fund, as well as any non-transferable financial instruments issued by the entity and held by the fund. [IAS 19 para 103].

Current assets of the scheme (such as contributions receivable) should be included in scheme assets. [FRS 17 para 15]. (FRS 17 para 47 also specifies that any unpaid contributions to the scheme are presented in the balance sheet as a creditor due within one year.)

Fair value should be market price if available. If no market price is available, fair value is estimated. [IAS 19 para 102].

Similar. [FRS 17 para 17].

Insurance policies that exactly match the amount and timing of some or all of the benefits payable under the scheme should be measured at the same amount as the related obligations. [IAS 19 para 104].

Same. [FRS 17 para 18].

Scheme liabilities, which include both contractual and constructive obligations, should be measured using the projected unit method. [IAS 19 paras 52, 64]. Actuarial assumptions should be unbiased and mutually compatible. [IAS 19 para 72]. Financial assumptions should reflect market expectations at the balance sheet date. [IAS 19 para 77].

Same. [FRS 17 paras 20, 23].

Scheme liabilities should be discounted at a rate equivalent to the current rate of return on a high quality corporate bond of equivalent currency and term. In countries where there is no deep market in such bonds, the market yield on government bonds should be used. [IAS 19 para 78].

Similar. However, FRS 17 specifies that for this purpose, a high quality corporate bond is a bond that has been rated at AA or equivalent status. If there is no liquid market in bonds of this type or duration, then a reasonable proxy should be used. This may be government bonds plus a margin for assumed credit risk. [FRS 17 para 33].

Obligations in respect of incapacity benefit are included with scheme liabilities if the level of benefit depends on the length of service. If the levelpigout of benefit is the same regardless of the period of service, the obligation is not recognised until disability occurs. [IAS 19 para 129].

Unless wholly insured, obligations in respect of death-in-service and incapacity benefits are included with scheme liabilities. If obligations are wholly insured, the cost recognised in each period is equal to the insurance premium payable. [FRS 17 paras 73, 74; UITF 35].

The value of scheme assets and liabilities must be determined with sufficient regularity that the amounts recognised in the financial statements do not differ materially from the amounts that would be determined at the balance sheet date. [IAS 19 para 56]. Valuations do not need to be performed by a qualified actuary. [IAS 19 para 57]. If a valuation is not at the balance sheet date it should be updated to that date. [IAS 19 para 57].

Full actuarial valuations by a professionally qualified actuary should be obtained at intervals not exceeding three years. In the intervening period, the most recent valuation should be updated at the balance sheet date. FRS 17 para 35]. Scheme assets should be valued at each balance sheet date. [FRS 17 para 14].

Current service cost

Current service cost is the increase in the present value of scheme liabilities resulting from employee service in the current period. [IAS 19 para 7].

Same. [FRS 17 para 2].

Past service costs

Past service costs are recognised in the profit and loss account on a straight-line basis over the period in which the benefit increases vest. [IAS 19 para 96].

Same. [FRS 17 para 60].

Past service costs arise when the employer makes a commitment to *change* benefits. [IAS 19 para 97]. Past service cost may be either positive or negative. [IAS 19 para 7].	Past service costs arise when the employer makes a commitment to *enhance* benefits. [FRS 17 para 61].
Any unrecognised past service costs are deducted from scheme liabilities and the balance sheet asset or liability adjusted accordingly. [IAS 19 para 54].	Same. [FRS 17 para 60].

Settlements and curtailments

Gains and losses arising on settlements and curtailments not allowed for in the actuarial assumptions should be recognised when they occur. [IAS 19 para 109] A curtailment occurs when the employer either is demonstrably committed to the transaction or it is reflected in amended scheme rules. [IAS 19 para 111] A settlement occurs when an employer enters into a transaction that eliminates all further obligation for part or all of benefits provided. [IAS 19 para 112].	Losses arising on settlements and curtailments not allowed for in the actuarial assumptions should be recognised in the profit and loss account when the employer becomes demonstrably committed to the transaction. [FRS 17 para 64]. Gains arising on settlements and curtailments not allowed for in the actuarial assumptions should be recognised in the profit and loss account when all parties whose consent is required are irrevocably committed to the transaction. [FRS 17 para 64].
The gain or loss on a settlement or curtailment reflects the change in the present value of scheme liabilities and the fair value of the plan assets, together with any related actuarial gains and losses and past service cost that have not previously been recognised in the profit and loss account. [IAS 19 para 109]. Before determining the effect of a settlement or curtailment, scheme assets and liabilities should be re-measured using current actuarial assumptions. [IAS 19 para 110].	The gain or loss on a settlement or curtailment reflects the change in the present value of scheme liabilities and the fair value of the plan assets. [FRS 17 para 50].

Interest cost and expected return on assets

Interest cost is based on the discount rate and present value of scheme liabilities at the beginning of the period, but should reflect changes in scheme liabilities during the period. [IAS 19 para 82].	Same. [FRS 17 para 53].
The expected return on assets is based on the average rate of return, including both income and changes in fair value, but net of scheme expenses and any tax payable by the plan itself, expected over the remaining life of the related obligation. [IAS 19 para 7].	Similar, but FRS 17 does not make reference to tax payable by the plan. [FRS 17 para 2].
Expected return is based on long-term expectations at the beginning of the period, but should reflect changes in the assets as a result of contributions paid in and benefits paid out. [IAS 19 para 106].	Same. [FRS 17 para 54].

Actuarial gains and losses

Under the 'corridor approach', a portion of actuarial gains and losses should be recognised in the profit and loss account if the net cumulative unrecognised actuarial gains and losses at the end of the previous reporting period exceed the greater of:	Actuarial gains and losses are recognised in the STRGL in the period in which they arise. [FRS 17 para 57].

- 10% of the present value of scheme liabilities; and

- 10% of the fair value of plan assets.

[IAS 19 para 92].

The portion to be recognised is at least the excess determined above divided by the expected average remaining working lives of employees participating in the scheme. Systematic methods that result in faster recognition are permissible. [IAS 19 para 93].

FRS 17 does not permit spreading of actuarial gains and losses.

If an entity adopts a policy of recognising actuarial gains and losses in the period in which they occur, it may recognise them outside profit or loss (in a 'statement of recognised income and expense'), providing it does so for:

This option in the amended IAS 19 is similar to the FRS 17 treatment.

(a) all of its defined benefit plans; and

(b) all of its actuarial gains and losses.

[IAS 19 paras 93A, 93B].

Balance sheet presentation

The pension asset/liability does not need to be presented separately on the face of the balance sheet, unless such presentation is relevant to an understanding of the employer's financial position. [IAS 1 paras 68, 69].

The pension asset/liability should be presented separately on the face of the balance sheet after all other net assets. [FRS 17 para 47].

Deferred tax assets and deferred tax liabilities should be presented as separate line items in the balance sheet. [IAS 1 para 68].

The pension asset/liability should be presented net of related deferred tax. [FRS 17 para 49].

Where an employer has more than one scheme, the total of any defined benefit assets and the total of any defined benefit liabilities should be shown separately on the face of the balance sheet, unless the employer:

Where an employer has more than one scheme, the total of any defined benefit assets and the total of any defined benefit liabilities should be shown separately on the face of the balance sheet. [FRS 17 para 47].

- has a legally enforceable right of set off; or

- intends either to settle the obligations on a net basis or to realise the surplus in one scheme and settle its obligation under the other scheme simultaneously.

[IAS 19 para 116].

Presentation in the performance statements

The net total of the following should be presented in profit or loss:

The following should be presented in the performance statements according to the rules described above:

- Current service cost.

- Past service cost.

- Settlements and curtailments.

- Interest cost.

- Expected return on assets.

- Actuarial gains and losses (as required by the entity's accounting policy).

- Current service cost.

- Past service cost.

- Settlements and curtailments.

- Interest cost.

- Expected return on assets.

- Actuarial gains and losses.

[FRS 17 para 50].

- The effect of the asset ceiling limit, unless it is recognised outside profit or loss in accordance the entity's policy

[IAS 19 para 61].

The standard does not specify whether an employer should present current service cost, interest cost and expected return on plan assets as components of a single line item on the face of the profit and loss account. [IAS 19 para 119].	Current service cost, past service cost, settlements and curtailments are recognised as operating items. [FRS 17 paras 51, 60]. The net of the interest cost and the expected return on assets should be presented as 'other finance costs/(income)' adjacent to interest. [FRS 17 para 56].
Net tax expense/(income) is presented on the face of the profit and loss account, unless it relates to transactions recognised in equity. [IAS 12 paras 58, 77].	Any tax relief on contributions payable is allocated first to the profit and loss account, unless it is clear that some other allocation is more appropriate. [FRS 17 para 71].

Disclosure

In December 2006, the ASB issued an amendment to FRS 17, replacing the disclosures required by FRS 17 with disclosures based on IAS 19. The amendment is effective for periods beginning on or after 6 April 2007. The summary below is based on the existing FRS 17 disclosures prior to the amendment.

The following disclosures are required by IAS 19, but not FRS 17:

- Accounting policy for recognising actuarial gains and losses. [IAS 19 para 120A(a)].

- An analysis of scheme liabilities into amounts arising from schemes that are wholly unfunded and amounts arising from schemes that are wholly or partly funded. [IAS 19 para 120A(d)].

- An analysis of the opening and closing scheme liabilities and scheme assets showing separately if applicable the movements in scheme assets and scheme liabilities. [IAS 19 para 120A(e)].

- Actuarial gains/losses and past service costs not yet recognised in the profit and loss account. [IAS 19 para 120A(f)].

- The principal actuarial assumptions used as at the balance sheet date. [IAS 19 para 120A(n)].

- The fair value of any asset recognised as a reimbursement right under paragraph 104A with a description of the link to the related obligation. [IAS 19 para 120A(f)].

- The actual and expected return and the expected rate of return on any asset recognised as a reimbursement right under IAS 19 paragraph 104A. [IAS 19 para 120A(g)(m)].

The following disclosures are required by FRS 17, but not IAS 19:

- The date of the most recent full actuarial valuation and a statement as to whether the actuary is an employee or officer of the employer. [FRS 17 para 76(b)].

- For closed schemes and those in which the age profile of the active membership is rising significantly, the fact that under the projected unit method the current service cost will increase as the members of the scheme approach retirement. [FRS 17 para 76(d)].

- The effects of changes in the demographic and financial assumptions underlying the present value of the scheme liabilities. [FRS 17 para 85].

- Expected rate of return assumed by class of asset. [FRS 17 para 80].

- The main financial assumptions at the beginning of the previous period. [FRS 17 para 91].

- The amount in reserves relating to the defined benefit asset/liability. [FRS 17 para 90].

- The effect of an increase of one percentage point and the effect of a decrease of one percentage point in the assumed medical cost trend rates on the net defined benefit cost and the defined benefit obligation. [IAS 19 para 120A(o)].

IAS 20 and SSAP 4 – Government grants

IAS 20, Government grants and assistance	SSAP 4, Accounting for government grants
Effective for accounting periods beginning on or after 1 January 1984.	*Effective for accounting periods beginning on or after 1 July 1990.*

Related pronouncements

SIC 10: Government assistance - No specific relation to operating activities	–

Overview

The requirements of IAS 20 are similar to those of SSAP 4. One difference in practice is that under IAS 20, grants that relate to recognised assets are presented in the balance sheet either as deferred income, or by deducting the grant from the cost of the asset. Although deduction from the cost of a fixed asset is possible in principle under SSAP 4, it is not permitted by UK company law for companies reporting under UK GAAP.

Convergence

The ASB is considering its plans for convergence with IFRS.

First-time adoption of IFRS

There are no specific rules in IFRS 1 in respect of IAS 20 and so the general rule of retrospective application will apply.

Summary of main points

Scope

IAS 20 applies to the accounting for, and disclosure of, government grants. It also applies to the disclosure of other forms of government assistance. [IAS 20 para 1].	No separate scope paragraph, however the general application as set out in the introduction (SSAP 4 paras 1 to 3) is consistent with IAS 20.
The standard states that it does not deal with certain situations, including:	No specific exclusions.

- Government assistance that takes the form of tax benefits.

- Government participation in the ownership of the entity.

- Government grants covered by IAS 41, 'Agriculture'. [IAS 20 para 2].

Definitions

IAS 20 provides the equivalent definitions to those in SSAP 4 for the terms 'government' and 'government grants', but also gives definitions for 'government assistance', 'grants related to assets' and 'grants related to income', 'forgivable loans' and 'fair value'.

Government refers to government, government agencies and similar bodies whether local, national or international. [IAS 20 para 3].	Same. [SSAP 4 para 21].
Government assistance is action by government designed to provide an economic benefit specific to an entity. It does not include benefits provided only indirectly, such as the provision of infrastructure in development areas or the imposition of trading constraints on competitors. [IAS 20 para 3].	Not specifically defined in SSAP 4.

Government grants are assistance by government in the form of transfers of resources to an entity in return for past or future compliance with certain conditions relating to the operating activities of the entity. They exclude those forms of government assistance which cannot reasonably have a value placed upon them and transactions with government which cannot be distinguished from the normal trading transactions of the enterprise. [IAS 20 para 3].

Same as IAS 20, except there is no clarification as to what types of government assistance would not constitute a government grant. [SSAP 4 para 22].

SIC 10 clarifies that government assistance to entities meets the definition of government grants, even if there are no conditions specifically relating to the operating activities of the entity other than the requirement to operate in certain regions or industry sectors. [SIC 10 para 3].

Not dealt with by SSAP 4.

Grants related to assets are government grants whose primary condition is that an entity qualifying for them should purchase, construct or otherwise acquire long-term assets. Further conditions may also be attached restricting the type or location of the assets or the periods during which they are to be acquired or held. [IAS 20 para 3].

Not specifically defined in SSAP 4, but similar applies.

Grants related to income are government grants other than those related to assets. [IAS 20 para 3].

Not specifically defined in SSAP 4, but similar applies.

Recognition

A government grant (including non-monetary grants at fair value) should not be recognised until there is reasonable assurance that the entity will comply with the conditions attaching to it and that the grant will be received. [IAS 20 para 7].

A government grant should not be recognised until the conditions for its receipt have been complied with and there is reasonable assurance that the grant will be received. [SSAP 4 para 24].

Government grants should be recognised as income over the periods necessary to match them with the related costs that they are intended to compensate, on a systematic basis. [IAS 20 para 12].

Similar. [SSAP 4 para 23].

A government grant that becomes receivable as compensation for expenses or losses already incurred or for immediate financial support (with no future related costs) should be recognised as income in the period in which it becomes receivable. [IAS 20 para 20].

Similar. [SSAP 4 para 23].

Not specifically stated in IAS 20, but similar applies.

Grants made to finance the general activities of an entity over a specific period or to compensate for a loss of current or future income should be recognised in the profit and loss account of the period in respect of which they are paid. [SSAP 4 para 23].

A government grant in the form of a transfer of a non-monetary asset is usually accounted for at fair value. [IAS 20 para 23]. IAS 20 also refers to the alternative of recording both asset and grant at a nominal amount, but it is generally considered preferable to treat monetary and non-monetary grants in the same way and to value all such grants at fair value.

Where a government grant takes the form of a transfer of non-monetary assets, the amount of the grant is the fair value of the assets transferred. [SSAP 4 para 16].

Once a government grant is recognised, any related contingency is treated in accordance with IAS 37. [IAS 20 para 11].

Similar. [SSAP 4 para 27]. SSAP 4 refers in places to SSAP 18, but this has now been superseded by FRS 12.

Presentation

Government grants relating to assets (including non-monetary grants at fair value) should be presented in the balance sheet either by setting up the grant as deferred income or by deducting the grant in arriving at the carrying amount of the asset. [IAS 20 para 24].

Similar. However the standard also says that in Counsel's opinion, the option to deduct government grants from the cost of fixed assets is not available to companies governed by the requirements of the Companies Act 1985. [SSAP 4 para 25].

Where government grants relating to assets are set up as deferred income, the grant is recognised as income on a systematic and rational basis over the useful economic life of the asset. [IAS 20 para 26].

Same. [SSAP 4 para 23].

Where government grants relating to assets are deducted from the carrying amount of the asset, the grant is recognised as income over the useful economic life of a depreciable asset by way of a reduced depreciation charge. [IAS 20 para 27].

Not relevant for companies under SSAP 4 (see above).

Not dealt with by IAS 20.

Tax-free grants that are available to the lessor against the purchase price of assets acquired for leasing should be spread over the period of the lease and dealt with by treating the grants as non-taxable income. [SSAP 4 para 26 , SSAP 21 (revised) para 41].

Grants related to income are sometimes presented as a credit in the income statement, either separately or under a general heading such as 'Other income'; alternatively, they are deducted in reporting the related expense. [IAS 20 para 29].

Not specifically referred to in SSAP 4. However, under UK company law, income and expenses cannot be offset. [CA85 4 Sch 5].

Repayment of grants

A government grant that becomes repayable should be accounted for as a revision to an accounting estimate (that is, in the current period as per IAS 8). [IAS 20 para 32].

Similar applies.

Repayment of a grant related to income should be applied first against any unamortised deferred credit set up in respect of the grant and then any excess recognised immediately as an expense. [IAS 20 para 32].

Same. [SSAP 4 para 27].

Repayment of a grant related to an asset should be recorded by increasing the carrying amount of the asset or reducing the deferred income balance by the amount repayable. The cumulative additional depreciation that would have been recognised to date as an expense in the absence of the grant should be recognised immediately as an expense. [IAS 20 para 32].	Same for deferred income, but the alternative of increasing the carrying amount of the asset is not relevant for companies under SSAP 4 (see above).

Disclosure

The accounting policy adopted for government grants, including the methods of presentation adopted in the financial statements. [IAS 20 para 39(a)].	Similar. [SSAP 4 para 28].
The nature and extent of government grants recognised in the financial statements and an indication of other forms of government assistance from which the entity has directly benefited. [IAS 20 para 39(b)].	Similar. [SSAP 4 para 28].
Unfulfilled conditions and other contingencies attaching to government assistance that has been recognised. [IAS 20 para 39(c)].	Similar, but there is no specific requirement to disclose unfulfilled conditions. [SSAP 4 para 29].

IAS 21 and SSAP 20 – Foreign currency

IAS 21, The effects of changes in foreign exchange rates	SSAP 20, Foreign currency translation
Effective for accounting periods beginning on or after 1 January 1995.	*Effective for accounting periods beginning on or after 1 April 1983.*
The revised standard (2003) is effective for annual periods beginning on or after 1 January 2005.	
Amendments in respect of net investment in a foreign operation are effective for annual periods beginning on or after 1 January 2006.	

Related pronouncements

IAS 29, Financial reporting in hyperinflationary economies.	UITF 9, Accounting for operations in hyper-inflationary economies.
IFRIC 7, Applying the restatement approach under IAS 29.	
IAS 39, Financial instruments: Recognition and measurement.	UITF 19, Tax on gains and losses on foreign currency borrowings that hedge an investment in a foreign enterprise.
SIC 7, Introduction of the euro.	UITF 21, Accounting issues arising from the proposed introduction of the euro.

Overview

In this summary, references to IAS 21 relate to the revised standard issued in December 2003. IAS 21's definition of functional currency is similar to SSAP 20's 'local currency', however, applying IAS 21 's detailed guidance on how to determine the functional currency of subsidiaries may lead to the selection of a functional currency that may be different from the local currency determined under UK GAAP. IAS 21 requires (like SSAP 20) that entities should measure their results in their functional currency. However, IAS 21 permits entities to present their financial statements in any currency, not necessarily their functional currency, and calls this the 'presentation' currency.

On initial recognition, both IAS 21 and SSAP 20 require transactions denominated in a foreign currency to be translated at the exchange rate in operation on the date of the transaction. However, SSAP 20 permits the use of the exchange rate specified in a related or matching forward contract. IAS 21 does not permit this. Monetary assets and liabilities denominated in a foreign currency are retranslated at the closing (period-end) rate.

IAS 21 requires the income and expense items of foreign entities, with a different functional currency to the group's presentation currency, to be translated at the transaction rate and suggests that the average rate may be a good approximation of that rate. IAS 21 does not permit the choice, allowed under SSAP 20, of using the closing rate for the profit and loss account when applying the closing rate/net investment method of translation.

IAS 21 contains specific rules requiring goodwill and fair value adjustments arising on the acquisition of a foreign operation to be treated as assets and liabilities of the foreign operation and translated at the closing rate. SSAP 20 does not specifically address this point, although current practice since publication of FRS 11 has increasingly been to regard goodwill as a currency asset in line with the requirements contained in IAS 21.

IAS 21 requires exchange differences on a monetary item forming part of a reporting entity's net investment in a foreign operation to be recognised in a separate component of equity in the reporting entity's consolidated financial statements. However, in the reporting entity's separate financial statements the differences should be recognised in profit or loss. SSAP 20 requires such exchange differences to be taken to reserves in the reporting entity's consolidated financial statements and, where recognised, in its separate financial statements.

Under IAS 21, net exchange differences classified as equity must be separately tracked and the cumulative amounts disclosed. On disposal of a foreign entity, the appropriate amount of cumulative translation difference relating to the entity is included in the gain or loss on sale in the income statement. SSAP 20 does not permit such 'recycling' of exchange gains and losses.

IAS 21 does not contain the requirements of SSAP 20 relating to the treatment of hedges of net investments in foreign operations. These matters are covered by IAS 39.

Under IAS 21, the financial statements of an entity whose functional currency is the currency of a hyper-inflationary economy must be restated under IAS 29 prior to translation into a different presentation currency. IAS 29 requires such an entity's results to be restated in terms of the measuring unit current at the balance sheet date. The alternative method of using a relatively stable currency as the functional currency of the relevant hyperinflationary economy, specified in UITF 9, is not permitted under IFRS.

IAS 21 has more extensive disclosure requirements than SSAP 20.

Convergence

In December 2004, the ASB issued FRS 23 (IAS 21), 'The effects of changes in foreign exchange rates', and FRS 24 (IAS 29), 'Financial reporting in hyper-inflationary economies', which derive from IAS 21 and IAS 29. In a change from the proposals in the preceding exposure draft (FRED 24), FRS 23 implements the requirement in IAS 21 that certain gains and losses should be recycled. FRS 23 and FRS 24's effective date is determined by reference to the application of FRS 26, 'Financial instruments: Measurement'.

First-time adoption of IFRS

IFRS 1 includes an exemption allowing the cumulative translation difference on retranslation of subsidiaries' net assets to be set to zero (for all subsidiaries) at the date of transition to IFRS so that it does not have to be separately disclosed and recycled in the income statement on disposal of the subsidiaries. This must, however, be done for translation differences arising from the date of transition. Also, the IAS 21 rules requiring retranslation of goodwill and fair value adjustments do not have to be applied retrospectively to business combinations that occurred before the date of transition to IFRS.

Summary of main points

Functional currency

Each individual entity, whether a stand-alone entity, an entity with foreign operations or a foreign operation, should determine its functional currency. This is defined as the currency of the primary economic environment in which the entity operates. IAS 21 gives some guidance on how to determine an entity's functional currency. Once the functional currency is determined it is changed only if there is a change in the underlying transactions, events or conditions relevant to it. [IAS 21 paras 9 to 13].

SSAP 20 uses the term 'local currency', which is defined as the currency of the primary economic environment in which the entity operates and generates net cash flows. This is similar to IAS 21's definition of functional currency, although SSAP 20 does not provide any further guidance on how to determine an entity's local/functional currency. [SSAP 20 para 39]. As a result, applying IAS 21's detailed guidance on how to determine the functional currency of subsidiaries may lead to the selection of a functional currency that may be different from the local currency determined under UK GAAP. SSAP 20 does not contain the same specific rules as IAS 21 on when local currency can be changed but IAS 21's explicit guidance is implicit in SSAP 20 and FRS 18, 'Accounting policies'.

Initial recognition

On initial recognition, foreign currency transactions should be recorded in the entity's functional currency using the spot rate at the date of the transaction. IAS 21 acknowledges that it may be more practical to use an average rate for a week or month rather than the actual spot rate on each transaction, however, it does state that where exchange rates fluctuate significantly the use of an average rate for a period would be inappropriate. [IAS 21 paras 21, 22].

Each asset, liability, revenue or cost arising from a foreign currency transaction should be translated into the local currency at the exchange rate at the date of the transaction (but see below). If the rates do not fluctuate significantly, an average rate for a period may be used as an approximation. [SSAP 20 para 46].

IAS 21 does not permit the use of contracted rates, or the rates in matching forward contracts, to translate foreign currency transactions. Many foreign currency derivative instruments are scoped out of IAS 21 and included in IAS 39, which also includes detailed rules for hedging foreign currency items.

SSAP 20 requires that where a transaction is to be settled at a contracted rate, that rate should be used. Where a trading transaction is covered by a related or matching forward contract, the rate of exchange specified in that contract may be used. [SSAP 20 para 46].

Reporting at subsequent dates

At each balance sheet date, subject to the hedging rules in IAS 39:

- Foreign currency monetary items should be translated using the closing rate. [IAS 21 para 23(a)].

- IAS 21 does not permit the use of contracted rates, or the rates in matching forward contracts, to translate foreign currency monetary items. Hedge accounting is dealt with in IAS 39.

- Generally, exchange differences arising on settlement of *monetary* foreign currency transactions and on translation of an entity's monetary items should be recognised as profit or loss in the period in which they arise (but see net investment rules below). [IAS 21 para 28].

- IAS 21 does not contain similar guidance to SSAP 20 in situations where there are doubts as to the convertibility of the currency of a long-term monetary item.

- Non-monetary items denominated in a foreign currency and measured at historical cost should be translated using the spot rate at the date of the transaction. [IAS 21 para 23(b)].

- Non-monetary items denominated in a foreign currency and measured at fair value should be translated using the exchange rates at the date when the value was determined. [IAS 21 para 23(c)].

At each balance sheet date:

- Foreign currency monetary assets and liabilities should be translated at the closing rate (but see below). [SSAP 20 para 48].

- Where a monetary item is to be settled at a contracted rate that rate should be used. Where there are related forward contracts in respect of trading transactions, the rates of exchange specified in those contracts may be used. [SSAP 20 para 48].

- Exchange gains or losses on settled transactions and on unsettled monetary items should normally be reported as part of the profit or loss for the year (but see net investment rules below). [SSAP 20 paras 49, 50].

- In exceptional situations, if an entity has doubts as to the convertibility of the currency of a long-term monetary item then it should restrict the amount of any gain recognised in the profit and loss account. [SSAP 20 para 50].

- Where a non-monetary item has been translated at the rate ruling when it was originally recorded, no subsequent translation of the asset is normally required (but see net investment rules below). [SSAP 20 para 47].

- SSAP 20 does not contain these specific requirements, but a similar treatment is used in practice.

- Any exchange component of gains or losses arising on non-monetary items should be recognised in equity or in the profit or loss depending on where the underlying gain or loss on the non-monetary item is recognised. [IAS 21 para 30].

- SSAP 20 does not contain these specific requirements, but a similar treatment is used in practice.

The associated tax effects of gains and losses on foreign currency transactions and translation should be accounted for in accordance with IAS 12, 'Income taxes'. [IAS 21 para 50].

The associated tax effects of gains and losses on foreign currency transactions and translation are accounted for in accordance with FRS 19, 'Deferred tax' and UITF 19.

Where there is a change in the functional currency of an entity, the translation procedures applicable to the new functional currency should be applied prospectively from the date of change. All items should be translated into the new functional currency using the exchange rate at the date of change. The resulting translated amounts for non-monetary items should be treated as their historical cost. Exchange differences arising on the translation of a foreign operation previously recognised in equity, will remain deferred in equity upon a change in functional currency. These exchange differences, deferred in equity, will not be recognised in profit or loss until the operation is sold. [IAS 21 paras 35 to 37].

This is not dealt with in SSAP 20, but, in practice, a change in local/functional currency is accounted for prospectively from the date of change. One difference from IAS 21 is that exchange differences arising on the translation of a foreign operation are not recycled on disposal under UK GAAP (see below).

Presentation currency

IAS 21 permits entities to present their financial statements in any currency, not necessarily their functional currency, and calls this the 'presentation' currency. [IAS 21 para 38]. If the presentation currency differs from the entity's functional currency, (an example would be where a group contains individual entities with different functional currencies and the results and financial position of each entity need to be expressed in a common currency), then the entity's financial statements need to be translated into the presentation currency as follows:

SSAP 20 does not include the concept of the use of a presentation currency. Under SSAP 20, financial statements are prepared in the entity's 'local' currency. However, when preparing consolidated financial statements using the closing rate/net investment method of translating a foreign entity's financial statements, the translation process is similar to the IAS 21 rules for translation into a presentation currency, as follows:

- Assets and liabilities for each balance sheet (that is, including comparatives) should be translated at the closing rate at the balance sheet date. [IAS 21 para 39(a)].

- A foreign entity's balance sheet should be translated into the group's reporting currency using the exchange rate ruling at the balance sheet date. [SSAP 20 para 16].

- Income and expenses for each income statement (that is, including comparatives) should be translated at exchange rates at the dates of the transactions (or an average rate, if appropriate). [IAS 21 paras 39(b), 40].

- A foreign entity's profit and loss account should be translated at the closing rate or at an average rate for the period, provided that the method selected is applied consistently from period to period. [SSAP 20 paras 54, 17].

- All resulting exchange differences should be recognised as a separate component of equity. [IAS 21 para 39(c)]. However, exchange differences arising on translation of intra-group monetary assets or liabilities should continue to be recognised as profit or loss in the reporting entity's consolidated financial statements providing they do not form part of an entity's net investment in a foreign operation.

- All resulting exchange differences should be recorded as a movement on reserves and included in STRGL. [SSAP 20 para 54]. However, exchange differences on translation of intra-group trading balances should continue to be recognised in the profit or loss account as they do not form part of an entity's net investment in the foreign entity.

Any goodwill and any fair value adjustments to the carrying amount of assets or liabilities arising on acquiring a foreign operation should be treated as the foreign operation's assets and liabilities and translated at the closing rate in accordance with the method for translation into an entity's presentation currency. [IAS 21 para 47].

SSAP 20 does not specifically address this point, although current practice since publication of FRS 11 has, increasingly, been to regard goodwill as a currency asset, similar to the requirements in IAS 21.

On disposal of a foreign operation the amount of any exchange differences relating to that operation that have been deferred in the separate component of equity relating to that foreign operation should be recognised in profit or loss when the gain or loss on disposal is recognised. [IAS 21 para 48].

SSAP 20 does not have a similar requirement. Exchange differences would not be recycled from the STRGL to the profit and loss account under FRS 3.

Temporal method

IAS 21 does not include the concept of the 'temporal method' for consolidated financial statements. Instead, each entity has to determine its functional currency. A foreign entity' whose trade is dependent on the economic environment of the investing company's currency will have the same functional currency as the investing entity.

Where a foreign entity's trade is more dependent on the economic environment of the investing company's currency than that of its own reporting currency, the temporal method should be used. Under the temporal method, the foreign entity's financial statements are included in the consolidated financial statements as if all its transactions had been entered into by the investing company itself. [SSAP 20 paras 55, 22].

Net investment in a foreign operation

Where an exchange difference arises on a monetary item forming part of a reporting entity's net investment in a foreign operation, IAS 21 requires that the gains or losses should be recognised initially in a separate component of equity in the consolidated financial statements and recognised in profit or loss on disposal of the net investment. [IAS 21 para 32].

Exchange differences on long-term intra-group loans that are regarded as part of the effective equity stake are dealt with as adjustments to reserves. [SSAP 20 para 20]. However, the exchange differences are not recycled to the profit and loss account on disposal of the investment.

Exchange differences arising on a monetary item that forms part of a reporting entity's net investment in a foreign operation should be recognised in profit or loss in the separate financial statements of the reporting entity or the individual financial statements of the foreign operation, as appropriate. [IAS 21 para 32].

Long-term intra-group loans that are regarded as part of the effective equity stake would not be retranslated in the parent's separate financial statements. However, if the long-term loan is financed by foreign borrowings, the loan would be retranslated and exchange differences taken to reserves to offset exchange differences on the borrowings (see below).

Equity investments financed by foreign borrowings

In consolidated financial statements, hedges of a net investment in a foreign operation are accounted for by translating the hedging instrument at the closing rate with the gain or loss on the effective hedge being taken to equity to match the gain or loss on the net assets. The ineffective portion is recognised in profit or loss. The gain or loss that has been recognised in equity is transferred to profit or loss on disposal of the foreign operation. [IAS 39 para 102]. There are onerous hedging criteria that must be met in order to achieve net investment hedge accounting.

Under IFRS, net investment hedging is only available in consolidated financial statements. It may be possible to achieve hedge accounting in the parent's separate financial statement if the relationship can be defined as a fair value hedge of foreign currency risk attributable to the equity investment. There are onerous hedging criteria that must be met in order to achieve fair value hedge accounting. However, exchange differences arising on the borrowing would be offset in profit or loss (and not reserves) by exchange differences arising on the related equity investment.

In consolidated financial statements, where foreign currency borrowings have been used to finance, or provide a hedge against, group equity investments in foreign entities, exchange gains or losses on the borrowings may, subject to certain conditions, be offset as reserve movements against exchange differences arising on the retranslation of the net investments. [SSAP 20 para 57]. The exchange differences are not recycled to the profit and loss account on disposal of the investment.

In a company's individual financial statements, where a company has used foreign currency borrowings to finance, or provide a hedge against, its foreign equity investments and certain conditions are met, the equity investments may be treated as foreign currency items and the carrying amounts retranslated at closing rates. Where investments are treated this way, any exchange differences arising should be taken to reserves and the exchange gains or losses on the foreign currency borrowings (which would otherwise have been taken to profit and loss account) should be offset against these, also as a reserve movement. [SSAP 20 para 51].

Hyper-inflationary economies

The financial statements of an entity whose functional currency is the currency of a hyper-inflationary economy must be restated under IAS 29 prior to translation into a different presentation currency. IAS 29 requires such an entity's results to be restated in terms of the measuring unit current at the balance sheet date. The alternative method specified under UK GAAP, of using a relatively stable currency as the functional currency of the relevant hyperinflationary economy, is not permitted under IFRS.

The financial statements of a foreign entity that operates in a country with a hyper-inflationary economy must be adjusted prior to consolidation, either by adjusting its local currency financial statements to reflect current price levels before the translation process is undertaken or by using a relatively stable currency as the functional currency. [UITF 9 para 6].

Disclosures

Some of the key disclosures required by IAS 21 include:

- The amount of exchange differences included in profit or loss for the period, except for those arising on financial instruments measured at fair value through profit or loss in accordance with IAS 39. [IAS 21 para 52(a)].

- If the presentation currency differs from the functional currency, that fact and the reason for using a different presentation currency. [IAS 21 para 53].

- Any changes in functional currency giving reasons for the change. [IAS 21 para 54].

The key disclosures under UK GAAP are:

- The net amount of exchange gains and losses on foreign currency borrowings less deposits, identifying separately (i) the amount offset in reserves and (ii) the net amount in the profit and loss account. In addition, disclosure is required of the net movement on reserves arising from exchange differences. [SSAP 20 para 60].

- SSAP 20 is silent on the use of a reporting currency/presentation currency that differs from the local/functional currency.

- No equivalent SSAP 20 requirement.

IAS 23 and FRS 15 – Borrowing costs

IAS 23, Borrowing costs	FRS 15, Tangible fixed assets (part)
Effective for accounting periods beginning on or after 1 January 1995.	*Effective for accounting periods ending on or after 23 March 2000.*

Related pronouncements

–	–

Overview

A policy of capitalisation is allowed under both IAS 23 and FRS 15 for borrowing costs that are directly attributable to the acquisition, construction or production of a qualifying asset. A qualifying asset is an asset that necessarily takes a substantial period of time to get ready for its intended use or sale.

Where specific borrowings are taken out to finance an asset, there are differences in the determination of the interest that can be capitalised. Under IAS 23, the amount of interest eligible for capitalisation is the actual costs incurred on the borrowings less any interest earned on the temporary reinvestment of funds not used. Under FRS 15, the amount of interest eligible for capitalisation is limited to costs incurred on borrowings in respect of expenditures to date.

Convergence

In May 2002, the ASB issued FRED 29 which proposes that IAS 23 should be implemented in the UK, replacing the FRS 15 rules on capitalisation of borrowing costs.

In May 2006, the IASB published an exposure draft proposing to require an entity to capitalise borrowing costs directly attributable to the acquisition, construction or production of a qualifying asset as part of the cost of that asset. The option of immediately expensing those borrowing costs would be removed.

The ASB is considering its plans for convergence with IFRS.

First-time adoption of IFRS

There are no specific rules in IFRS 1 in respect of IAS 23 and so the general rule of retrospective application will apply. An entity adopting IFRS will adopt a policy of either capitalising borrowing costs or not and should apply this retrospectively. However, in situations where a deemed cost has been established for an asset, and used at the date of transition (see IAS 16 summary), then any borrowing costs incurred prior to the asset's measurement should be included in the asset's deemed cost on transition to IFRS.

Summary of main points

Scope

Applies to qualifying assets, whether current assets (that is, inventories) or fixed assets (including tangible and intangible fixed assets). [IAS 23 para 6].	FRS 15 applies to tangible fixed assets. SSAP 9 applies to inventories. In addition, the rules in the Act apply to fixed and current assets. [CA85 4 Sch 26(3)].

Definitions

A qualifying asset is an asset that necessarily takes a substantial period of time to get ready for its intended use or sale. [IAS 23 para 4].	No similar definition, although the Act requires a 'period of production', so the effect is the same in practice. [CA85 4 Sch 26(3)(b)].
Borrowing costs are interest and other costs incurred by an entity in connection with the borrowing of funds. [IAS 23 para 4].	FRS 15 defines finance costs as the difference between the net proceeds of an instrument and the total amount of payments that the issuer may be required to make in respect of that instrument. [FRS 15 para 2]. In practice there are unlikely to be significant differences.

Borrowing costs include:

• Interest on borrowings. [IAS 23 para 5(a)].	Same. [FRS 15 para 2].
• Amortisation of discounts and premiums on borrowings. [IAS 23 para 5(b)].	Same. [FRS 15 para 2].
• Amortisation of issue costs. [IAS 23 para 5(c)].	Same. [FRS 15 para 2].
• Finance lease costs. [IAS 23 para 5(d)].	Same. Finance lease costs are determined in accordance with SSAP 21 and are capitalised where applicable.
• Exchange differences on foreign currency borrowings to the extent that they are regarded as an adjustment to interest costs. [IAS 23 para 5(e)].	• Not mentioned in FRS 15, but under SSAP 20, exchange differences that relate to borrowings are included in interest payable.

Recognition

Benchmark treatment

Borrowing costs should be recognised as an expense in the period in which they are incurred. [IAS 23 para 7].

Similarly, UK GAAP permits a choice in respect of the policy of capitalisation of interest. Expensing borrowing costs as incurred is one option. [FRS 15 paras 19 and 20].

Allowed alternative treatment

Borrowing costs that are directly attributable to the acquisition, construction or production of a qualifying asset should be capitalised as part of the cost of that asset. [IAS 23 para 11].

FRS 15 is similar. [FRS 15 para 9]. Also, the Act permits the capitalisation of interest on capital borrowed to finance the production of an asset to the extent that it accrues in respect of the period of production. [CA85 4 Sch 26(3)(b)].

If such a policy is adopted it should be applied consistently to all qualifying assets. [IAS 8 para 13].

FRS 15 requires a policy of capitalisation to be adopted consistently across all tangible fixed assets. [FRS 15 para 20].

SSAP 9 is silent in respect of capitalisation of interest on stock, other than a reference in the appendix that it is not normally appropriate to include interest in the cost of long-term contracts, but it may be appropriate where sums are borrowed to finance specific contracts.

Not mentioned in IAS 23.

Finance costs are capitalised on a gross basis, that is, before the deduction of any tax relief to which they give rise. [FRS 15 para 21].

Borrowing costs eligible for capitalisation

Where funds are borrowed specifically for the purpose of obtaining a qualifying asset, the amount of borrowing costs eligible for capitalisation on that asset should be the actual borrowing costs incurred on that borrowing during the period less any investment income on the temporary investment of those borrowings (that is, the net interest on total specific borrowings is capitalised). [IAS 23 para 15].

FRS 15 requires the capitalisation of interest incurred on specific borrowings based on the actual expenditures incurred to date on the asset (that is, gross interest payable is capitalised, but interest on 'excess' (or unspent) borrowings is ignored). [FRS 15 para 22].

General borrowings should be capitalised by applying a capitalisation rate to the expenditures on those assets funded by general borrowings. [IAS 23 para 17].

Same. [FRS 15 para 23].

The capitalisation rate is the weighted average of borrowing costs applicable to non-specific borrowings. [IAS 23 para 17].	Same. [FRS 15 para 23].
The amount of borrowing costs capitalised in a period should not exceed the borrowing costs incurred during that period. [IAS 23 para 17].	Same. [FRS 15 para 19].

Capitalisation period

Capitalisation of borrowing costs should commence when: • expenditures for the asset are being incurred; • borrowing costs are being incurred; and • activities that are necessary to prepare the asset for its intended use or sale are in progress. [IAS 23 para 20].	Same. [FRS 15 para 25].
Capitalisation should be suspended during extended periods in which active development is interrupted. [IAS 23 para 23].	Same. [FRS 15 para 27].
Capitalisation should cease when substantially all the activities necessary to prepare the asset for its intended use or sale are complete. . [IAS 23 para 25].	Same. [FRS 15 para 29].
When construction is completed in parts and each part is capable of being used while construction continues on other parts, capitalisation of borrowing costs should cease when substantially all the activities necessary to complete each part are completed. [IAS 23 para 27].	Similar. FRS 15 is clearer in that it refers to the finance costs 'relating to a part' should cease when substantially all the activities that are necessary to get that part ready for use are completed. [FRS 15 para 29].

Disclosure

Disclose the accounting policy adopted for borrowing costs. [IAS 23 para 29(a)].	Same under UK GAAP. [FRS 15 para 31(a) and CA85 4 Sch 26(3)].
Where a policy of capitalisation is adopted, disclose:	
• Amount of borrowing costs capitalised during the period. [IAS 23 para 29(b)].	Same. [FRS 15 para 31(c)].
• The capitalisation rate used to determine the amount of borrowing costs eligible for capitalisation. [IAS 23 para 29(c)].	Same. [FRS w15 para 31(e)].
No similar requirement.	The aggregate amount of interest included in the cost of tangible fixed assets [FRS 15 para 31(b)] and other assets [CA85 4 Sch 26(3)].
No similar requirement in IAS 23. IAS 1 requires disclosure of 'finance costs' on the face of the income statement. [IAS 1 para 81].	The amount of finance costs recognised in the profit and loss account during the period. [FRS 15 para 31(d)].

IAS 24 and FRS 8 – Related party disclosures

IAS 24, Related party disclosures	FRS 8, Related party disclosures
Effective for accounting periods beginning on or after 1 January 2005.	*Effective for accounting periods beginning on or after 23 December 1995.*

Related pronouncements

For UK companies, Schedule 6 and Schedule 7A to the Companies Act 1985.	Schedule 6 and Schedule 7A to the Companies Act 1985.

Overview

In this summary, references to IAS 24 relate to the revised standard issued in December 2003 and consequential amendments in subsequent standards. IAS 24 contains similar requirements and definitions to FRS 8. However, IAS 24 does not include most of the exemptions available under FRS 8.

IAS 24 does not exempt subsidiaries from disclosing related party transactions. Under FRS 8, there is no requirement to disclose transactions with other group entities (or other related party investees) in the financial statements of 90 per cent (or more) owned subsidiaries, provided the parent's consolidated financial statements in which those subsidiaries are included are publicly available.

Also, IAS 24 requires disclosure of related party transactions in the separate financial statements of parent entities. Under FRS 8, there is an exemption when the parent's own financial statements are presented with its consolidated financial statements.

IAS 24 requires the disclosure of key management compensation in aggregate, split into various categories. All directors are regarded as key management, but the definition of key management is not confined to directors. Senior employees may also be regarded as key management for related party disclosure purposes if they have authority and responsibility for planning, directing and controlling the entity's activities. FRS 8 excludes management compensation from its scope. The structure of the disclosures required by IAS 24 differs from that required for directors' remuneration by the Companies Act 1985, so even where the key management of a company consists solely of its directors, separate analyses of their remuneration is usually required to satisfy each requirement.

IAS 24 does not include the exemption in FRS 8 whereby the related party disclosure rules do not apply if this conflicts with the reporting entity's duties of confidentiality arising by the operation of the law.

There is no specific requirement in IAS 24 to disclose the name of the related party (other than the controlling and ultimate parties). However, this disclosure may be necessary in order to meet the requirement to disclose the information necessary for an understanding of the potential effect of the related party relationship on the financial statements

The specific guidance in FRS 8 on determining whether a related party transaction is material for disclosure purposes and particularly the specification that a related party transaction is material if regarded as material for individual related parties is not included in IAS 24. IAS 24 gives no guidance on the materiality of related party transactions requiring disclosure, but general guidance on materiality in respect of disclosures is included in IAS 1.

Convergence

In May 2002, the ASB issued FRED 25 proposing that FRS 8 should be replaced by the then proposed revisions to IAS 24. However, a new UK standard has not yet been issued and this now forms part of the wider debate on convergence with IFRS.

First-time adoption of IFRS

There are no specific rules in IFRS 1 in respect of IAS 24 and so the general rule of retrospective application will apply.

Summary of main points

Scope

Applies to the financial statements of each entity. [IAS 24 para 1].	Applies to all financial statements intended to give a true and fair view. [FRS 8 para 3].
No similar confidentiality exemption.	Related party disclosure rules do not apply if this conflicts with the reporting entity's duties of confidentiality arising by the operation of the law (but this does not include the effects of terms stipulated in a contract). [FRS 8 para 16].
IAS 24 does not address materiality in the context of the disclosure requirements. IAS 1 includes guidance on materiality.	Applies to all material related party transactions. [FRS 8 para 6]. FRS 8 defines 'materiality' in paragraph 20 – it is judged in relation to both the reporting entity and an individual related party. [FRS 8 para 20].

Related parties

A party is related to an entity if:	The definition of related parties is wider and includes common influence. Two or more parties are related when at any time during the financial period:
a) The party, directly or indirectly:	
iii. Controls, is controlled by, or is under common control with, the entity (this includes parents, subsidiaries and fellow subsidiaries).	• One party has direct or indirect control of the other; or the parties are under common control from the same source. This includes parent undertakings, subsidiaries and fellow subsidiaries. [FRS 8 paras 2.5(a), 2.5(b)(i)].
iii. Has an interest in the entity that gives it significant influence over the entity.	• One party has influence over the financial and operating policies of the other to inhibit the other from pursuing its separate interests. This includes the investor in respect of which the reporting entity is an associate and persons controlling over 20 per cent of voting rights (presumed rather than deemed to be a related party). [FRS 8 paras 2.5(a), 2.5(b)(iii), 2.5(c)(ii)].
iii. Has joint control over the entity.	It also includes the venturer in respect of which the reporting entity is a joint venture. [FRS 8 para 2.5(b)(iii)].
	• the parties are subject to common influence in entering into a transaction to the extent that one party has subordinated its own interests. [FRS 8 para 2.5(a)].
b) The party is an associate of the entity (see IAS 28, Investments in associates').	Associates are deemed to be related parties. [FRS 8 para 2.5(b)(ii), (iii)].
c) The party is a joint venture in which the entity is a venturer (see IAS 31, 'Interests in joint ventures').	Joint ventures and the venturer in respect of which the reporting entity is a joint venture. [FRS 8 para 2.5(b)(ii), (iii)].

d) The party is a member of key management of the entity or its parent. Key management includes executive and non-executive directors.	Directors of the entity and of its parents are deemed to be related parties. [FRS 8 paras 2.5(b)(iv)]. Key management are presumed (rather than deemed) to be a related party. [FRS 8 para 2.5(c)(i)].
e) The party is a close family member of an individual related to an entity under categories (a) or (d).	Close family of directors or individuals with a controlling interest. [FRS 8 para 2.5(d)].
f) The party is an entity that is controlled, jointly controlled or significantly influenced by an individual referred to in categories (d) or (e).	Other parties such as companies, partnerships, trusts connected to directors or individuals with a controlling interest. [FRS 8 para 2.5(d)].
g) The party is a post-employment benefit plan for the benefit of employees of the entity, or of any entity that is a related party of the entity.	Pension funds for the benefit of employees of the reporting entity (or of any entity that is a related party of the reporting entity) are a related party. [FRS 8 para 2.5(b)(v)].

[IAS 24 para 9].

IAS 24 does not deal with persons acting in concert. If they were, however, there would probably be a requirement to give disclosure, because IAS 24 does not specifically limit disclosure to situations where the controlling party is a single individual or entity.	Persons acting in concert so as to control or influence the reporting entity are presumed (rather than deemed) to be a related party. [FRS 8 para 2.5(c)(iii)].
Not included in IAS 24.	An entity managing or managed by the reporting entity under a management contract is presumed (rather than deemed) to be a related party. [FRS 8 para 2.5(c)(iv)].
If at any time during the reporting period, two parties were related for the purposes of IAS 24, the standard applies and the reporting entity should report any transactions with the other party for the period when the two parties were related.	Disclosure more extensive. The definition of related parties captures a relationship that exists at any time during the financial year. Therefore, even though a relationship may cease during the year, transactions between the parties throughout the year are disclosable if they are material.
Control is the power to govern the financial and operating policies of an entity so as to obtain benefits from its activities. [IAS 24 para 9].	*Control* is the ability to direct the financial and operating policies with a view to gaining economic benefits. [FRS 8 para 2.2].
Significant influence is the power to participate in the financial and operating policy decisions of an entity (but not control). Significant influence may be gained by share ownership, statute or agreement. [IAS 24 para 9].	There is no definition of *influence* in the standard. It envisages influence that inhibits or causes subordination of interests, depending on the context (see the definition of related parties in FRS 8 paragraph 2.5(a)).
Close members of the family of an individual are those who may be expected to influence, or be influenced by, that individual in their dealings with the entity. [IAS 24 para 9]. This is interpreted to include members of the same household.	Close members of the family of an individual are those family members, or members of the same household, who may be expected to influence, or be influenced by, that person in their dealings with the reporting entity. [FRS 8 para 2.1].
The following are not necessarily related parties:	The following are not necessarily related parties:
• Two entities simply because they have a director or key manager in common. [IAS 24 para 11(a)].	• Two companies with a director in common and common influence relationships – unless this leads to subordination of interests in a transaction. [FRS 8 para 14(a)-(c)].

- Two venturers simply because they share joint control over a joint venture. [IAS 24 para 11(b)].

- Providers of finance, trade unions, public utilities, and government bodies, simply by virtue of their normal dealings with the entity. [IAS 24 para 11(c)].

- A customer, supplier, franchisor, distributor or general agent with whom an entity transacts a significant volume of business, merely by virtue of the resulting economic dependence. [IAS 24 para 11(d)].

- Not specified by FRS 8, but the same applies.

- Providers of finance in course of business, utility companies and government bodies, simply as a result of their role in that capacity. [FRS 8 para 4(a)-(c)].

- A customer, supplier, franchisor, distributor or general agent with whom the entity transacts a significant volume of business, simply as a result of their role in that capacity. [FRS 8 para 4(d)].

Exemptions

- No disclosure of transactions is required in consolidated financial statements in respect of intra-group transactions as these are eliminated in those financial statements. [IAS 24 para 4].

- There is no exemption for the parent's own financial statements. IAS 24 requires disclosure of related party transactions and balances in the separate financial statements of a parent, venturer or investor presented in accordance with IAS 27, 'Consolidated and separate financial statements'. [IAS 24 para 3].

- There is no exemption for a subsidiary's financial statements. IAS 24 requires related party transactions and balances with other group entities to be disclosed in an entity's financial statements. [IAS 24 para 4].

No similar exemption.

No similar exemption.

- No disclosure is required in consolidated financial statements of any transactions or balances between group entities that have been eliminated on consolidation. [FRS 8 para 3(a)].

- No disclosure is required in a parent's own financial statements when these are presented with its consolidated financial statements. [FRS 8 para 3(b)].

- No disclosure is required in financial statements of 90 per cent subsidiaries if these are included in consolidated financial statements which are publicly available, of transactions with group entities and investees qualifying as related parties. [FRS 8 para 3(c)]. A statement is required that this exemption has been taken. [FRS 8 para 3].

- No disclosure is required of pension contributions paid to a pension fund. [FRS 8 para 3(d)].

- No disclosure is required of emoluments for services as an employee of the reporting entity. [FRS 8 para 3(e)].

There may be circumstances, however, where, in order to give a true and fair view, it is necessary to give certain disclosures that would otherwise be exempt from disclosure under FRS 8.

Related party transactions

A *related party transaction* is the transfer of resources, services or obligations between related parties, regardless of whether a price is charged. [IAS 24 para 9].

Examples are purchases or sales, rendering or receiving services, leases, transfer of research and development, licence agreements, finance arrangements, settlement of liabilities and provision of guarantees and collateral. [IAS 24 para 20].

A *related party transaction* is the transfer of assets or liabilities or the performance of services by, to or for a related party irrespective of whether a price is charged. [FRS 8 para 2.6].

FRS 8 has a similar list. [FRS 8 para 19]. FRS 8 also specifies that agency arrangements and management contracts are related party transactions.

Disclosure

Control

Irrespective of the existence of transactions, must disclose:

- Name of the entity's parent.

- Name of ultimate controlling party, if different.

- Name of the next most senior parent that produces financial statements available for public use, if neither the entity's parent nor the ultimate controlling party does so.
[IAS 24 para 12].

Irrespective of the existence of transactions, must disclose:

- Name of ultimate controlling party, if different.

- Name of ultimate controlling party if different.

- Not required by FRS 8, but would be required under Schedule 5 to the Companies Act 1985 [FRS 8 para 5].

Transactions

The aggregate of key management compensation should be disclosed, showing the split between: short-term employee benefits, post-employment benefits, other long-term benefits, termination benefits and share-based payment. [IAS 24 para 16].

FRS 8 has an exemption for emoluments for services as an employee of the reporting entity. [FRS 8 para 3(e)].

The disclosure requirements for directors' remuneration in the Companies Act 1985 (and, if applicable, the Listing Rules) also have to be given by UK companies reporting under EU-adopted IFRS. The structure of the IAS 24 disclosures differs from that required by the Act for directors' remuneration, so even where the key management of a company consists solely of its directors, separate analyses of their remuneration is usually required to satisfy each requirement.

There are disclosure requirements for directors' remuneration in the Companies Act 1985 (and, if applicable, the Listing Rules).

If there have been related party transactions, must disclose:

If there have been material related party transactions, must disclose:

- Names of the transacting related parties.

- Information about the transactions and outstanding balances.

- Description of the transactions.

- The nature of the related party relationship.

- Description of related party relationship.

- The amount of transaction. (Disclosure of proportions of transactions and outstanding balances is no longer sufficient.)

- Amounts involved.

- The amount of outstanding balances, including their terms and conditions, whether they are secured, the nature of consideration to be provided and details of guarantees.

- Amounts due to and from related parties at the balance sheet date.

- Provisions for bad and doubtful debts and the expense recognised during the period.

- Amounts written off.

- Any other information necessary for an understanding of the potential effect of the relationship on financial statements.
[IAS 24 para 17].

- Any other elements necessary for an understanding of the financial statements (for example, transfers at non-commercial rates).
[FRS 8 para 6].

IAS 24 does not include a specific requirement to disclose the name of the related party. However, this disclosure may be necessary in order to disclose the information necessary for an understanding of the potential effect of the relationship on financial statements as required by IAS 24 paragraph 17.	Disclosure required by FRS 8.
Disclosure that transactions were made on arm's length terms can only be made if such terms are capable of substantiation. [IAS 24 para 21].	Not specified by FRS 8.
Related party disclosures should be made separately for different categories of related parties. Aggregation is permitted for items of a similar nature, unless separate disclosure is necessary for an understanding of the effects of the transactions on the financial statements. [IAS 24 paras 18, 22].	Similar. Aggregation is permitted for similar transactions by type of related party, unless disclosure of individual transactions is necessary for an understanding of the impact of the transactions on the financial statements. [FRS 8 para 6].

IAS 27 and FRS 2 – Consolidated financial statements

IAS 27, Consolidated and separate financial statements	FRS 2, Accounting for subsidiary undertakings
Effective for accounting periods beginning on or after 1 January 1990.	*Effective for accounting periods ending on or after 23 December 1992.*
The revised standard (2003) is effective for annual periods beginning on or after 1 January 2005.	*Amendments to FRS 2 effective for accounting periods beginning on or after 1 January 2005.*

Related pronouncements

IAS 32, Financial instruments: Disclosure and presentation (for certain 'minority interests' - para AG29).	FRS 25, Financial instruments: Disclosure and presentation (para AG29) (for certain 'minority interests').
SIC 12, Consolidation - special purpose entities.	FRS 5, Reporting the substance of transactions.
IFRIC amendment to SIC 12.	TF 43, The interpretation of equivalence for the purposes of section 228A of the Companies Act 1985.
IFRIC 5, Rights to interests arising from decommissioning, restoration and environmental rehabilitation funds.	

Overview

In this summary, references to IAS 27 relate to the revised standard issued in December 2003 and the consequential amendments to IAS 27 by subsequent standards. The scope of IAS 27 and FRS 2 is similar, except that IAS 27 includes guidance on the treatment of investments in subsidiaries in the parent's separate financial statements, whereas FRS 2 does not. In addition, FRS 2 details the accounting required for changes in stake, wher eas this is dealt with in IFRS 3, 'Business combinations', not IAS 27.

IAS 27 does not specify that the parent of wholly-owned or partially-owned subsidiaries must be located in a particular country for the exemption from the requirement to produce consolidated financial statements to apply. Instead, the ultimate or any intermediate parent must produce consolidated IFRS financial statements available for public use. In the past, FRS 2 required the immediate parent to be established under the law of an EC Member State. However, for accounting periods beginning on or after 1 January 2005, the exemption is extended to intermediate parent undertakings that are majority-owned subsidiaries of parents that are not governed by the law of a European Economic Area (EEA) State. This is subject to various conditions, including the foreign parent preparing consolidated financial statements in a manner equivalent to the Seventh Directive. In October 2006, the UITF published Abstract 43 to provide guidance on the interpretation of 'equivalence' for the purposes of section 228A of the Companies Act 1985.

IAS 27's definition of a subsidiary is simply "*an entity, including an unincorporated entity such as a partnership, that is controlled by another entity (known as the parent)*". Control is defined as the "*power to govern the financial and operating policies of an entity so as to obtain benefits from its activities*". The circumstances where there is control are similar to most of those contained within FRS 2.

IAS 27 states that the existence and effect of potential voting rights that are currently exercisable or convertible should be considered when assessing whether an entity controls another entity. This is a subtle difference from the UK position where options are taken into account in determining whether a party has a majority of the voting rights only when the option has been exercised. However, in practice other factors, such as dominant influence, may well make the decision to consolidate the same under both sets of accounting standards

FRS 2 requires a subsidiary to be excluded from consolidation where severe long-term restrictions substantially hinder the exercise of the parent undertaking's rights over the assets or management of the subsidiary undertaking. IAS 27 does not have such an exclusion exemption. However, severe restrictions would be considered in determining whether control exists. Control must be lost for exclusion to occur.

The method of consolidation of subsidiaries is broadly the same under IFRS as it is under UK GAAP. Also, both IAS 27 and FRS 2 specify that consolidated financial statements should be prepared using uniform accounting policies for like transactions and other events in similar circumstances.

Under both UK GAAP and IFRS, the reporting periods of the reporting entity and its subsidiaries should be consistent. Where this is not possible, UK GAAP allows consolidation of the subsidiary's reported results where the subsidiary's period end is no more then three months before the parent's reporting year end. IAS 27 is more flexible and allows consolidation of non-coterminous reported financial statements where the subsidiary's period end is within three months of the period end of the parent (that is, subsidiary financial statements for a period ending after the group's period end may be consolidated).

SIC 12, 'Consolidation – Special purpose entities', deals with the accounting for a special purpose entity (SPE). Similar to FRS 5 under UK GAAP, SIC 12 requires SPEs to be consolidated where the substance of the relationship is that of control.

The calculation of the gain or loss on disposal of a subsidiary differs. Under IAS 27, it excludes goodwill previously written off to equity. Under FRS 2, goodwill previously written off to reserves is included in the calculation of the gain or loss on disposal.

Convergence

The IASB is undertaking a project concerned with the circumstances in which an entity should consolidate another and with consolidation procedures. The project's objective is to issue a new consolidation standard to replace IAS 27 and SIC 12. The new standard will address consolidation of all controlled entities including SPE's. In the meantime, the DTI has issued SI 2004/2947, which amends the Companies Act 1985 for accounting periods beginning on or after 1 January 2005. The SI amends the definition of a subsidiary and the exemption from preparing consolidated financial statements to bring these more in line with IAS 27.

As a result, in December 2004, the ASB issued an amendment to FRS 2, applicable for accounting periods beginning on or after 1 January 2005, which deletes references to 'participating interest' in the definition of a subsidiary; adds 'the power to exercise dominant influence or control' to the definition of a subsidiary (expanding on 'actually exercises dominant influence'); reflects the DTI's exemption from the requirement to prepare consolidated financial statements for an intermediate parent whose parent is not governed by the law of a European Economic Area State; and deletes the exclusion from consolidation of subsidiaries with dissimilar operations to the parent.

In June 2005, the IASB published proposed amendments to IAS 27 as part of phase II of the project on business combinations. The IASB is proposing that transactions with minority shareholders should be treated as if they are transactions with owners. In July 2005, the ASB published similar amendments to FRS 2. The ASB is considering its plans for convergence with IFRS

First-time adoption of IFRS

IFRS 1 specifies that if an entity becomes a first-time adopter later than its subsidiary, joint venture or associate it should measure the assets and liabilities of its subsidiary, joint venture or associate in its consolidated financial statements at the same carrying amount as in the separate financial statements of the subsidiary (or joint venture or associate). IFRS 1 also contains guidance for situations where a subsidiary was not consolidated under an entity's previous GAAP.

Summary of main points

Scope

Applies in the preparation and presentation of consolidated financial statements for a group of entities under the control of a parent. [IAS 27 para 1].

Applies to parent undertakings preparing consolidated financial statements intended to give a true and fair view. [FRS 2 para 18].

Applies in accounting for investments in subsidiaries, jointly controlled entities and associates when an entity elects, or is required by local regulations, to present separate financial statements. [IAS 27 para 3].	Does not deal with the individual financial statements of a parent undertaking. [FRS 2 para 18].
Changes in stake are dealt with in IFRS 3.	FRS 2 details the accounting required for changes in stake. [FRS 2 paras 50 to 52].

Classification

A *parent* is an entity that has one or more subsidiaries. [IAS 27 para 4].	A group is defined as a parent undertaking and its subsidiary undertakings. [FRS 2 para 9].
A *subsidiary* is an entity, including an unincorporated entity such as a partnership, that is controlled by another entity (known as the parent). [IAS 27 para 4].	Similar. *An undertaking* is a body corporate, partnership or unincorporated association carrying on a trade or business with or without a view to profit. An undertaking is a subsidiary of another undertaking if certain control criteria apply (see below). [FRS 2 paras 14, 16].
Control is the power to govern the financial and operating policies of an entity so as to obtain benefits from its activities. [IAS 27 para 4].	Similar. Control is the ability of an undertaking to direct the financial and operating policies of another undertaking with a view to gaining economic benefits from its activities. [FRS 2 para 6].
Control is presumed to exist when the parent owns more than half of the entity's voting power, unless in exceptional circumstances it can be clearly demonstrated that such ownership does not constitute control. The circumstances where control exists when the parent owns half or less of the entity's voting power are when there is:	Similar. An undertaking is a parent undertaking of another undertaking (a subsidiary undertaking) where any of the following apply:
• power over more than half of the voting rights by virtue of an agreement with other investors;	• It holds majority of voting rights.
	• It is a member and can appoint or remove directors holding a majority of voting rights.
• power to govern the financial and operating policies under statute or agreement;	• It has the right to exercise dominant influence through provisions in the memorandum or articles or by control contract.
• power to appoint/remove majority of board; or equivalent governing body; or	• It is a member and controls through agreement majority of voting rights.
	• It has a participating interest and actually exercises dominant influence or it and the undertaking managed on unified basis. For accounting periods beginning on or after 1 January 2005, this criterion changes to: Has the power to exercise, or actually exercises, dominant influence or control over the undertaking; or it and the undertaking are managed on a unified basis.
• power to cast majority of votes at board or equivalent government body meetings.	• A parent is also treated as the parent undertaking of the subsidiary undertakings of its subsidiary undertakings.
[IAS 27 para 13].	[FRS 2 para 14].
Potential voting rights (options and convertible instruments) that are currently exercisable or convertible should be considered, in addition to other factors, when assessing whether an entity has the power to govern the financial and operating policies of another entity. [IAS 27 para 14].].	Options are taken into account in determining whether a parent has a majority of voting rights only when the option has been exercised.

Accounting for subsidiaries in consolidated financial statements

Presentation

A parent should present consolidated financial statements in which it consolidates all its subsidiaries. [IAS 27 paras 9, 12].

A parent should prepare consolidated financial statements, unless an exemption from this requirement is available. [FRS 2 para 20]. The consolidated financial statements should include the parent and all subsidiaries, except those required to be excluded. [FRS 2 para 23].

Exemption

A parent is exempt from the requirement to present consolidated financial statements if all the following apply:

- is a wholly-owned subsidiary.

- It is a partially-owned subsidiary and its other owners have been informed about, and do not object to, the parent not presenting consolidated financial statements.

- Its debt or equity securities are not traded in a public market or it is not issuing any class of instruments in a public market.

- The ultimate or any intermediate parent produces consolidated financial statements available for public use that comply with IFRS.

Exemption is on the following grounds:

- It is a wholly-owned subsidiary, its immediate parent is established under the law of an EEA State, none of its securities are traded on an EEA regulated market and it is included in the consolidated financial statements of a larger group drawn up to the same or earlier date in accordance with the 7th Directive or IFRS.

- It is a wholly-owned subsidiary of a parent that is not established under the law of an EEA State, none of its securities are traded on an EEA regulated market and it is included in the consolidated financial statements of a larger group drawn up to the same or earlier date in accordance with the 7th Directive or equivalent (applies for accounting periods beginning on or after 1 January 2005).

- It is a majority-owned subsidiary, it meets the conditions for exemption as a wholly-owned subsidiary and no notice has been served on the company to prepare consolidated financial statements.

[IAS 27 para 10].

No similar exemption. All subsidiaries are required to be consolidated.

[FRS 2 para 21(b) to (e)].

A parent is also exempt from preparing consolidated financial statements if all of its subsidiaries are required or permitted to be excluded. [FRS 2 para 21(f)].

No similar exemption.

If the group is small or medium-sized and is not an ineligible group, it is exempt from preparing consolidated financial statements. [FRS 2 para 21(a)].

Exclusions from consolidation

No similar exclusion permitted. Control must be lost for exclusion to occur. However, severe restrictions would be considered in determining whether control exists.

A subsidiary is excluded from consolidation if severe long-term restrictions substantially hinder the exercise of the parent undertaking's rights over the subsidiary's assets or management. Such a subsidiary is treated as a fixed asset investment. If the restrictions came into force after acquisition, the subsidiary would be carried at a fixed amount calculated using the equity method at that date. [FRS 2 paras 25(a), 27].

If on acquisition, a subsidiary meets the criteria for classification as held for sale in IFRS 5, it is accounted for in accordance with that standard. [IAS 27 para 12].

A subsidiary is excluded from consolidation where it is held exclusively with a view to subsequent resale (that is, a purchaser has been identified or is being sought and it is reasonably expected to be sold within one year of acquisition or it is acquired as a result of the enforcement of a security) and it has not previously been consolidated. Such investments are recorded as a current asset at the lower of cost and net realisable value. [FRS 2 paras 25(b), 29].

Dissimilar activities are not a basis for non-consolidation. [IAS 27 para 20].

Similar. There was previously an exemption for dissimilar activities, however this was repealed under SI 2004/2947, 'The Companies Act 1985 (International Accounting Standards and Other Amendments) Regulations 2004'.

Subsidiaries held by venture capital organisations, mutual funds, unit trusts and similar entities are not excluded from consolidation. [IAS 27 para 19].

No specific mention in FRS 2.

No specific mention in IAS 27, but similar would apply as all subsidiaries are required to be consolidated.

Disproportionate expense or undue delay in obtaining the information necessary is not a basis for excluding subsidiary undertakings from consolidation. [FRS 2 para 24].

Consolidation procedures

Method

Consolidated financial statements are prepared by combining the parent and its subsidiaries on a line-by-line basis, adding together those items of assets, liabilities, equity, income and expenses that are alike. The carrying amount of parent's investment and the parent's share of equity in each subsidiary are eliminated. [IAS 27 para 22].

Similar. [FRS 2 para 5].

The subsidiary's income and expenses are included in the consolidated financial statements from the date of acquisition (as defined in IFRS 3) to the date on which the parent ceases to have control. [IAS 27 para 30].

Similar. [FRS 2 para 45].

Minority interests

Minority interests in consolidated subsidiaries' profit or loss are separately disclosed from the parent shareholder's interest (and are not income or expense). Minority interests in consolidated subsidiaries' net assets are presented in the consolidated balance sheet within equity separate from the parent shareholders' equity. [IAS 27 paras 22, 33, 34].

The aggregate capital and reserves attributable to the minority are shown separately in the consolidated balance sheet. The aggregate profit or loss attributable to the minority is also shown separately. [FRS 2 paras 35, 36].

Losses applicable to the minority in excess of the minority's interest in the subsidiary's equity are allocated against the majority, except to the extent that the minority has a binding obligation and is able to make an additional investment to cover the losses. [IAS 27 para 35].

Losses in excess of the minority's interest in the subsidiary's equity are attributed to the minority, except that the group should make a provision to the extent it has any commercial or legal obligation to provide finance that may not be recoverable in respect of the accumulated losses attributable to the minority interest. [FRS 2 para 37].

Similar. [IFRS 3 para 40].

The amounts attributable to the minority are based on the same carrying amounts of assets and liabilities attributable to the majority (that is, including fair value adjustments). However, goodwill is recognised only in respect of the majority interest and no goodwill is attributable to the minority. [FRS 2 para 38].

Options and convertible shares

The proportions of profit or loss and changes in equity allocated to the parent and minority interests are based on present ownership interests. [IAS 27 para 23].

No specific mention, although the same basis is applied in practice.

Intra-group transactions

All intra-group balances, transactions, income and expenses are eliminated in full. Intra-group losses may indicate an impairment. [IAS 27 paras 24, 25].

Similar. Intra-group transactions, balances and unrealised profits are eliminated in full. Unrealised profits are eliminated proportionally between group and minority interest. [FRS 2 para 39].

Subsidiary financial statements

A subsidiary's financial statements drawn up to the same date as for the parent are used for the purpose of preparing consolidated financial statements. [IAS 27 para 26].

Similar. [FRS 2 para 42].

If it is impractical for the subsidiary to prepare statements to the parent's reporting date, a different reporting date (no more than three months before or after) may be used, but the length of the reporting periods must be consistent from one period to the next. [IAS 27 para 27].

FRS 2 is more restrictive. The subsidiary's reporting date can be no more than three months before that of the parent's. [FRS 2 para 43].

Where different reporting dates are used, adjustments should be made for any significant transactions that occur between the date of the subsidiary's financial statements and that of the parent. [IAS 27 para 27].

Similar. [FRS 2 para 43].

Adjustments should be made to the subsidiary's financial statements where the subsidiary applies different accounting policies to the parent such that uniform accounting policies are used. [IAS 27 paras 28, 29].

Similar. Uniform accounting policies should be used except in exceptional cases. [FRS 2 paras 40, 41].

Changes in stake

The gain or loss on disposal of a subsidiary, recognised in the consolidated income statement, is the difference between the proceeds from disposal and the subsidiary's carrying amount as at the date of disposal The carrying amount does not include goodwill previously written off to equity. [IAS 27 para 30; IFRS 1 App B para B2(i)(i); IFRS 3 para 80].

The calculation of the gain or loss on disposal of a subsidiary differs from IAS 27. Under FRS 2, goodwill not previously written off through the profit and loss account is included in the calculation of gain or loss on disposal. [FRS 2 paras 46, 47; FRS 10 para 71(c)].

An investment in an entity is accounted for in accordance with IAS 39 from the date it ceases to be a subsidiary, provided that it does not become an associate or jointly controlled entity. The investment's carrying amount at that date should be regarded as its cost on initial measurement as a financial asset in accordance with IAS 39. [IAS 27 paras 31, 32].

Not dealt with in FRS 2.

Not dealt with in IAS 27.

If an interest in a subsidiary is increased, goodwill arising on the increase in stake is calculated by reference to the fair values at the date of the increase in stake. [FRS 2 para 50, 51].

Parent's separate financial statements

Separate financial statements are a parent's own financial statements in which investments are accounted for on the basis of the direct equity interest (rather than on the basis of the reported results and net assets of investees). They are presented in addition to consolidated financial statements and economic entity financial statements of investors that do not have subsidiaries, but do have investments in associates and joint ventures. Parents that are exempt from presenting consolidated financial statements may present separate financial statements as their only financial statements. [IAS 27 paras 3 to 8].

There is no guidance in FRS 2 on the treatment in the parent's separate financial statements.

IAS 27 does not mandate which entities produce separate financial statements, but specifies the accounting when an entity elects or is required by local regulations to present separate financial statements. [IAS 27 para 38].

In separate financial statements, investments in subsidiaries, jointly controlled entities and associates (that are not classified as held for sale under IFRS 5) are accounted for either at cost or in accordance with IAS 39. [IAS 27 para 37].

Under the cost method, distributions received in respect of accumulated profits arising before the date of acquisition are recognised as a reduction in the cost of investment, such distributions being regarded as a recovery of the investment. [IAS 27 para 4].

Not dealt with in FRS 2. However, when a subsidiary pays a cash dividend out of pre-acquisition profits, it is normally recorded in the parent's profit and loss account. Following the payment of the dividend, it is necessary to consider whether the carrying amount of the investment in the subsidiary is impaired. [FRS 11 para 8].

Disclosures in consolidated financial statements

Excluded subsidiaries

Not applicable as subsidiaries are not permitted to be excluded.

Names of subsidiary undertakings excluded, reasons for exclusion and certain financial information. [FRS 2 paras 26, 31; CA85 5 Sch 15, 17].

The reasons why the investor concludes that it does not have control when it holds more than half of voting (or potential voting) power of the investee. [IAS 27 para 40(d)].

Disclosures for severe long-term restrictions would apply.

Consolidated subsidiaries

No similar requirement in IAS 27, but Schedule 5 disclosures will have to be given by UK companies reporting under EU-adopted IFRS.

Particulars of subsidiary undertakings, including name, country of incorporation (if not UK), principal place of business if unincorporated and whether consolidated. Also, the identity and percentage holding of each class of shares held. [CA85 5 Sch 15, 16].

No similar requirement in IAS 27.

Indication of nature of business and proportion of voting rights held by the parent and its subsidiaries. [FRS 2 para 33(a),(b)].

The nature of the relationship between the parent and subsidiary should be disclosed when the parent does not own (directly or indirectly) more than half of the voting power. [IAS 27 para 40(c)].

The specific conditions by virtue of which the entity meets the definition of a subsidiary undertaking (unless majority of voting rights held) should be disclosed. [CA85 5 Sch 15(5)]. Also, FRS 2 requires disclosure of the basis of the parent's dominant influence or control where an entity is a subsidiary because the parent has the power to exercise, or actually exercises, dominant influence or control over it. [FRS 2 para 34].

Reporting dates

The reporting date of the subsidiary's financial statements used, if the date or period differs from that of the parent, and the reason for using a different reporting date or different period. [IAS 27 para 40(e)].

Similar. The name of the subsidiary also needs to be disclosed. [FRS 2 para 44].

Restrictions

The nature and extent of any significant restrictions on the ability of subsidiaries to transfer funds to the parent. [IAS 27 para 40(f)].

Similar. [FRS 2 para 53].

Separate financial statements

Exempt from preparing consolidated financial statements

A parent taking advantage of the exemption from preparing consolidated financial statements is required to disclose in its separate financial statements:

- The fact that they are separate financial statements and that the exemption from consolidation has been used. The name and country of incorporation or residence of the parent that publishes consolidated IFRS financial statements and where those financial statements can be obtained. [IAS 27 para 41(a)].

  Similar. [CA85 Sec 228 (2)(c),(d), 228A 2(d),(e); 5 Sch 1(4), 11(4); FRS 2 para 22].

- A list of significant investments in subsidiaries, jointly controlled entities and associates, including the name; country of incorporation or residence; proportion of ownership interest; and proportion of voting power held (if different). [IAS 27 para 41(b)].

  Similar. [CA85 5 Sch 1(2),(3), 2(1)].

- The method used to account for the above investments. [IAS 27 para 41(c)].

  No similar specific requirement.

No similar requirement in IAS 27, but Schedule 5 disclosures will have to be given by UK companies reporting under EU-adopted IFRS.

The capital and reserves and profit or loss of subsidiaries, unless the parent is exempt from producing consolidated financial statements by virtue of section 228 or the investment is included using the equity method of valuation. [CA85 5 Sch 3(1)].

Other separate financial statements

A parent (other than those taking advantage of the exemption from preparing consolidated financial statements), a venturer in a jointly controlled entity or an investor in an associate that prepares separate financial statements are required to disclose:

- The fact the financial statements are separate and why they are prepared (if not required by law). [IAS 27 para 42(a)]. Individual financial statements will be required by law for UK companies reporting under EU-adopted IFRS.

  No similar disclosure requirement. The requirement to produce individual accounts is set out in section 226 of the Companies Act 1985.

- A list of significant investments in subsidiaries, jointly controlled entities and associates, including the name; country of incorporation or residence; proportion of ownership interest; and proportion of voting power held (if different).[IAS 27 para 42(b)].

  Similar. [CA85 5 Sch 1(2),(3), 2(1)].

- The method used to account for the above investments [IAS 27 para 42(c)].

  No similar specific requirement.

- Identification of the parent's consolidated financial statements or venturer's or investor's economic entity financial statements to which the separate financial statements relate. [IAS 27 para 42].

  No similar requirement. Individual and consolidated financial statements are required to be published together. [CA85 Sec 240(2)].

No similar requirement in IAS 27, but Schedule 5 disclosures will have to be given by UK companies reporting under EU-adopted IFRS.

The capital and reserves and profit or loss of subsidiaries, unless the parent is exempt from producing consolidated financial statements by virtue of section 228 or the investment is included using the equity method of valuation. [CA85 5 Sch 3(1)].

IAS 28 and FRS 9 – Associates

IAS 28, Investments in associates	S 9, Associates and joint ventures
Effective for accounting periods beginning on or after 1 January 1990.	*Effective for accounting periods ending on or after 23 June 1998.*
The revised standard (2003) is effective for annual periods beginning on or after 1 January 2005.	

Related pronouncements

—	UITF 31, Exchanges of businesses or other non-monetary assets for an interest in a subsidiary, joint venture or associate.

Overview

In this summary, references to IAS 28 relate to the revised standard issued in December 2003 and consequential amendments in subsequent standards. Under IAS 28, the definition of an associate is similar to that in FRS 9, although FRS 9's definition is more restrictive as it requires that the investor must actually exercise significant influence for an associate relationship to exist. Under IAS 28, an investor has to have significant influence, which is defined as the power to participate in the financial and operating policy decisions of the investee, regardless of whether that power is actually exercised. Consequently, some associates under IAS 28 would not be classified as such under FRS 9.

Both IAS 28 and FRS 9 use the equity method of accounting for associates. The investor presents its share of the associate's profits or losses in its income statement. IAS 28 requires the investor's share of profit or loss of associates to be separately disclosed, but does not specify where in the income statement this should be presented. This is dealt with in IAS 1, which presents the share of the associate's profits or losses (net of tax and minority interests) after the line item for finance costs, but before the line item for tax expense. FRS 9 is more detailed and does require the investor's share of the associate's operating profit, exceptional items, interest and tax to be presented separately.

The requirements under IAS 28 to equity account associates include those investors that do not have subsidiaries, but do have interests in associates. The only exception to this requirement is for those investors that are exempt from the requirement to prepare consolidated financial statements or those that would be exempt under similar conditions had they interests in subsidiaries. This is different to the treatment under FRS 9, as such interests are dealt with by additional disclosure rather than inclusion. Under FRS 9, an investor that is not required to produce consolidated financial statements because it has no subsidiaries, treats interests in associates as investments and carries them at cost or valuation. FRS 9 requires additional disclosures of the relevant equity accounted amounts for these associate interests. Such disclosures are not required for those associates not included because the investor was exempt from the requirement to prepare consolidated financial statements (or would be if the investor had subsidiaries).

FRS 9 exempts investment funds (for example, venture capitalists) from the requirement to equity account those investments over which they have significant influence or joint control. IAS 28 excludes from its scope investments in associates held by venture capital organisations, mutual funds, unit trusts and similar entities including investment-linked insurance funds that upon initial recognition are designated as at 'fair value through profit or loss' or are classified as held for trading and accounted for in accordance with IAS 39.

FRS 9 requires extensive additional disclosures in aggregate or individually where certain measurement thresholds are exceeded. IAS 28 requires summarised aggregated financial information disclosures for all associates.

Convergence

The ASB is considering its plans for convergewnce with IFRS.

First-time adoption of IFRS

If there are entities that are classified as associates under IFRS, but not UK GAAP, then a first-time adopter may elect to apply the business combinations exemption in IFRS 1. This sets out how to determine the goodwill, without requiring a retrospective fair value exercise.

Summary of main points

Scope

Applies in accounting by an investor for investments in associates. [IAS 28 para 1].	The scope of FRS 9 is wider and covers joint ventures and other joint arrangements. [FRS 9 para 1]. These are dealt with separately in the IAS 31 comparisons summary.
IAS 28 does not apply to investments in associates held by venture capital organisations, mutual funds, unit trusts and similar entities (including investment-linked insurance funds) that upon initial recognition are designated as at 'fair value through profit or loss' or are classified as held for trading and accounted for in accordance with IAS 39, 'Financial instruments: Recognition and measurement'. Changes in such an investment's fair value are recognised in profit or loss in the period of the change. [IAS 28 para 1].	Certain investment funds are permitted to include all investments in their investment portfolio (including those over which they have significant influence) in the same way (that is, at cost or market value). [FRS 9 para 49].

Classification

An *associate* is an entity (other than a subsidiary or a joint venture) over which the investor has significant influence. [IAS 28 para 2].	An associate is an entity (other than a subsidiary) in which the investor has a participating interest and exercises significant influence. [FRS 9 para 4].
Significant influence is the power to participate in the financial and operating policy decisions of the investee, but is not control or joint control over those policies. [IAS 28 para 2].	*Exercise of significant influence* is where the investor is actively involved and is influential in policy decisions, including strategic issues. [FRS 9 para 4]. The decisive feature is the actual relationship between investor and investee. [FRS 9 para 17].
Similar, as there is an exception to equity accounting for those associate investments that are classified as held for sale in accordance with IFRS 5 (see below). [IAS 28 para 13(a)].	*Participating interest* is an interest held on a long term basis for the purpose of securing a contribution to the investor's activities by the exercise of influence. [FRS 9 para 4].
A direct or indirect holding of more than 20 per cent of an investee's voting power is presumed to give significant influence, unless it can be demonstrated that this is not the case. Holding less than 20 per cent (directly or indirectly) is presumed not to give significant influence, unless it can be clearly demonstrated. [IAS 28 para 6].	FRS 9 and IAS 28 differ on the issue of the rebuttable presumption. FRS 9 states that the holding of 20 per cent or more of the voting rights in another entity suggests, but does not ensure, that the investor exercise significant influence. [FRS 9 para 16]. The presumption is rebutted if the interest is either not long-term (as defined in FRS 9 para 4) or not beneficial. [FRS 9 para 4].
A substantial or majority ownership by another investor does not necessarily preclude an investor from having significant influence. [IAS 28 para 6].	No specific mention in FRS 9.

Significant influence is usually evidenced in one or more of the following ways - board representation, participation in policy-making, material transactions between the investor and investee, or the exchange of managerial personnel or technical information. [IAS 28 para 7].

The investor's involvement in its associate is usually achieved through nomination to the board of directors (or its equivalent), but may result from any arrangement that allows the investor to participate effectively in policy-making decisions. [FRS 9 para 16].

Potential voting rights (options and convertible instruments) that are currently exercisable or convertible should be considered, in addition to other factors, when assessing if there is significant influence. [IAS 28 para 8].

An interest in the shares of another entity includes an interest convertible into an interest in shares or an option to acquire shares. [FRS 9 para 4].

Accounting for associates

An investment in an associate should be accounted for under the equity method (see below), with the following exceptions. [IAS 28 para 13].

An investment in an associate should be accounted for in consolidated financial statements under the equity method. [FRS 9 para 26].

An investment classified as held for sale in accordance with IFRS 5 is accounted for in accordance with that standard. The fact that it is not accounted for using the equity method should be disclosed. [IAS 28 paras 13(a), 14, 37(h)].

No specific exclusions. However, if an investment is being actively marketed with a sale expected to take place within 12 months, it is unlikely that the definition of participating interest will be met, that is, holding the interest on a long-term basis (as defined in FRS 9 para 4).

An investor is exempt from equity accounting if all of the following apply:

An investor is exempt from equity accounting if it is not required to produce consolidated financial statements (see below). [FRS 9 para 26]. An investor is not required to produce consolidated financial statements if:

- It is a subsidiary of another entity and its owners do not object.

- It has no subsidiaries.

- Its debt or equity instruments are not traded in a public market or it is not issuing any class of instruments in a public market.

- The group is small or medium-sized and is not an ineligible group.

- The investor's ultimate or any intermediate parent produces consolidated financial statements available for public use that comply with IFRS.

- It is a wholly-owned subsidiary and its immediate parent is established under the law of an EEA Member State.

[IAS 28 paras 13(b), (c)].

- It is a wholly-owned subsidiary of a parent that is not established under the law of an EEA State (applies for accounting periods beginning on or after 1 January 2005).

- It is a majority-owned subsidiary, it meets the conditions for exemption as a wholly-owned subsidiary and no notice has been served on the company to prepare consolidated financial statements.

The exemption is conditional on certain other factors as set out in sections 228(2) and 228A(2) of the Companies Act 1985. [FRS 2 para 21].

The requirement to equity account applies to both investors that also have subsidiaries and produce consolidated financial statements and to those investors that do not have subsidiaries, but do have investments in associates. [IAS 28 para 13].

The requirement to equity account only applies to consolidated financial statements. [FRS 9 para 26]. Where an investor does not prepare consolidated financial statements, it should present the relevant amounts for associates as additional information. Investing entities that are exempt from preparing consolidated financial statements, or would be exempt if they had subsidiaries, are exempt from this requirement. [FRS 9 para 48].

Equity method

Under the equity method, the investment is initially recorded at cost and adjusted thereafter for the post-acquisition change in the investor's share of net assets of the investee. [IAS 28 para 2].

Similar definition applies. [FRS 9 para 4].

This involves increasing or decreasing the carrying amount of the investment to recognise the investor's share of the investee's post-acquisition profits or losses. Distributions received from an investee reduce the carrying amount of the investment. [IAS 28 para 11].

Similar, but under FRS 9, the carrying amount of the investment is adjusted by the investor's share of the results of its investee less any amortisation of goodwill. [FRS 9 para 4]. Goodwill is not amortised under IFRS.

Adjustments to the carrying amount of the investment may also be necessary for changes in the investor's interest in the investee that have not been included in profit or loss (for example, revaluation of fixed assets). [IAS 28 para 11].

Same. FRS 9 says that the carrying amount of the investment is adjusted by the investor's share of any relevant gains or losses. [FRS 9 para 4].

The investor's share of its associate's profit or loss should be separately disclosed. [IAS 28 para 38]. IAS 1 shows the share of the associate's profits or losses (after tax and minority interests) presented after the line item for finance costs, but before the line item for tax expense. [IAS 1 para 81, IG]. The investor's share of any discontinued operations of an associate is also required to be separately disclosed. [IAS 28 para 38].

FRS 9 requires a more detailed split in the income statement. The investor's share of its associate's operating results are included immediately after group operating profit (but after its share of operating results of its joint ventures, if any). The investor's share of any non-operating exceptional items, interest and tax should be shown separately from the amounts for the group. [FRS 9 para 27].

Associates accounted for using the equity method should be classified as non-current assets and separately disclosed. Goodwill relating to the associate is included in the carrying amount of the investment. Goodwill is not amortised. [IAS 28 paras 23, 38].

The investor's share of the net assets of its associates should be shown as a separate item in fixed asset investments. Goodwill less any amortisation should be included in the carrying amount for the associates, but should be disclosed separately. [FRS 9 para 29].

The investor's share of changes recognised directly in the associate's equity should be recognised directly in equity by the investor and disclosed in the statement of changes. [IAS 28 para 39; IAS 1 para 98(b)].

The investor's share of its associate's total recognised gains and losses should be included in the consolidated STRGL. If the amounts included are material, they should be shown separately under each heading either in the statement or in a note that is referred to in the statement. [FRS 9 para 28].

There is no separate heading in an IAS cash flow statement for dividends received from associates. See separate summary for comparison of IAS 7 and FRS 1.	The investor's consolidated cash flow statement should include dividends received from associates as a separate item between operating activities and returns on investments and servicing of finance. [FRS 9 para 30].

Application of the equity method

Acquisitions

Many of the procedures for the application of the equity method are similar to the consolidation procedures set out in IAS 27. Also, the concepts underlying the consolidation procedures used in the acquisition of a subsidiary are used on the acquisition of an investment in an associate. [IAS 28 para 20].	Same. [FRS 9 para 31].
An investment in an associate is accounted for under the equity method from the date on which it becomes an associate. [IAS 28 para 23].	Same. [FRS 9 para 40].
Adjustments to the investor's share of post-acquisition profits or losses are made to account for example, for depreciation and impairment losses, based on fair values at the acquisition date. [IAS 28 para 23].	Similar. [FRS 9 para 31(a)].

Associate's financial statements

The most recent available financial statements of the associate are used, drawn up to the date of the investor's financial statements. [IAS 28 para 24].	Same. [FRS 9 para 31(d)].
If it is impractical for the associate to prepare statements to the investor's reporting date, a different reporting date (no more than three months before or after) may be used, but the length of the reporting periods must be consistent from one period to the next. [IAS 28 para 25].	Where it is not practicable to use the same reporting date, the associate should be included on the basis of financial statements prepared for a period ending not more than three months before the investor's period-end (or six months for price-sensitive information). [FRS 9 para 31(d)].
Where different reporting dates are used, adjustments should be made for any significant transactions that occur between the date of the associate's financial statements and that of the investor. [IAS 28 para 25].	Similar. [FRS 9 para 31(d)].
Adjustments should be made to the associate's financial statements where the associate applies different accounting policies to the investor such that uniform accounting policies are used. [IAS 28 paras 26, 27].	Same. In arriving at the amounts to be included by the equity method, the same accounting policies as those of the investor should be applied. [FRS 9 para 31(c)].

Transactions with associates

Under the equity method, profits and losses resulting from 'upstream' and 'downstream' transactions between an investor (or its consolidated subsidiaries) and associates are recognised only to the extent of the unrelated investors' interests in the associate. The investor's share in the associate's profits and losses resulting from these transactions is eliminated. [IAS 28 para 22].	Same. Where profits and losses resulting from transactions between the investor and its associate are included in the carrying amount of assets in either entity, the part relating to the investor's share should be eliminated. [FRS 9 para 31(b)].

IAS 28 contains separate rules on impairment losses (see below).

Share of associate's losses

Where an investor's share of losses of an associate equals or exceeds its interest in the associate, the investing group should discontinue recognising its share of further losses. The amount to be reduced to nil includes not only the carrying amount of the associate under the equity method, but also other long-term interests that in substance form part of the investors' net investment in the associate. Additional losses are provided for only to the extent that the investor has incurred legal or constructive obligations or made payments on behalf of the associate. [IAS 28 paras 29, 30].

Impairment

If, based on applying the requirements of IAS 39, there is an indication that an investment in an associate may be impaired, IAS 36 on impairment of assets should be applied. IAS 28 includes some guidance on determining value in use. Because goodwill included in the carrying amount of an investment in an associate is not separately recognised, IAS 28 states that it is not tested for impairment separately. Instead, the entire carrying amount of the investment is tested under IAS 36 for impairment. [IAS 28 paras 31 to 34].

Contingencies

IAS 28 refers to the need to disclose contingent liabilities (see disclosure below).

Associate's sub-group

When an associate itself has subsidiaries, associates, or joint ventures, the profits or losses and net assets to be taken into account in the equity method are those recognised in the associate's financial statements (including the associate's share of the profits or losses and net assets of its associates and joint ventures), after any adjustments for uniform accounting policies. [IAS 28 para 21].

IAS 28 refers to the need to disclose contingent liabilities (see disclosure below).

Where the transaction provides evidence of the impairment of those assets or any similar assets, this should be taken into account. [FRS 9 para 31(b)].

Under FRS 9, losses continue to be equity accounted. The investor should continue to use the equity method even if this results in an interest in net liabilities. The only exception is where there is sufficient evidence that an event has irrevocably changed the relationship between the investor and its investee, marking its irreversible withdrawal from its investee as its associate. [FRS 9 para 44].

Where there has been an impairment in goodwill attributable to an associate, the goodwill should be written down. [FRS 9 para 38]. Any impairment in the underlying net assets of an associate would normally be reflected at the level of the entity itself (that is, by writing down the relevant assets) or in the adjustments made to apply the equity method. [FRS 9 para 39].

Where an investor has an interest in a non-corporate associate, the investor should ensure that all its liabilities (for example, as a result of joint and several liability) with respect to that entity are reflected appropriately in its financial statements. [FRS 9 para 46]. It may be necessary either to include an additional amount for that liability or to report it as a contingent liability. [FRS 9 para 47].

Same. [FRS 9 para 32].

Options and convertible shares

Where the investor holds options or convertible shares in its associate, the investor's share is determined based on present ownership interests and does not reflect the possible exercise or conversion of potential voting rights. [IAS 28 para 12].

Where the investor holds options or convertible shares in its associate, these should be taken into account in determining the investor's share where the conditions attaching to such holdings indicate that this is appropriate. [FRS 9 para 33].

Cessation of the equity method

An investor should discontinue the use of the equity method from the date that it ceases to have significant influence over an associate, but retains, either in whole or in part, its investment. [IAS 28 para 18].

The date on which an investment ceases to be an associate is the date on which it ceases to fulfil the definition of an associate. [FRS 9 para 40].

The carrying amount of the investment at that date should be regarded as its cost on initial measurement as a financial asset in accordance with IAS 39. [IAS 28 para 19].

Similar. When an entity ceases to be either an associate, the initial carrying amount of any retained interest is based on the final carrying amount for the former associate at the date the entity ceased to qualify as such (written down, if necessary, to its recoverable amount). [FRS 9 para 42].

Disclosure

Required disclosures include the following:

The fair value of investments in associates for which there are published price quotations. [IAS 28 para 37(a)].

The aggregate market value of listed investments where this differs from the amount at which they are stated in the balance sheet. [CA85 4 Sch 45(2)(a)].

Summarised financial information of associates, including the aggregated amounts of assets, liabilities, revenues and profit or loss. In addition, the same summarised financial information is required, either individually or in groups, for associates that are not accounted for using the equity method. [IAS 28 paras 37(b), 37(i)].

FRS 9 requires additional disclosure in respect of the investor's share of certain financial statement items where associates in aggregate have excess of 15 per cent of gross assets, gross liabilities, turnover or operating result (on a three-year average) of the investing group. Also, further disclosure is required for each individual associate that exceeds 25 per cent of gross assets, gross liabilities, turnover or operating result (on a three-year average) of the investing group. [FRS 9 paras 57, 58].

The reasons why the investor concludes that it has significant influence when it holds less than 20 per cent of the voting (or potential voting power) of the investee. [IAS 28 para 37(c)].

No similar requirement.

The reasons why the investor concludes that it does not have significant influence when it holds more than 20 per cent of the voting (or potential voting power) of the investee. [IAS 28 para 37(d)].

Reasons where the presumption that an investor holding 20 per cent or more of the voting rights of another entity has significant influence or a participating interest is rebutted. [FRS 9 para 56].

The reporting date of the associate's financial statements used, if the date or period differs from that of the investor and the reason for using a different reporting date or different period. [IAS 28 para 37(e)].

Similar. The accounting period or date of the financial statements used if they differ from those of the investing group. [FRS 9 para 52(b)].

The nature and extent of any significant restrictions on the ability of associates to transfer funds to the investor. [IAS 28 para 37(f)].	Similar. If there are significant statutory, contractual or exchange control restrictions on the ability of an associate or joint venture to distribute reserves, the extent of the restrictions should be indicated. [FRS 9 para 54].
The unrecognised share of losses of an associate, both for the period and cumulatively, if an investor has discontinued recognising its share of losses of an associate. [IAS 28 para 37(g)].	Not applicable as an investor continues to recognise its share of an associate's losses under FRS 9.
No similar requirement.	The proportion of the issued shares in each class held by the investing group, indicating any special rights or constraints attaching to them. [FRS 9 para 52(a)].
No equivalent.	An indication of the nature of its business. [FRS 9 para 52(c)].
The investor's share of an associate's contingent liabilities and those contingent liabilities that arise because the investor is severally liable for all or part of the liabilities of an associate. [IAS 28 para 40].	Similar [FRS 9 para 53].
No equivalent in IAS 28, but IAS 24 requires disclosure of the amounts payable to and receivable from associates. [IAS 24 para 18].	The amounts owing and owed between an investor and its associates should be analysed into amounts relating to loans and amounts relating to trading balances. This disclosure may be combined with those required by FRS 8. [FRS 9 para 55].

Investor's separate financial statements

Separate financial statements are the investor's own financial statements in which investments are accounted for on the basis of the direct equity interest (rather than on the basis of the reported results and net assets of the investees). [IAS 28 para 2]. They are presented in addition to consolidated financial statements and economic entity financial statements of investors that do not have subsidiaries but do have investments in associates where an entity elects or is required by local regulations to present separate financial statements [IAS 28 paras 4, 36].	'Separate' financial statements are the equivalent of the investor's 'individual' financial statements prepared under UK GAAP.
IAS 28 cross-refers to paragraphs 37 to 42 of IAS 27 as that standard specifies the accounting and disclosures required for investments in associates in an investor's separate financial statements. [IAS 28 para 35]. IAS 27 requires that such investments (that are not classified as held for sale under IFRS 5) should be accounted for either at cost or in accordance with IAS 39. [IAS 27 para 37].	In the investor's individual financial statements, its interests in associates should be treated as fixed asset investments and shown either at cost less any amounts written off, or at valuation. [FRS 9 para 26].

IAS 31 and FRS 9 – Joint ventures

IAS 31, Interests in joint ventures	FRS 9, Associates and joint ventures
Effective for accounting periods beginning on or after 1 January 1992.	*Effective for accounting periods ending on or after 23 June 1998.*
The revised standard (2003) is effective for annual periods beginning on or after 1 January 2005.	

Related pronouncements

SIC 13, Jointly controlled entities – Non-monetary contributions by venturers.	UITF 31, Exchanges of businesses or other non-monetary assets for an interest in a subsidiary, joint venture or associate.

Overview

In this summary, references to IAS 31 relate to the revised standard issued in December 2003 and consequential amendments in subsequent standards. IAS 31 identifies three types of joint ventures, namely jointly controlled 'entities', jointly controlled operations and jointly controlled assets. Under FRS 9, only jointly controlled 'entities' are classified as joint ventures and the definition is more restrictive than IAS 31. Under IAS 31, 'entities' can be corporations, partnerships or other entities. This is similar to FRS 9, but such undertakings are only treated as joint ventures under FRS 9 if they carry on their own trade or business. Jointly controlled operations or assets fall within the FRS 9 category of 'joint arrangements that are not entities'.

For jointly controlled entities, IAS 31 requires use of either proportionate consolidation or the equity method. FRS 9 does not permit proportionate consolidation and requires use of the 'gross equity' method for joint ventures (that is, use of the equity method, but with separate presentation of the venturer's share of gross assets and liabilities and turnover on the face of the balance sheet and income statement).

The requirements under IAS 31 to either proportionately consolidate or equity account interests in jointly controlled entities include those venturers that do not have subsidiaries, but do have interests in jointly controlled entities. The only exception to this requirement is for those venturers that are exempt from the requirement to prepare consolidated financial statements or those that would be exempt under similar conditions had they interests in subsidiaries. This is different to FRS 9 as such interests are dealt with by additional disclosure rather than inclusion. Under FRS 9, a venturer that is not required to produce consolidated financial statements because it has no subsidiaries treats interests in joint ventures as investments and carries them at cost or valuation. Additional disclosures are required of the relevant gross equity accounted amounts for these joint venture interests, although this does not apply when the joint venture is not included because the venturer was exempt from the requirement to prepare consolidated financial statements (or would be if the venturer had subsidiaries).

FRS 9 exempts investment funds (for example, venture capitalists) from the requirement to gross equity account those investments over which they have joint control. IAS 31 excludes from its scope investments in jointly controlled entities held by venture capital organisations, mutual funds, unit trusts and similar entities including investment-linked insurance funds that upon initial recognition are designated as at 'fair value through profit or loss' or are classified as held for trading and accounted for in accordance with IAS 39.

IAS 31 does not include the same detailed disclosure requirements of FRS 9, in particular, it does not include the extensive additional disclosures required in aggregate or individually where certain measurement thresholds are exceeded. IAS 31 does require additional aggregate disclosures when the line-by-line reporting format for proportionate consolidation or the equity method is used for reporting interests in jointly controlled entities.

Convergence

IAS 31 is currently under review as part of the US/IFRS convergence project. The key proposal is to remove the option of proportional consolidation for jointly controlled entities. This will bring IFRS more in line with current UK GAAP. The IASB may also decide to carry out a more fundamental review of accounting for joint ventures. The ASB is considering its plans for convergence with IFRS.

If there are entities that are classified as jointly controlled entities under IFRS, but not UK GAAP, then a first-time adopter may elect to apply the business combinations exemption in IFRS 1. This sets out how to determine the goodwill, without requiring a retrospective fair value exercise.

Summary of main points

Scope

Interests in joint ventures and the reporting of joint venture assets, liabilities, income and expenses in the financial statement of venturers and investors. [IAS 31 para 1].

IAS 31 does not apply to investments in jointly controlled entities held by venture capital organisations, mutual funds, unit trusts and similar entities (including investment-linked insurance funds) that upon initial recognition are designated as at 'fair value through profit or loss' or are classified as held for trading and accounted for in accordance with IAS 39, 'Financial instruments: Recognition and measurement'. Changes in such an investment's fair value are recognised in profit or loss in the period of the change. [IAS 31 para 1].

The scope of FRS 9 is wider and also covers associates. [FRS 9 para 1]. These are dealt with separately in the IAS 28 comparisons summary.

Certain investment funds are permitted to include all investments in their investment portfolio (including those over which they have joint control) in the same way (that is, at cost or market value). [FRS 9 para 49].

Classification

IAS 31 identifies three broad types of joint ventures. [IAS 31 para 7]. These all meet the definition of joint ventures:

FRS 9 is more restrictive and only jointly controlled 'entities' (with a trade or business of their own) meet the definition of joint ventures. [FRS 9 para 4]. There is a separate classification for 'joint arrangement that is not an entity'.

- Jointly controlled operations.

Equivalent to a joint arrangement that is not an entity.

- Jointly controlled assets.

Equivalent to a joint arrangement that is not an entity.

- Jointly controlled entities.

Equivalent to a joint venture.

A *joint venture* is a contractual arrangement whereby two or more parties undertake an economic activity which is subject to joint control. [IAS 31 para 3].

A *joint venture* is an entity in which the reporting entity holds an interest on a long-term basis and which is jointly controlled by the reporting entity and one or more other venturers under a contractual agreement. The definition of entity means carrying on a trade or business of its own. [FRS 9 para 4].

Joint control is the contractually agreed sharing of control over an economic activity, and exists only when the strategic financial and operating decisions relating to the activity require the unanimous consent of the parties sharing control (the venturers). [IAS 31 para 3].

A reporting entity jointly controls a venture with others if no one entity alone can control it, but all together they can do so and decisions on financial and operating policy essential to the activities, economic performance and financial position of that venture require each venturer's consent. [FRS 9 para 4].

An *investor* is a party to a joint venture, but does not have joint control. [IAS 31 para 3].

FRS 9 uses the term 'investor' both in the context of an investor that shares control over a joint venture and an investor that is a party to the joint venture, but does not have joint control. [FRS 9 para 10].

A *venturer* is a party to a joint venture and has joint control over it. [IAS 31 para 3].

Similar implied in the definition of joint venture. [FRS 9 para 4].

The common characteristics of a joint venture are that two or more venturers are bound by a contractual agreement and the contractual agreement establishes joint control. [IAS 31 para 7].

Similar. The definition of a joint venture refers to joint control under a contractual arrangement. [FRS 9 para 4].

Contractual arrangement

The contractual arrangement may be evidenced in a number of ways, for example by contract, minutes of discussion, or the articles of joint venture. The contractual arrangement is usually in writing, and deals with the activity, duration and reporting obligations of the joint venture, board appointments and voting rights, capital contributions, and the sharing of income and expenses of the joint venture. [IAS 31 para 10].

Similar concept implied in the definitions of an agreement governing the arrangement.

Activities that have no contractual arrangement to establish joint control are not joint ventures. The contractual arrangement establishes joint control over the joint venture and ensures that no single venturer is in a position to control the activity unilaterally. [IAS 31 paras 9, 11].

Each venturer that shares control should play an active role in setting the joint venture's operating and financial policies, at least at a general strategy level. Each venturer has a veto on high-level strategic decisions. However, the requirement for each venturer's consent to high-level strategic decisions does not have to be set out in the joint venture agreement, provided that the joint venture works in practice on the basis of securing such consent. [FRS 9 paras 11, 12].

Jointly controlled operations

This involves the use of the venturers' own assets and other resources rather than setting up a separate corporation, partnership or other entity. [IAS 31 para 13].

Joint arrangement that is not an entity

A *'joint arrangement that is not an entity'* is a contractual arrangement under which the participants engage in joint activities that do not create an entity because it would not be carrying on a trade or business of its own. [FRS 9 para 4].

An example is where two or more venturers combine their operations, resources and expertise in order to manufacture, market and distribute jointly a particular product. Each venturer bears its own costs and takes a share of the revenue from the sales, such share being determined in accordance with the contractual agreement. [IAS 31 para 14].

Similar. [FRS 9 paras 8, 9]. Carrying on a trade or business normally denotes a continuing activity with repetition of the buying and selling activities and, therefore, a joint arrangement carrying out a single project is unlikely to be carrying on a trade or business of its own, being instead a facility or agent in its participants' trades or businesses. [FRS 9 para 9].

A contractual arrangement where all significant matters of operating and financial policy are predetermined does not create an entity because the policies are those of its participants, not of a separate entity. [FRS 9 para 4].

Accounting treatment

In respect of its interests in jointly controlled operations, a venturer should recognise in its financial statements:

Participants in a joint arrangement that is not an entity should account for their own assets, liabilities and cash flows, measured according to the terms of the agreement governing the arrangement. [FRS 9 para 18].

- The assets that it controls and the liabilities that it incurs.

- The expenses that it incurs and its share of the income that it earns from the sale of goods and services by the joint venture.

[IAS 31 para 15].

Because the assets, liabilities, income and expenses are recognised in the venturer's financial statements, no adjustments are required for the consolidated financial statements. [IAS 31 para 16].	Same.

Jointly controlled assets

Some joint ventures involve the joint control by the venturers of an asset contributed to or acquired for the purposes of the joint venture. [IAS 31 para 18]. Each venturer has control over its share of future economic benefits through its share in the jointly controlled asset. [IAS 31 para 19].	Under FRS 9 this would be a 'joint arrangement that is not an entity' (see above).
An example is an oil pipeline where each venturer uses the pipeline to transport its own product in return for which it bears an agreed proportion of the expenses of operating the pipeline. [IAS 31 para 20].	Similar. [FRS 9 para 9].

Accounting treatment

In respect of its interests in jointly controlled assets, a venturer should recognise in its financial statements:	As above, participants in a joint arrangement that is not an entity should account for their own assets, liabilities and cash flows, measured according to the terms of the agreement governing the arrangement. [FRS 9 para 18].

- Its share of jointly controlled assets, classified according to the nature of the assets.

- Any liabilities that it has incurred.

- Its share of liabilities incurred jointly with other venturers.

- Any income from the sale or use of its share of the output of joint venture, together with its share of any expenses incurred by joint venture.

- Any expenses which it has incurred in respect of its interest in the joint venture.

[IAS 31 para 21].

Because the asset, liabilities, income and expenses are recognised in the venturer's financial statements, no adjustments are required for the consolidated financial statements. [IAS 31 para 22].	Same.

Jointly controlled entities	Joint venture
A jointly controlled entity is a joint venture which involves the establishment of a corporation, partnership or other entity in which the venturer has an interest. It operates in the same way as other entities, except that a contractual arrangement between the venturers establishes joint control over the economic activity of the entity. [IAS 31 para 24].	The definition of a joint venture is based on having joint control over an entity. [FRS 9 para 4].
IAS 31 does not require a jointly controlled 'entity' to carry out a business of its own.	An 'entity' is a body corporate, partnership or unincorporated association carrying on a trade or business of its own, with or without a view to profit. [FRS 9 para 4].
An example is when two entities combine their activities in a particular line of business by transferring the relevant assets and liabilities into a jointly controlled entity. [IAS 31 para 26].	Similar, provided that the jointly controlled entity has a business of its own.
Many jointly controlled entities are similar in substance to jointly controlled operations and jointly controlled assets, except that the jointly controlled elements are 'housed' within a separate entity. [IAS 31 para 27].	Jointly controlled operations or jointly controlled assets 'housed' in an entity will be classified as a 'joint arrangement that is not an entity' under FRS 9 if they do not carry out a trade or business of their own.

Accounting treatment

A venturer's interest in a jointly controlled entity should be recognised using either proportionate consolidation or the equity method. [IAS 31 paras 30, 38].	FRS 9 requires use of the gross equity method (see below) and does not permit use of proportionate consolidation.
The requirement to proportionately consolidate or to equity account applies to both venturers that also have subsidiaries and produce consolidated financial statements and to those venturers that do not have subsidiaries, but do have investments in jointly controlled entities. [IAS 31 paras 31, 39].	The requirement to gross equity account only applies to consolidated financial statements. [FRS 9 para 20]. Where a venturer does not prepare consolidated financial statements, it should present the relevant amounts for joint ventures as additional information. Venturers that are exempt from preparing consolidated financial statements, or would be exempt if they had subsidiaries, are exempt from this requirement. [FRS 9 para 48].

Proportionate consolidation | *Gross equity method*

A venturer should recognise its interest in a jointly controlled entity using one of the two reporting formats for proportionate consolidation. [IAS 31 para 30].	In its consolidated financial statements, an investor should include its joint ventures using the gross equity method in all its primary financial statements. [FRS 9 para 20].
Proportionate consolidation means that the venturer's financial statements include its share of the assets, liabilities, income and expenses of the jointly controlled entity. [IAS 31 para 33].	The gross equity method is an expansion of the equity method used to account for associates. The investor's share of the aggregate gross assets and liabilities underlying the net amount included for the investment is shown on the face of the balance sheet and, in the profit and loss account, the investor's share of the investee's turnover is noted. [FRS 9 para 4].

There are two different reporting formats for proportionate consolidation:

- The venturer's share of the assets, liabilities, income and expenses of a jointly controlled entity is combined on a line-by-line basis with similar items in the venturer's financial statements.

- The venturer's share of the assets, liabilities, income and expenses of a jointly controlled entity is reported as separate line items in the venturer's financial statements.

Both these formats result in the reporting of identical amounts of net income and major classification of assets, liabilities, income and expenses. [IAS 31 para 34].

A venturer should discontinue the use of proportionate consolidation from the date on which it ceases to have joint control. [IAS 31 para 36].

Equity method

IAS 31 permits the use of the equity method as an alternative for the accounting of jointly controlled entities. [IAS 31 para 38]. It prefers the proportionate consolidation method as this better reflects the substance and economic reality of the venturer's interests in a jointly controlled entity. [IAS 31 para 40].

Under the equity method, the investment is initially recorded at cost and adjusted thereafter for the post-acquisition change in the venturer's share of net assets of the jointly controlled entity. The venturer's profit or loss includes its share of the jointly controlled entity's profit or loss. [IAS 31 para 3].

A venturer should discontinue the use of the equity method from the date on which it ceases to have joint control (or significant influence). [IAS 31 para 41].

Exceptions

An interest in a jointly controlled entity classified as held for sale in accordance with IFRS 5 is accounted for in accordance with that standard. [IAS 31 paras 2(a), 42].

A venturer with an interest in a jointly controlled entity is exempt from proportionately consolidating or equity accounting if all of the following apply:

- It is a subsidiary of another entity and its owners do not object.

Not applicable.

Same. The date on which an investment ceases to be a joint venture is the date on which the investor ceases to have joint control. [FRS 9 para 40].

No choice of methods allowed. FRS 9 requires use of the gross equity method (see above) in consolidated financial statements.

Similar. [FRS 9 para 4].

Same. [FRS 9 para 40].

No specific exclusions. However, if an investment is being actively marketed with a sale expected to take place within 12 months, it is unlikely that the definition of a joint venture (held on a long-term basis) will be met.

A venturer is exempt from gross equity accounting if it is not required to produce consolidated financial statements (see above). [FRS 9 para 20]. An investor is not required to produce consolidated financial statements if:

- It has no subsidiaries.

- Its debt or equity instruments are not traded in a public market or it is not issuing any class of instruments in a public market.

- The venturer's ultimate or any intermediate parent produces consolidated financial statements available for public use that comply with IFRS.

[IAS 31 paras 2(b), (c)].

- The group is small or medium sized and is not an ineligible group.

- It is a wholly owned subsidiary and its immediate parent is established under the law of an EEA Member State.

- It is a wholly-owned subsidiary of a parent that is not established under the law of an EEA State (applies for accounting periods beginning on or after 1 January 2005).

- It is a majority owned subsidiary, it meets the conditions for exemption as a wholly-owned subsidiary and no notice has been served on the company to prepare consolidated financial statements.

The exemption is conditional on certain other factors as set out in sections 228(2) and 228A(2) of the Companies Act 1985. [FRS 2 para 21].

Changes in classification

From the date on which a jointly controlled entity becomes a subsidiary of the venturer, it is accounted for in accordance with IAS 27. [IAS 31 para 45].

Similar. An interest in a subsidiary would be accounted for under FRS 2.

From the date on which a jointly controlled entity becomes an associate of the venturer, it is accounted for in accordance with IAS 28. [IAS 31 para 45].

Similar. An interest in an associate would be accounted for under FRS 9.

Transactions between a venturer and a joint venture

When a venturer contributes or sells assets to a joint venture and where the assets are retained by the joint venture, the venturer should recognise only the proportion of the gain or loss that is attributable to the interests of the other venturers. [IAS 31 para 48].

Similar. Where profits and losses resulting from transactions between the investor and its joint venture are included in the carrying amount of assets in either entity, the part relating to the investor's share is eliminated. [FRS 9 para 31(b)].

The venturer should recognise the full amount of any loss when the contribution or sale provides evidence of a reduction in the net realisable value of the current assets or an impairment loss. [IAS 31 para 48].

Similar. Where the transaction provides evidence of impairment of those assets or any similar assets, this should be taken into account. [FRS 9 para 31(b)].

SIC 13 provides additional guidance. It requires recognition of the portion of a gain or loss attributable to the other venturers' interests when non-monetary assets are contributed to a jointly controlled entity in exchange for an equity interest in that entity. This is subject to limited exceptions, one of which is where the contribution transaction lacks commercial substance (as described in IAS 16). [SIC 13 para 5].

UITF 31 has guidance for exchanges of businesses or other non-monetary assets for an interest in a joint venture.

When a venturer purchases assets from a joint venture, the venturer should not recognise its share of the profits of the joint venture until it resells the asset to an independent third party. Losses should be similarly recognised, except where losses represent a reduction in net realisable value of current assets or an impairment when losses should be recognised immediately. [IAS 31 para 49].

Similar. [FRS 9 para 31(b)].

Operators of joint ventures

A venturer may act as the operator or manager of the joint venture and receive a fee for such duties. The operator or manager would account for the fee in accordance with IAS 18. [IAS 31 para 52]. The fees are accounted by the joint venture as an expense. [IAS 31 para 53].

Not dealt with in FRS 9.

Disclosure

A venturer should disclose:

- The aggregate amount of contingent liabilities, unless the probability of loss is remote, separate from other contingent liabilities. [IAS 31 para 54].

Similar. [FRS 9 para 53].

- The aggregate amount of commitments in respect of its interest in joint ventures, separate from other commitments. [IAS 31 para 55].

Similar [FRS 9 para 53].

- A listing and description of interests in significant joint ventures and the proportion of ownership interest held in jointly controlled entities. [IAS 31 para 56].

Similar [FRS 9 para 52(a)].

- The method it uses to recognise its interests in jointly controlled entities. [IAS 31 para 57].

Not applicable as FRS 9 does not permit a choice of methods.

No equivalent.

The accounting period or date of the financial statements used if they differ from those of the investing group. [FRS 9 para 52(b)].

No equivalent.

An indication of the nature of the joint venture's business. [FRS 9 para 52(c)].

No equivalent in IAS 31, but IAS 24 requires disclosure of the amounts payable to and receivable from joint ventures. [IAS 24 para 18].

The amounts owing and owed between an investor and its joint ventures should be analysed into amounts relating to loans and amounts relating to trading balances. This disclosure may be combined with those required by FRS 8. [FRS 9 para 55].

A venturer that recognises its interest in a joint venture using the line by line reporting format of proportionate consolidation or the equity method should disclose the aggregate amounts of each of current assets, long-term assets, current liabilities, long-term liabilities, income and expenses related to its interests in joint ventures. [IAS 31 para 56].

FRS 9 requires additional disclosure in respect of the venturer's share of certain financial statement items where joint ventures in aggregate have in excess of 15 per cent of gross assets, gross liabilities, turnover or operating results (on a three year average) of the reporting group. Also, further disclosure is required for each individual joint venture that exceeds 25 per cent of gross assets, gross liabilities, turnover or operating results (on a three-year average) of the reporting group. [FRS 9 paras 57 and 58].

Venturer's separate financial statements

Separate financial statements are the venturer's own financial statements in which investments are accounted for on the basis of the direct equity interest (rather than on the basis of the reported results and net assets of the investees). [IAS 31 para 3]. They are presented in addition to consolidated financial statements and economic entity financial statements of venturers that do not have subsidiaries but do have investments in jointly controlled entities where an entity elects or is required by local regulations to present separate financial statements [IAS 31 paras 5, 47].

'Separate' financial statements are the equivalent of the venturer's 'individual' financial statements prepared under UK GAAP.

Contributions (cash or other resources) made by the venturer are recognised in the venturer's separate financial statements as an investment in a jointly controlled entity. [IAS 31 para 29]. IAS 31 cross-refers to paragraphs 37 to 42 of IAS 27 as that standard specifies the accounting and disclosures required for investments in jointly controlled entities in an venturer's separate financial statements. [IAS 31 para 46]. IAS 27 requires that such investments (that are not classified as held for sale under IFRS 5) should be accounted for either at cost or in accordance with IAS 39. [IAS 27 para 37]

In the investor's individual financial statements, investments in joint ventures should be treated as fixed asset investments and shown either at cost, less any amounts written off, or at valuation. [FRS 9 para 20].

IAS 32 , IFRS 7 and FRS 25, FRS 29 – Financial instruments: Presentation

IAS 32, IFRS 7	FRS 25, FRS 29 Financial instruments: Disclosure and presentation

FRS 25 derives from IAS 32 and is almost identical to that standard. FRS 25 also includes certain paragraphs of IAS 1, 'Presentation of financial statements. FRS 29 largely replicates IFRS 7's requirements. It supersedes FRS 13 and FRS 25's disclosure requirements.

For a comparison of the disclosure requirements in IFRS 7 (FRS 29), IAS 32 (FRS 25) and the Companies Act 1985, see the table 'Financial instrument disclosures: Comparison of UK GAAP v IFRS v New Companies Act requirements'.

The scope and effective date criteria are complicated. The flow chart FRS 25 on page 147 will help identify which entities are within the scope of FRS 25 and when they will have to implement it. In addition, the flow chart incorporates the scoping and implementation dates for the Companies Act 1985's new fair value accounting rules and the new disclosure requirements.

Comparison of UK GAAP vs. IFRS vs. New Companies Act Requirements

Disclosure	UK GAAP			IFRS GAAP		CA
	FRS 13	FRS 25	FRS 29	IAS 32	IFRS 7	Sch. 4/7
	α	β	γ	δ	ε	ζ

General						
Objective of the standard		51,52	1, 7, 31, Appendix A	51,52	1, 7, 31, Appendix A	
Level of disclosures		54	B3, IG 5	54	B3, IG 5	
Classes of financial instruments		55	B1, B2	55	B1, B2	
Objectives, policies and strategies for financial instruments, significance, nature and extent of risks arising from financial instruments by class	13	56, 57 60(a)	33(b), 34(c)	56,57, 60(a)	33(b), 34(c)	7Sch 5A(1)
Explanation of changes in above from prior periods	16		7		7	
Explanation if period-end numerical disclosures are not representative of the position	20		7		7	
General information of hedged items and hedging instruments and associated risk for each type of hedge	21	58	22, 23(a), 23(b)	56, 58	22, 23(a), 23(b)	7Sch 5A(1)
Hedging policy for each type of forecast transaction	59					
Exposure to price, credit, liquidity and cash flow risks – Change from previous period			33(a), 33(c)		33(a), 33(c)	7Sch 5A(1) (η)
Objectives, policies and processes for managing risk and methods used to measure risk – change from previous period	13	56	33(b), 33(c)	56	33(b), 33(c)	7Sch 5A(1) (η)
Detailed disclosures of terms and conditions of individual or class of financial instruments that create a potentially significant exposure to risk		63		63		
Disclosure on risk concentration		83-5	34(c)	83-5	34(c)	
Disclose for each category of financial asset whether regular purchases and sales recorded at trade or settlement date		61		61	B5(c)	

	UK GAAP			IFRS GAAP		CA
Disclosure	FRS 13	FRS 25	FRS 29	IAS 32	IFRS 7	Sch. 4/7
	α	β	γ	δ	ε	ζ

Interest rate risk

Financial liabilities - Carrying amount split by fixed and floating	26, 32	67(a), 71 74(a)-(c)	40-42, B18 –B22	67(a), 71 74(a)-(c)	40-42, B18 –B22	
Financial liabilities - Weighted average interest rate disclosures	30, 32	74(d)	40-42, B18 –B22	74(d)	40-42, B18 –B22	
Contractual re-pricing or maturity dates (the earlier of)		67, 70, 74(a)	40-42, B18 –B22	67, 70, 74(a)	40-42, B18 –B22	
Financial assets and liabilities exposed and not exposed to fair value interest rate risk and cash flow interest rate risk		71, 74(d)	40-42, B18 –B22	71, 74(d)	40-42, B18 –B22	
The effective interest rates		67(b)		67(b)		
Sensitivity analysis, basis on which it has prepared information and significant assumptions, changes from previous periods		75	40-42, B18 –B22	75	40-42, B18 –B22	

Currency risk

Net monetary assets and liabilities split by main currencies	34	52(a), 60(a)	1(b), 21, 31, B5, Appendix A	52(a), 60(a)	1(b), 21, 31, B5, Appendix A	

Liquidity risk

Maturity profile of carrying amount of financial liabilities – showing remaining contractual maturities	38	74(a)	39(a)	74(a)	39(a)	
Maturity profile of material undrawn committed borrowing facilities	40					
Description of how entity manages risk			39(b)		39(b)	

Disclosure	UK GAAP			IFRS GAAP		CA
	FRS 13	FRS 25	FRS 29	IAS 32	IFRS 7	Sch. 4/7
	α	β	γ	δ	ε	ζ

Credit risk

Disclosure	FRS 13	FRS 25	FRS 29	IAS 32	IFRS 7	Sch. 4/7
Quantitative disclosure for each type of credit risk			34(a), 34(b)		34(a), 34(b)	
Maximum credit exposure (excl collateral including a description of collateral and other credit enhancements) includes effect of transactions not recognised on balance sheet		76(a), 79-82	36(a) 36(b), B9, B10	76(a), 79-82	36(a) 36(b), B9, B10	
Significant concentrations of credit risk		76(b), 83-85	34(c), B8, IG18, IG19	76(b), 83-85	34(c), B8, IG18, IG19	
Information about credit quality of financial assets that are neither past due or impaired			36(c)		36(c)	
Carrying amount of financial assets that would otherwise be past due or impaired whose terms have been renegotiated			36(d)		36(d)	
Effect of master netting agreement on credit risk		81	36(a)	81	36(a)	
An analysis of the age of financial assets that are past due as at the reporting date but not impaired plus a description of collateral or other credit enhancements available and estimate of their fair value			37(a)(c)		37(a)(c)	
An analysis of financial assets individually determined to be impaired as at the reporting date, including factors the entity considered in determining impairment plus description of collateral or other credit enhancements and estimate of their fair value			37(b)(c)		37(b)(c)	
Where possession is taken of collateral or other credit enhancements are called on during the period, the nature and carrying amount of assets obtained and, when not readily convertible to cash, policies for disposing of them or using them in the entity's operations			38		38	

Disclosure	UK GAAP			IFRS GAAP		CA
	FRS 13	FRS 25	FRS 29	IAS 32	IFRS 7	Sch. 4/7
	α	β	γ	δ	ε	ζ

Market risk

Disclosure	FRS 13	FRS 25	FRS 29	IAS 32	IFRS 7	Sch. 4/7
Numerical disclosures that show the magnitude of market price risk	66		40-1		40-1	
Approach to market price risk to set numerical information in context	67		40-1		40-1	
Explanation of methods, objectives, main parameters, assumptions and changes from the previous periods for market risk analysis	69		40-1		40-1	

Derivatives

Disclosure	FRS 13	FRS 25	FRS 29	IAS 32	IFRS 7	Sch. 4/7
Extent, nature, terms, conditions of derivatives		60	21	60	21	4Sch 45A(2)
Extent, nature and fair value for each class of derivatives not recorded at fair value						4Sch 45B
For each class of derivatives, extent of the instrument, including significant terms and conditions that may affect amount, timing and certainty of the future cash flows						4Sch 45A(2)(c)

Fair value

Disclosure	FRS 13	FRS 25	FRS 29	IAS 32	IFRS 7	Sch. 4/7
Aggregate fair value and carrying amount for each class of financial assets and financial liabilities	44a	86-89	25, 26, 29(a)	86-89	25, 26, 29(a)	4Sch 45A(2)(b) 45B(a),(b)
Reason for not recording provision on financial fixed assets whose carrying amount exceeds fair value and evidence to support expected recovery of carrying amount. Disclosure of fair value amount and excess of carrying amount over fair value						4Sch 45C
Aggregate fair value and carrying amounts split between positive and negative fair values	44b					
Fair value methods and assumptions	51	92(a), 93	27(a)	92(a), 93	27(a)	4Sch 45A(2)(a)

Disclosure	UK GAAP			IFRS GAAP		CA
	FRS 13	FRS 25	FRS 29	IAS 32	IFRS 7	Sch. 4/7
	α	β	γ	δ	ε	ζ

Fair value *continued*

Disclosure	FRS 13	FRS 25	FRS 29	IAS 32	IFRS 7	Sch. 4/7
Whether fair values are determined by reference to active market process or valuation techniques		92(b)	27(b)	92(b)	27(b)	
Whether valuation techniques are determined in whole or part using assumptions not supportable by prices from observable current market data		92(c)	27(c)	92(c)	27(c)	
Total change in fair value estimated where valuation techniques are employed that use non observable market data		92(d)	27(d)	92(d)	27(d)	
Where the initial transaction price is different from the valuation using non observable data at initial recognition disclosure of the accounting policy for amortising the difference to the P&L and the unamortized difference at the beginning and end of the period and reconciliation of the changes			28		28	
Disclosure exemption when carrying amount approximates fair value, non quoted equity investments, derivatives such investments, contracts with discretionary participating features when fair value cannot be measured reliably	53	90, 91	29(b), 30	90, 91	29(b), 30	
For instruments with discretionary participation features (IFRS 4) if fair value cannot be measured disclose this fact, a description of the contract, carrying amount, why fair value is not measurable, plus highly likely range of fair values, market information, intention and method of disposal, carrying amount and gains and losses on de-recognition		91A	29(c), 30	91A	29(c), 30	

Disclosure	UK GAAP			IFRS GAAP		CA
	FRS 13	FRS 25	FRS 29	IAS 32	IFRS 7	Sch. 4/7
	α	β	γ	δ	ε	ζ
Financial instruments held for trading						
Net gain or loss recognised in P&L split by category	57		20(a)		20(a)	4Sch 45A(2)(b)
Carrying amount of assets and liabilities held for trading	57(c)	94(e)(i)	8(a), 8(e)	94(e)(i)	8(a), 8(e)	4Sch 45C(2)(b)
Carrying amounts of financial assets and liabilities designated at inception at fair value through the P&L			8(a), 8(e)	94(e)(i)	8(a), 8(e)	
Hedges						
All hedges						
Cumulative aggregate gains/losses not recognised	59(a)					
Cumulative aggregate gains/losses carried forward in the balance sheet pending P&L recognition	59(b)					
Extent to which gains and losses disclosure above are expected to be recognised in the P&L in the next accounting period	59(c)					
Amount of gains or losses in the P&L that arose in previous years and either unrecognised or carried forward in the balance sheet at the start of the period	59(d)					
Cash flow hedges						
Periods when the cash flows are expected to occur and when they are expected to affect profit or loss		58(d)	23(a)	58(d)	23(a)	
A description of any forecast transaction for which hedge accounting had previously been used, but which is no longer expected to occur		58(d)	23(b)	58(d)	23(b)	
Amount recognised in equity during the period			23(c)	59(a)	23(c)	4Sch 45A(2)(b)
Amount of gains/losses previously in equity removed and included in P&L for period	62		23(d)	59(b)	23(d)	4Sch 45A(2)(b)

Disclosure	UK GAAP			IFRS GAAP		CA
	FRS 13	FRS 25	FRS 29	IAS 32	IFRS 7	Sch. 4/7
	α	β	γ	δ	ε	ζ
Cash flow hedges continued						
Amount of gains/losses removed from equity during the period and included in the initial cost or other carrying amount of a non-financial asset or non-financial liability whose acquisition / incurrence was a hedged highly probable forecast transaction			23(e)	59(c)	23(e)	
The ineffectiveness recognised in profit or loss that arises from cash flow hedges			24(b)		24(b)	
Fair value hedges						
Gains or losses on the hedging instrument and on the hedged item attributable to the hedged risk			24(a)		24(a)	
Hedge of net investment in foreign operations						
The ineffectiveness recognised in profit or loss that arises from hedges of net investments in foreign operations			24(c)		24(c)	
Financial assets and liabilities at fair value through profit or loss (AFVTPL)						
Carrying amount of financial assets and financial liabilities fair valued split by (i) trading and (ii) upon initial recognition designated as AFVTPL		94(e) 94(f)	8(a), 8(e)	94(e) 94(f)	8(a), 8(e)	
Loan or receivable designated as AFVTPL						
Maximum exposure to credit risk of the loan or receivable at the reporting date				94(g)(i)	9(a)	
Amount by which any related credit derivative or similar instruments mitigate that maximum exposure to credit risk				94(g)(ii)	9(b)	
Amount of change during the period and cumulatively in the fair value of the loan or receivable				94(g)(iii)	9(c)	
Amount of change in the fair value of any related credit derivatives or similar instruments during the period and cumulatively				94(g)(iv)	9(d)	

Disclosure	UK GAAP			IFRS GAAP		CA
	FRS 13	FRS 25	FRS 29	IAS 32	IFRS 7	Sch. 4/7
	α	β	γ	δ	ε	ζ

Financial liability designated as AFVTPL

Disclosure	FRS 13	FRS 25	FRS 29	IAS 32	IFRS 7	Sch. 4/7
Amount of change during the period and cumulative in the fair value not attributable to changes in the benchmark rate		94(h)(i)		94(h)(i)	9 (c)(i), (ii)	
Amount of change during the period and cumulative in the fair value attributable to credit risk			10(a)		10(a)	
Difference between the financial liability's carrying amount and the amount the entity would contractually be require to pay at maturity		94(h)(ii)	10(b)	94(h)(ii)	10(b)	
Method used to determine the fair value attributable to credit risk		94(i)	11	94(i)	11	

Balance sheet

Disclosure	FRS 13	FRS 25	FRS 29	IAS 32	IFRS 7	Sch. 4/7
Carrying amount split by the IAS39 classification of financial instruments		55	B1, B2	55	B1, B2	

Capital disclosures

Disclosure	FRS 13	FRS 25	FRS 29	IAS 32	IFRS 7	Sch. 4/7
Disclose objectives, policies and processes for managing entity's capital			E1 (i)			
Qualitative information describing capital managed and any external capital requirements and process to meet requirements			E2(a) (i)			
Summary quantitative data including charges from previous paid and compliance with extremely exposed capital requirements			E2(b) to (e) (i)			

Income statement and equity

Disclosure	FRS 13	FRS 25	FRS 29	IAS 32	IFRS 7	Sch. 4/7
Net gains/losses split by IAS 39 classification of financial instruments disclose separately those held for trading and those designated as AFVTPL)			20(a)	94(h)	20(a)	4Sch 45A(2)(b)
Total interest and total expense (calculated using EIR method) for financial assets and financial liabilities not AFVTPL		94(k)(i)	20(b)	94(k)(i)	20(b)	

Disclosure	UK GAAP			IFRS GAAP		CA
	FRS 13	FRS 25	FRS 29	IAS 32	IFRS 7	Sch. 4/7
	α	β	γ	δ	ε	ζ

Income statement and equity
continued

Disclosure	FRS 13	FRS 25	FRS 29	IAS 32	IFRS 7	Sch. 4/7
Fee income and expense arising from financial assets and financial liabilities not at FVTPL or trust and other fiduciary duties		94(k)(ii)	20(c)	94(k)(ii)	20(c)	
Interest income accrued on impaired financial assets		94(k)(iii)	20(d)	94(k)(iii)	20(d)	
Disclose total interest expense recognised in profit or loss on contracts with discretionary participation features			20A (θ)			
Amount of impairment loss by class of financial assets		94(l)	20(e)	94(l)	20(e)	
Total gain/loss recognised directly in reserves and amount removed from reserves and recycled to the P&L for available for sale assets		94(k)(ii)	20(a)(ii)	94(k)(ii)	20(a)(ii)	4Sch 45A(3) (κ)
Where any amount is transferred to or from the fair value reserve, state in tabular form: (a) amount of reserve at beginning and end of period; (b) amount transferred to or from reserve during period; and (c) source and application of amounts transferred.						4Sch 45A(3)

Accounting policies

Disclosure	FRS 13	FRS 25	FRS 29	IAS 32	IFRS 7	Sch. 4/7
Accounting policies relating to financial instruments	74-6	60(b), 61, 66	21, B5	60(b), 61, 66	21, B5	
Additional specific disclosures for entities not applying FRS26			21A			
Basis for reporting realised and unrealised gains and losses, interest and other items of income and expense on financial assets and financial liabilities, including hedging instruments and reason for any net presentation of income and expense in profit and loss			21B			

Disclosure	UK GAAP			IFRS GAAP		CA
	FRS 13	FRS 25	FRS 29	IAS 32	IFRS 7	Sch. 4/7
	α	β	γ	δ	ε	ζ

Compound financial instruments with multiple derivatives

Disclosure	FRS 13	FRS 25	FRS 29	IAS 32	IFRS 7	Sch. 4/7
Disclose the existence of the features		94(d)	17	94(d)	17	
Disclose the effective interest rate on the liability component		94(d)		94(d)		

Reclassifications

Disclosure	FRS 13	FRS 25	FRS 29	IAS 32	IFRS 7	Sch. 4/7
Disclose amounts and explain any reclassified financial instruments from fair value to cost/amortised cost method or vice versa		94(j)	12	94(j)	12	

Collateral

Disclosure	FRS 13	FRS 25	FRS 29	IAS 32	IFRS 7	Sch. 4/7
Carrying amount of financial assets pledged as collateral for liabilities/ contingent liabilities, terms and conditions		94(b)	14	94(b)	14	
For pledged collateral that the entity is permitted to sell or repledge in the absence of default by the owner of the collateral the fair value of collateral available, fair value of such collateral sold or repledged, whether this is an obligation to return it and terms/ conditions associated with its use of this collateral		94(c)	15	94(c)	15	

Allowance account for credit losses

Disclosure	FRS 13	FRS 25	FRS 29	IAS 32	IFRS 7	Sch. 4/7
Where assets are impaired by credit losses and the impairment is recorded in a separate account reconciliation of changes during the period for each class of financial asset			16		16	

Disclosure	UK GAAP			IFRS GAAP		CA
	FRS 13	FRS 25	FRS 29	IAS 32	IFRS 7	Sch. 4/7
	α	β	γ	δ	ε	ζ

Defaults and breaches

Details of the default, carrying amount of the loan in default at reporting date and whether the default has been remediated or terms renegotiated before the financial statements are authorised		94(k), 95	18-19, IG12	94(k), 95	18-19, IG12	
If there are breaches of terms other than those above, disclose the same information as above unless remediated or the terms of the loan renegotiated on or before the reporting date			19		19	

De-recognition

Where part of a financial asset does not qualify for de-recognition disclose the nature of the asset, risk and rewards, carrying amount of retained interest and associated liability		FRS4	FRS4	94(a)	13	

Notes:

α) Applicable to banks and listed companies for accounting periods ending on or after 23 March 1999. Superseded for entities applying the disclosure requirements in FRS 25 or FRS 29.

β) Paragraphs 51 to 95 are applicable to entities within the scope of FRS 26 from the date of application of FRS 26. Effective for accounting periods beginning on or after 1 January 2005. Voluntary application permitted. Paragraphs 51 to 95 are superseded for entities applying FRS 29.

γ) Applicable to entities within the scope of FRS 26. Supersedes paragraphs 51 to 95 in FRS 25. Effective for accounting periods beginning on or after 1 January 2007. Earlier application encouraged. Voluntary application permitted.

δ) Applicable for annual accounting periods beginning on or after 1 January 2005. Earlier application permitted. Paragraphs 51 to 95 are superseded for entities applying IFRS 7.

ε) Applicable for annual accounting periods beginning on or after 1 January 2007. Earlier application encouraged. Supersedes paragraphs 51 to 95 in IAS 32.

ζ) Schedule 4 disclosures required only for UK GAAP reporters. Schedule 7 disclosures required for both UK GAAP and IFRS reporters. Certain disclosure requirements in the Act are similar but not identical to the disclosure requirements in FRS25/FRS29 and IAS32/IFRS7. Entities within the scope of both the Act and FRS25/FRS29 or IAS32/IFRS7 will need to ensure that they comply with the requirements of both. Schedule 4/7 disclosures must be presented in comparatives when FRS 25/29 or IAS 32/IFRS 7 are not applied in the comparative period.

η) Changes from previous period are not required explicitly but would be part of the general discussion on risk which is require the Act.

θ) Identical to disclosure required by IFRS4

ι) This disclosure is required in IAS 1.124A-C

κ) Must be presented in tabular form.

Scope and effective date and Companies Act requirements for a UK GAAP reporter

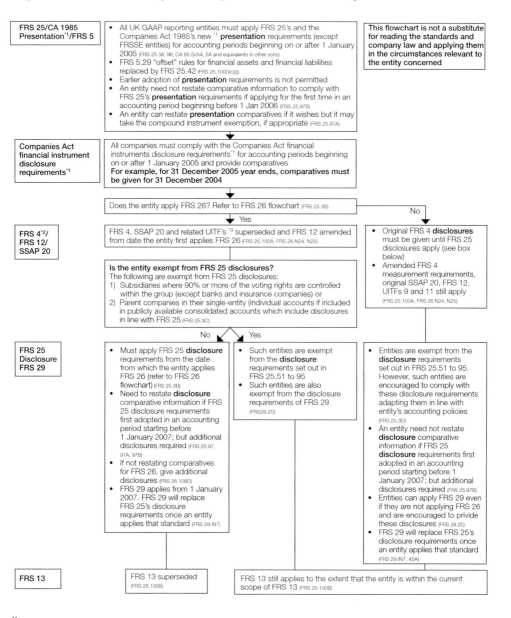

FRS 25/CA 1985 Presentation*1/FRS 5	
	• All UK GAAP reporting entities must apply FRS 25's and the Companies Act 1985's new *1 **presentation** requirements (except FRSSE entities) for accounting periods beginning on or after 1 January 2005 (FRS 25.3A, 96; CA 85 Sch4, 5A and equivalents in other schs)
	• FRS 5.29 "offset" rules for financial assets and financial liabilities replaced by FRS 25.42 (FRS 25.100D(c)(i))
	• Earlier adoption of **presentation** requirements is not permitted
	• An entity need not restate comparative information to comply with FRS 25's **presentation** requirements if applying for the first time in an accounting period beginning before 1 Jan 2006 (FRS 25.97B)
	• An entity can restate **presentation** comparatives if it wishes but it may take the compound instrument exemption, if appropriate (FRS 25.97A)

This flowchart is not a substitute for reading the standards and company law and applying them in the circumstances relevant to the entity concerned

Companies Act financial instrument disclosure requirements*1

All companies must comply with the Companies Act financial instruments disclosure requirements*1 for accounting periods beginning on or after 1 January 2005 and provide comparatives
For example, for 31 December 2005 year ends, comparatives must be given for 31 December 2004

Does the entity apply FRS 26? Refer to FRS 26 flowchart (FRS 25.3B) — No

↓ Yes

FRS 4*2/ FRS 12/ SSAP 20

FRS 4, SSAP 20 and related UITF's *3 superseded and FRS 12 amended from date the entity first applies FRS 26 (FRS 25.100A, FRS 26.N24, N25)

• Original FRS 4 **disclosures** must be given until FRS 25 disclosures apply (see box below)
• Amended FRS 4 measurement requirements, original SSAP 20, FRS 12, UITFs 9 and 11 still apply (FRS 25.100A, FRS 26.N24, N25)

Is the entity exempt from FRS 25 disclosures?
The following are exempt from FRS 25 disclosures:
1) Subsidiaries where 90% or more of the voting rights are controlled within the group (except banks and insurance companies) or
2) Parent companies in their single-entity (individual accounts if included in publicly available consolidated accounts which include disclosures in line with FRS 25 (FRS 25.3C)

No ↙ ↘ Yes

FRS 25 Disclosure FRS 29

• Must apply FRS 25 **disclosure** requirements from the date from which the entity applies FRS 26 (refer to FRS 26 flowchart) (FRS 25.3B)
• Need to restate **disclosure** comparative information if FRS 25 disclosure requirements first adopted in an accounting period starting before 1 January 2007; but additional disclosures required (FRS 25.97, 97A, 97B)
• If not restating comparatives for FRS 26, give additional disclosures (FRS 26.108D)
• FRS 29 applies from 1 January 2007. FRS 29 will replace FRS 25's disclosure requirements once an entity applies that standard (FRS 29.IN7)

• Such entities are exempt from the **disclosure** requirements set out in FRS 25.51 to 95
• Such entities are also exempt from the disclosure requirements of FRS 29 (FRS29.2D)

• Entities are exempt from the **disclosure** requirements set out in FRS 25.51 to 95. However, such entities are encouraged to comply with these disclosure requirements adapting them in line with entity's accounting policies (FRS 25.3D)
• An entity need not restate **disclosure** comparative information if FRS 25 disclosure requirements first adopted in an accounting period starting before 1 January 2007; but additional disclosures required (FRS 25.97B)
• Entities can apply FRS 29 even if they are not applying FRS 26 and are encouraged to privide these disclosures (FRS 29.2E)
• FRS 29 will replace FRS 25's disclosure requirements once an entity applies that standard (FRS 29.IN7, 45A)

FRS 13

FRS 13 superseded (FRS 25.100B)

FRS 13 still applies to the extent that the entity is within the current scope of FRS 13 (FRS 25.100B)

---

*1 Refers to the presentation and disclosures requirements inserted into the Companies Act 1985 by the Companies Act 1985 (International Accounting Standards and Other Accounting Amendments) Regulations 2004.

*2 FRS 25 substantially amends FRS 4 'Capital instruments' to remove the concept of non-equity shares as all capital instruments (or components thereof) must be presented as equity or debt for accounting periods starting from 1 January 2005.

*3 Related UITF's are as follows: FRS 26 supersedes UITF 11 Capital instruments: issuer call options for those applying FRS 26, FRS 25 presentation requirements supersede UITF 33 Obligations in capital instruments and UITF 37 Purchases and sales of own shares for accounting periods starting from 1 January 2005. FRS 24 supersedes UITF 9 for those applying FRS 24.

IAS 33 and FRS 22 – Earnings per share

IAS 33, Earnings per share	FRS 22, Earnings per share
The revised standard (2003) was effective for annual periods beginning on or after 1 January 2005.	*Effective for accounting periods beginning on or after 1 January 2005.*

Related pronouncements

–	–

Overview

In this summary, references to IAS 33 relate to the revised standard issued in December 2003 and consequential amendments in subsequent standards.

In December 2004, the ASB issued FRS 22 (IAS 33), 'Earnings per share' (following on from FRED 26 issued in May 2002) which replaced FRS 14. FRS 22 is based on the revised IAS 33, 'Earnings per share'. FRS 22 applies to listed companies and those in the process of listing and is effective for accounting periods beginning on or after 1 January 2005.

The requirements, scope and effective date of FRS 22 are identical to IAS 33 except that:

- Early adoption is not permitted consistent with FRS 25 (IAS 32), Financial Instruments: Disclosure and Presentation.

- The guidance on earnings per share for business combinations accounted for as mergers under FRS 6, Acquisitions and Mergers, that was exposed in FRED 26, Earnings per share, has been retained in an appendix. The references to other IASs and IFRSs in IAS 33 have been amended where necessary to enable the standard to be applied in the UK context. The ASB believes that those amendments do not change the requirements of IAS 33 in any way.

Convergence

FRS 22 is based on the revised IAS 33, 'Earnings per share'.

First-time adoption of IFRS

There are no specific rules in IFRS 1 in respect of IAS 33 and so the general rule of retrospective application will apply.

Summary of main points

Objective

Sets out principles for calculating and presenting EPS. Focus is on the denominator of the EPS calculation. [IAS 33 para 1].	Same. [FRS 22 para 1].

Scope

Applies to entities whose ordinary shares or potential ordinary shares are publicly traded and to entities that are in the process of issuing ordinary shares or potential ordinary shares in public markets. [IAS 33 para 2].	Same. [FRS 22 para 1].
Not dealt with in IAS 33.	Reporting entities applying the Financial Reporting Standard for Smaller Entities currently applicable are exempt from FRS 22. [FRS 22 para 2A].
Not applicable as IFRS 3 prohibits merger accounting for business combinations within its scope.	Entities that use merger accounting as required or permitted by FRS 6, Acquisitions and Mergers, should follow the requirements in Appendix C, Application to Merger Accounting.

A potential ordinary share is a financial instrument or other contract that may entitle its holder to ordinary shares, for example:

- Convertible debt or preference shares.

- Share warrants and options.

- Deferred consideration in the form of shares (for example, for the purchase of a business).

[IAS 33 paras 5, 7].

Same. [FRS 22 paras 5, 7].

Measurement: Basic EPS

Basic EPS is the profit or loss attributable to the parent entity's ordinary equity holders divided by the weighted average number of ordinary shares outstanding during the period. [IAS 33 para 10].

Same. [FRS 22 para 10].

Earnings – Basic

Profit or loss attributable to the parent entity's ordinary equity holders is the profit or loss for the period adjusted for the after-tax amounts of preference dividends and differences arising on the settlement of preference shares classed as equity. [IAS 33 para 12].

Same. [FRS 22 para 12].

Number of shares – Basic

The weighted average number of ordinary shares outstanding during the period is the number of ordinary shares outstanding at the beginning of the period, adjusted by the number of ordinary shares bought back or issued during the period multiplied by a time-weighting factor. [IAS 33 para 20].

Same. [FRS 22 para 20].

The time-weighting factor is the number of days that the specific shares are outstanding as a proportion of the total number of days in the period. [IAS 33 para 20].

Same. [FRS 22 para 20].

In most cases, shares are included in the weighted average number of shares from the date consideration is receivable (which is generally the date of their issue). [IAS 33 para 21]. A list of examples in given in IAS 33 paragraph 21.

Same. [FRS 22 para 21].

Ordinary shares issued as part of the cost of a business combination are included in the weighted average number of shares from the acquisition date. [IAS 33, paragraph 22].

Same [FRS 22, para 22], except for a business combination that is merger accounted under FRS 6. [FRS 22 para C2]. Basic and diluted EPS for all periods presented should be restated for the effects of such a combination.

Weighted average number of ordinary shares outstanding during the period and for all periods presented should be adjusted for events (other than the conversion of potential ordinary shares) that have changed the number of ordinary shares outstanding, without a corresponding change in resources. [IAS 33 para 26].

Same. [FRS 22 para 26].

Events that change the number of ordinary shares outstanding, without a corresponding change in resources include:

- A capitalisation or bonus issue.

- A bonus element in any other issue, for example in a rights issue.

- A share split.

- A share consolidation.

[IAS 33 para 27].

Same. [FRS 22 para 27].

The bonus element inherent in a rights issue is measured by the following fraction:

Same. [FRS 22 para A2].

$$\frac{\textit{Fair value per share immediately before the exercise of rights}}{\textit{Theoretical ex-rights fair value per share}}$$

Guidance on determining the theoretical ex-rights fair value per share is given in an appendix to the standard. [IAS 33 para A2].

The weighted average number of shares in prior periods is not adjusted for a share consolidation combined with a special dividend where the overall commercial effect is that of a share repurchase at fair value. The weighted average number of shares for the period in which the combined transaction takes place is adjusted for the reduction in the number of shares from the date the special dividend is recognised. [IAS 33 para 29].

Same. [FRS 22 para 29].

Measurement: Diluted EPS

Profit attributable to the parent entity's ordinary equity holders and weighted average number of ordinary shares outstanding should be adjusted for the effects of all dilutive potential ordinary shares outstanding during the period. [IAS 33 para 31].

Same. [FRS 22 para 31].

Earnings – Diluted

Profit or loss for the period attributable to the parent entity's ordinary equity holders (as in basic EPS) should be adjusted for the after-tax effects of:

Same. [FRS 22 para 33].

- Any dividends or other items related to dilutive potential ordinary shares deducted in arriving at the profit attributable to ordinary equity holders for basic EPS.

- Interest recognised in the period related to the dilutive potential ordinary shares.

- Any other changes in income or expense that would result from the conversion of the dilutive potential ordinary shares.

[IAS 33 para 33].

Number of shares – Diluted

Weighted average number of ordinary shares as for basic EPS should be increased by the weighted average number of additional ordinary shares that would be issued on the conversion of all dilutive potential ordinary shares into ordinary shares. [IAS 33 para 36].	Same. [FRS 22 para 36].
IAS 33 provides specific guidance in respect of purchased options and written put options. [IAS 33 paras 62, 63].	Same. [FRS 22 paras 62, 63].

Dilutive potential ordinary shares

Dilutive potential ordinary shares should be deemed to have been converted into ordinary shares at the beginning of the period, or, if later, the date of issue of the potential ordinary share. [IAS 33 para 36].	Same. [FRS 22 para 36].
The number of dilutive potential ordinary shares is determined independently for each period presented and is not a weighted average of the dilutive potential ordinary shares included in each interim computation. [IAS 33 para 37].	Same. [FRS 22 para 37].
Potential ordinary shares are weighted for the period they were outstanding as follows:	Same. [FRS 22 para 38].

- Those that lapsed during the reporting period are included in diluted EPS only for the portion of the period during which they were outstanding.

- Those that have been converted into ordinary shares during the reporting period are included in diluted EPS up to the date of conversion; from the date of conversion, the resulting ordinary shares are included in both basic and diluted EPS.

[IAS 33 para 38].

Potential ordinary shares should be treated as dilutive when, and only when, their conversion to ordinary shares would decrease EPS or increase loss per share from continuing operations. [IAS 33 para 41].	Same. [FRS 22 para 41].
The profit or loss from continuing operations is the profit (or loss) after adjusting for preference dividends (and similar items) and excludes items relating to discontinued operations. [IAS 33 para 42].	Same. [FRS 22 para 42].
In determining, whether potential ordinary shares are dilutive or antidilutive, each issue or series of potential ordinary shares is considered separately rather than in aggregate. In order to maximise diluted EPS, each series is considered in sequence from the most dilutive to the least dilutive. [IAS 33 para 44].	Same. [FRS 22 para 44].

Share warrants and options

Exercise of dilutive options and warrants should be assumed. The assumed proceeds should be regarded as having been received from the issue of ordinary shares at the average market price of ordinary shares during the period. [IAS 33 para 45]. The difference between the number of shares issued and the number of shares that would have been issued at the assumed proceeds should be treated as an issue of ordinary shares for no consideration. [IAS 33 para 45].	Same. [FRS 22 para 45].

Employee share and incentive plans

Share-based remuneration schemes give rise to potential ordinary shares. Employee share options with fixed or determinable terms are treated as options in the calculation of diluted EPS. Performance-based employee share options are treated as contingently issuable shares. [IAS 33 para 48].	Same. [FRS 22 para 48].
For share options and other share-based payment arrangements to which IFRS 2 applies, the assumed proceeds used in the diluted EPS calculation includes the fair value of any goods or services to be supplied to the entity in the future under the arrangement. [IAS 33 para 47A].	Same. [FRS 22 para 47A].

Contingently issuable shares

Ordinary shares that are issuable for little or no cash or other consideration upon the satisfaction of specified conditions are included in the computation of basic EPS from the date when all necessary conditions have been satisfied. [IAS 33 paras 5, 24].	Same. [FRS 22 paras 5, 24].
Shares that are issuable solely after the passage of time are not contingently issuable shares, because the passage of time is a certainty. [IAS 33 para 24].	Same. [FRS 22 para 24].
Contingently issuable shares are included in the calculation of diluted EPS based on the number of shares that would be issued if the end of the reporting period was the end of the contingency period. [IAS 33 para 52].	Same. [FRS 22 para 52].
They are included from the beginning of the period or as of the date of the contingent share agreement. [IAS 33 para 52].	Same. [FRS 22 para 52].
Restatement is not permitted if the conditions are not met when the actual contingency period expired. [IAS 33 para 52].	Same. [FRS 22 para 52].

Contracts that may be settled in shares or cash

Contracts that may be settled in ordinary shares or in cash at the *entity's option* are presumed to be settled in ordinary shares and the resulting potential ordinary shares are included in diluted EPS if the effect is dilutive. For contracts that may be settled in ordinary shares or in cash at the holder's option, the more dilutive of cash settlement and share settlement is used in calculating diluted EPS. [IAS 33 paras 58, 60].

Same. [FRS 22 paras 58, 60].

Presentation

An entity should disclose both basic and diluted EPS on the face of the income statement for profit or loss from continuing operations (if presented) and for profit or loss for the period for each class of ordinary shares that has a different right to share in profit for the period. [IAS 33 paras 9, 30, 66].

Same. [FRS 22 paras 9, 30, 66].

An entity that reports a discontinued operation should disclose the basic and diluted EPS for the discontinued operation either on the face of the income statement or in the notes to the financial statements. [IAS 33 para 68].

Same. [FRS 22 para 68].

Basic and diluted EPS should be presented with equal prominence for all periods presented. [IAS 33 para 66].

Same. [FRS 22 para 66].

Both basic and diluted EPS should be presented even if the amounts are negative (a loss per share). [IAS 33 para 69].

Same. [FRS 22 para 69].

Disclosure

An entity should disclose the following:

- The earnings amounts used as the numerator in calculating basic and diluted EPS, and a reconciliation of those earnings amounts to the profit or loss for the period. [IAS 33 para 70(a)].

  Same. [FRS 22 para 70(a)].

- The weighted average number of shares used as the denominator in calculating basic and diluted EPS, and a reconciliation of these denominators to each other. [IAS 33 para 70(b)].

  Same. [FRS 22 para 70(b)].

- Instruments (including contingently issuable shares) that could potentially dilute basic EPS in the future, but not included in diluted EPS as they are antidilutive for the period(s) presented. [IAS 33 para 70(c)].

  Same. [FRS 22 para 70(c)].

- Details of post balance sheet ordinary or potential ordinary share transactions, not resulting in restated EPS (see below), that significantly change the number of ordinary or potential ordinary shares outstanding. [IAS 33 para 70(d)].

  Same. [FRS 22 para 70(d)].

When a change in accounting policy has an effect on the current period or any prior period, or would have such an effect except that it is impracticable to determine the amount of the adjustment, or might have an effect on future periods, an entity should disclose for the current period and each prior period presented, to the extent practicable, the amount of the adjustment for basic and diluted EPS. [IAS 8 paras 28(f)(ii), 29(c)(ii)].

Not dealt with in FRS 22.

Similarly, for the retrospective correction of material prior period errors, an entity should disclose for each prior period presented, to the extent practicable, the amount of the correction for basic and diluted EPS. [IAS 8 para 49(b)(ii)].

Not dealt with in FRS 22.

Additional EPS

If an entity discloses, in addition to basic and diluted EPS, amounts per share using a reported component of the income statement other than one required by IAS 33 (see 'Presentation' above), such amounts should be calculated using the weighted average number of shares used in the standard calculations. [IAS 33 para 73].

Same. [FRS 22 para 73].

Additional basic and diluted EPS should be disclosed with equal prominence to each other and should be presented in the notes to the financial statements. [IAS 33 para 73].

Same. [FRS 22 para 73].

The basis for determining the numerator for additional EPS should be indicated, including whether amounts per share are before or after tax. [IAS 33 para 73].

Same. [FRS 22 para 73].

If a component of the income statement is used that is not reported as a line item in the income statement, a reconciliation should be provided between the component used and a line item that is reported in the income statement. [IAS 33 para 73].

Same. [FRS 22 para 73].

Restatement

Basic and diluted EPS for all periods presented should be restated for:

- Events occurring during the current period and those occurring after the balance sheet date but prior to approval of the financial statements that change the number of shares without a corresponding change in the resources of the entity (for example, bonus issue, share split or share consolidation). [IAS 33 para 64].

  Same. [FRS 22 para 64].

- The effects of errors and adjustments resulting from changes in accounting policies accounted for retrospectively. [IAS 33 para 64].

  Same. [FRS 22 para 64].

• Not applicable as IFRS 3 prohibits merger accounting for business combinations within its scope.	Basic and diluted EPS for all periods presented should be restated for the effects of a business combination that is merger accounted under FRS 6. [FRS 22 para C2].

No restatement

Diluted EPS of any prior period should not be adjusted for changes in the assumptions used or for the conversion of potential ordinary shares into ordinary shares. [IAS 33 para 65].	Same. [FRS 22 para 65].
Prior period's EPS should not be adjusted for a share consolidation combined with a special dividend where the overall commercial effect is that of a share repurchase at fair value. [IAS 33 para 29].	Same. [FRS 22 para 29].

IAS 34 and ASB's statement – Interim reports

IAS 34, Interim financial reporting	ASB statement, Interim reports
Effective for financial statements covering periods beginning on or after 1 January 1999.	*No effective date as it is a voluntary best practice statement.*

Related pronouncements

IFRIC 10, Interim financial reporting and impairment. Note – the Listing Rule/AIM Rule references given in the 'ASB column' also apply to UK listed/AIM companies reporting under IFRS.	Listing Rules (chapter 9) – mandatory for listed companies. On 21 December 2006, the FSA published new rules following the implementation of the EU Transparency Directive in the UK. These apply for accounting periods commencing on or after 20 January 2007, and are not yet included in this summary. AIM Rules – mandatory for AIM companies.

Overview

In this summary, references to IAS 34 include consequential amendments in subsequent standards. There is no requirement under IFRS to publish an interim financial report. However, entities that are required by local regulators or elect voluntarily to publish an interim financial report in accordance with IFRS, must apply IAS 34. In the UK, listed companies are required by the Listing Rules to publish half-yearly interim reports. The Listing Rules set out minimum requirements for interim reports and, under UK GAAP, are supplemented by the ASB's statement of best practice.

IAS 34 defines the minimum content of an interim report, including disclosures together with the recognition and measurement principles to be applied. The requirements are broadly consistent with the UK requirements.

One difference is that, under IAS 34, comparatives for the balance sheet are required to be disclosed as at the end of the previous full financial year, whereas in the UK, the Listing Rules require balance sheet comparatives for the corresponding interim date in the prior year. The Listing Rules do not require disclosure for the previous full financial year, but it is recommended by the ASB's statement and, in practice, this disclosure is given by UK companies that publish interim reports.

Furthermore, under IAS 34, quarterly interim reports must contain figures (other than for the balance sheet) for the cumulative period to date and for the corresponding period of the preceding year. This is not specified under UK GAAP.

IAS 34 requires detailed disclosures, in accordance with the requirements of IFRS 3, 'Business combinations', in respect of business combinations during the period. The ASB's interim statement refers only to narrative commentary in respect of major acquisitions in the period.

Convergence

The IASB has indicated its intention to review IAS 34 as part of the IFRS/US convergence project.

First-time adoption of IFRS

IFRS 1 applies to interim financial statements, presented in accordance with IAS 34, covering part of the period in an entity's first IFRS financial statements. IFRS 1 requires additional disclosures, including the same reconciliations as in the annual financial statements and a reconciliation of the profit for the comparative interim period and of the equity at the end of that period.

Summary of main points

Scope

IAS 34 does not require entities to publish an interim report, but it applies if an interim report is published in accordance with IFRS. Publicly traded entities are encouraged to provide interim financial reports. [IAS 34 para 1].	Listed companies are required to prepare an interim report for the first six months of the financial year. [LR 9.9.1 R; AIMR 18]. Use of the ASB's statement is encouraged as best practice, but is not mandatory.

Timing of publication

Publication within 60 days of the interim period end is encouraged. [IAS 34 para 1].	The ASB's statement is the same as IAS 34. [IR para 3]. The Listing Rules require publication within 90 days of the interim period end. [LR 9.9.3 R]. The new Listings Rules act to shorten filing periods for half yearly reports to two months. They also make preliminary announcements voluntary and introduce interim management statements for those companies that do not report quarterly. The AIM Rules require publication within three months of the interim period end. [AIMR 18].

Content

An interim report should include, as a minimum, the following components:	The Listing Rules set out the minimum requirements for interim reports. The ASB's statement recommends additional content as best practice.
• Condensed balance sheet.	• Same. [LR 9.9.8 R (1); AIMR 18; IR para 52].
• Condensed income statement.	• Same. [LR 9.9.8 R (3); AIMR 18; IR para 40].
• Condensed statement showing either all changes in equity or changes in equity other than transactions with owners.	• Same. [LR 9.9.8 R (5)]. Also, the ASB's statement recommends inclusion of a STRGL and reconciliation of movement in shareholders' funds. [IR paras 49, 51].
• Condensed cash flow statement.	• Same. [LR 9.9.8 R (2); AIMR 18; IR para 53].
• Selected explanatory notes (see below). [IAS 34 para 8].	• Explanatory notes are also required. [LR 9.9.8 R (6)]. However, there are some differences (see below).
Basic and diluted earnings per share should be presented on the face of the income statement. [IAS 34 para 11].	Similar. [LR 9.9.8 R (3)(k); IR para 48].
The notes to the interim report should include the information set out below, if material:	
• A statement that the accounting policies and methods are the same as in the most recent annual financial statements, or a description of the changes.	• Similar. [LR 9.9.2 R; IR para 10].
• Explanation of the effects of seasonality or cyclicality of interim operations.	• Explanation relating to the activities over the last interim period (including any special factors), enabling users to assess trends and make a comparison with the corresponding period of the prior year. [LR 9.9.8 R(6)].

• Nature and amount of items that are unusual because of nature, size or incidence.	• Similar disclosure recommended by ASB's statement. [IR paras 45 to 47].
• Changes in estimates of previously reported amounts.	• No specific mention of changes in estimates.
• Movements in debt and equity.	• Explanation recommended of movements in working capital, liquidity and net debt. [IR para 38].
• Dividends paid.	• Similar. [LR 9.9.8 R (3)(i); IR para 40].
• Segment revenue and result for the primary segment.	• Similar recommended, but the segmental analysis should be given for both geographical and business segments. [IR para 43].
• Material events subsequent to the interim period end.	• Similar disclosure recommended. [IR para 39].
• Effects of changes in the composition of the group. In the case of business combinations, the entity should disclose the information required by paragraphs 66 to 73 of IFRS 3.	• Recommended that the narrative commentary should give details of acquisitions and disposals of major fixed assets or investments during the period. [IR para 39]. Also, FRS 3 analysis (continuing and discontinued) of turnover and operating profit on the face of the profit and loss account is recommended. [IR para 41].
• Changes in contingencies since the last balance sheet date. [IAS 34 para 16].	• Similar disclosure recommended. [IR para 39].
No specific requirement in IAS 34.	Listing Rules require disclosure, so far as possible, of the group's prospects. [LR 9.9.8 R (6)].
No specific requirement in IAS 34.	Other recommended disclosures include discussion of the effective tax rate, the period covered by the report and the date the report was approved by the directors. [IR paras 22, 58].
If an interim report complies with IFRS, that fact should be disclosed. [IAS 34 para 19].	No requirement for a statement of compliance.

Periods for which interims are required to be presented

Balance sheet – current interim period end and comparatives for the last full financial year end. [IAS 34 para 20(a)].	Listing Rules require current interim period end and comparatives for corresponding prior year interim period end. [LR 9.9.8 R (4); also AIMR 18]. The ASB's statement also recommends comparatives from the last annual financial statements. [IR para 56].
Income statement – current interim period and cumulatively for the current year to date with corresponding comparative periods for both. [IAS 34 para 20(b)].	Listing Rules require current interim period and comparatives for corresponding prior year interim period. [LR 9.9.8 R (4); also AIMR 18]. The ASB's statement also recommends comparatives for the preceding full year. [IR para 55]. There is no requirement to report year-to-date information.
Statement of changes in equity and cash flow statement – cumulatively for the current year to date and corresponding comparative period. [IAS 34 para 20(c),(d)].	Same as for income statement.

Highly seasonal businesses are encouraged to present financial information for the twelve months to date, together with comparatives. [IAS 34 para 21].	No equivalent requirement or recommendation.

Materiality

Materiality should be assessed in relation to the interim period financial data. [IAS 34 para 23].	Same. [IR para 28].

Disclosure in annual financial statements

Significant changes in previously reported estimates should be disclosed in the annual financial statements if no separate interim report is published for the final interim period. [IAS 34 para 26].	The ASB's best practice statement on preliminary announcements recommends separate presentation of the final interim period figures, together with their corresponding amounts. [PA para 35].

Recognition and measurement

The same accounting policies should be used in the interim period as are used in the last full year, except for changes in accounting policies to be reflected in the next annual financial statements. [IAS 34 para 28].	Similar, but applies to presentation as well as policies. The Listing Rules require adoption of changes in accounting policies to be made in the interim report. [LR 9.9.2 R; also AIMR 18].
Measurements should be made on a year-to-date basis (that is, the frequency of interim reports should not affect the annual results). [IAS 34 para 28].	No specific mention.
Any impairment losses recognised in an interim financial statement may not be reversed in subsequent interim or annual financial statements. [IFRIC 10 para 8].	No specific mention.
The same principles should be applied as at the year end. Seasonal, cyclical or occasional revenues or uneven costs should not be anticipated or deferred, unless this would be appropriate at the end of the financial year. [IAS 34 paras 37, 39].	The ASB's statement recommends the same – that is, the 'discrete method'. [IR para 8].
Appendix B to IAS 34 includes examples of applying the recognition and measurement principles, including provisions, year end bonuses, pensions, tax, inventories and foreign currency.	Similar guidance is given in the ASB's statement.
Interim reports will generally require a greater use of estimation methods than annual reports. [IAS 34 para 41].	Similar.
Appendix C to IAS 34 includes examples of the use of estimates in interim periods.	Similar examples are given in the ASB's statement.
Where fixed assets are carried at revalued amounts, an entity may rely on professionally qualified valuers at annual reporting dates though not at interim reporting dates. [IAS 34 App C para 7].	The ASB's statement says that interim valuations are not normally necessary. [IR para 26].

Taxation

Income tax expense is recognised in each interim period based on the best estimate of the weighted average annual income tax rate expected for the full financial year. [IAS 34 para 30(c)].	Similar. [IR para 18].

Restatement of previously reported interim periods

Changes in accounting policy (other than where a new standard has transitional provisions) should be reflected by:

• restating prior interim periods of the current year and comparable interim periods of any prior years that will be restated in the annual financial statements in accordance with IAS 8; or	Similar. [IR para 12].
• when it is impracticable to determine the cumulative effect of applying a new accounting policy to all prior periods, adjusting the financial statements of prior interim periods of the current year and comparable interim periods of prior years to apply the new accounting policy prospectively from the earliest date practicable.	There is no exception for impracticability in the ASB's statement or in FRS 3.

[IAS 34 para 43].

Method of publication

Not dealt with in IAS 34.	The Listing Rules require an interim report to be notified to a Regulatory Information Service. [LR 9.9.4 R; also AIMR 18]. It must also be sent to holders of listed securities or an advert placed in the national press. [LR 9.9.5 R].

Auditors' review

Not dealt with in IAS 34.	Where the figures in the half-yearly report have been audited or reviewed by auditors under APB bulletin 99/4, the auditors' review report must be reproduced in full. [LR 9.9.9 R].

IAS 36 and FRS 11 – Impairment of assets

IAS 36, Impairment of assets	FRS 11, Impairment of fixed assets and goodwill
Effective for accounting periods beginning on or after 1 July 1999.	*Effective for accounting periods ending on or after 23 December 1998.*
The revised standard (2004) applies to goodwill and intangible assets acquired in business combinations on or after 31 March 2004 and to all other assets for annual periods beginning on or after 31 March 2004.	

Related pronouncements

IFRS 3, Business combinations.	FRS 10, Goodwill and intangible assets.
	FRS 7, Fair values in acquisition accounting.

Overview

In this summary, references to IAS 36 relate to the revised standard issued in March 2004. The basic approach in IAS 36 is the same as that in FRS 11 – impairment is measured by comparing the carrying value of fixed assets and goodwill with the higher of fair value less costs to sell (equivalent to net realisable value) and value in use. Value in use is calculated by discounting the cash flows that are expected to be generated from the assets.

However, there are some differences between IAS 36 and FRS 11 arising from the UK view of intangible assets as being of a similar nature to goodwill, whereas under IFRS, intangible assets are treated as akin to tangible fixed assets. The main implications of this arise in:

- The allocation of impairment losses, which under IAS 36 are allocated first to goodwill and then pro-rata to intangible assets and other tangible fixed assets. Under FRS 11, losses are allocated first to goodwill, then to intangible assets and then to other tangible fixed assets.

- Under IAS 36, reversals of impairment of goodwill are prohibited. Reversals of impairments on intangible assets are permitted where there are indicators that the impairment no longer exists or is reduced. FRS 11 permits reversals of impairments of goodwill and intangible assets in restricted circumstances.

Goodwill is not amortised under IFRS. Instead, IAS 36 requires an annual impairment review, which should take place at the same time each year (not necessarily the year end, although if there is a trigger event subsequent to an impairment test being performed on goodwill, then the impairment test must be updated). UK GAAP requires a review of goodwill at the end of the first full year after acquisition, but then only requires such reviews when there has been a trigger event or where goodwill is amortised over more than 20 years (or carried indefinitely without being amortised).

Where acquired entities are merged with existing operations, FRS 11 requires calculation of the internally generated goodwill of the pre-existing operation to facilitate a more accurate assessment of whether acquired goodwill has been subsequently impaired. There is no similar requirement in IAS 36.

Both standards require that in determining value in use, future cash flows should be estimated for the asset in its current condition and should not include estimated cash flows from future restructuring to which the entity is not yet committed or future expenditure that will improve or enhance the asset. However, FRS 11 includes an exception for newly-acquired income generating units and permits these future cash flows to be taken into account if they were anticipated at the time of performing the impairment review in the first full year after acquisition and were consistent with plans and budgets at that time.

The accuracy of previous value in use calculations over the last five years have to be monitored under FRS 11 ('look-back test'), with any impairment that should have been recognised being required to be charged when actual cash flows are substituted. IAS 36 requires management to assess the reasonableness of the assumptions in its current cash flow projections by examining the causes of differences between past cash flow projections and actual cash flows, but there is no requirement to recognise losses that would have arisen in the past (but which have since reversed).

FRS 11 requires impairments of revalued assets that are clearly caused by the consumption of economic benefits to be recognised in the profit and loss account, whereas IAS 36 requires such impairments to be recognised in the profit and loss account only to the extent that the loss exceeds the balance on the revaluation reserve relating to the specific asset.

IAS 36 requires extensive disclosure of impairments by segment and, where material, by cash-generating unit. In addition there is extensive narrative disclosure required on the impairment testing process and, in certain circumstances, disclosure of the key assumptions made in impairment tests and sensitivity analysis.

Convergence

In July 2005, the ASB published FRED 38, proposing that FRS 11 should be replaced by IAS 36. However, a new UK standard has not yet been issued and this forms part of the wider debate on convergence to IFRS.

First-time adoption of IFRS

There are no specific transitional rules in IFRS 1 in respect of the revised version of IAS 36 and so the general rule of retrospective application will apply. Also, under IFRS 1, capitalised goodwill should be tested for impairment at the date of transition, regardless of whether there is any indication of impairment.

Summary of main points

Objective

IAS 36 does not apply to:	Similar. FRS 11 applies to fixed assets and so the various current asset categories are not within its scope. FRS 11 also specifies that it does not apply to costs capitalised under the oil and gas SORP. [FRS 11 para 5].
• Inventories (see IAS 2).	
• Construction contracts (see IAS 11).	
• Deferred tax assets (see IAS 12).	
• Assets arising from employee benefits (see IAS 19).	
• Financial assets within the scope of IAS 39.	
• Investment property measured at fair value (see IAS 40).	
• Certain biological assets (see IAS 41).	
• An insurer's deferred acquisition costs and intangible assets arising under insurance contracts within the scope of IFRS 4.	
• Non-current assets (or disposal groups) classified as held for sale under IFRS 5.	
[IAS 36 para 2].	
IAS 36 applies to investments in subsidiaries, joint ventures and associates. [IAS 36 para 4].	Same. [FRS 11 para 6].

Recognition of asset impairment

General rules

An asset is impaired when its carrying amount exceeds its recoverable amount. [IAS 36 para 8].	Same. [FRS 11 para 2].
An asset's recoverable amount is defined as the higher of 'fair value less costs to sell' and value in use. [IAS 36 para 6].	Similar. FRS 11 uses the terminology 'net realisable value'. [FRS 11 para 2].

Level at which the impairment test should be undertaken

The starting point for an impairment test is the individual asset. If it is not possible to estimate the recoverable amount of the individual asset, an entity should determine the recoverable amount of the cash-generating unit to which the asset belongs. [IAS 36 para 66].

Similar. A fixed asset's value in use should be estimated individually where reasonably practicable. Otherwise, value in use should be calculated at the level of income-generating units. These should be identified by dividing the total income of the entity into as many largely independent income streams as is reasonably practicable. [FRS 11 paras 24, 27].

A cash-generating unit is the smallest identifiable group of assets that generates cash inflows that are largely independent of cash inflows from other assets or groups of assets. [IAS 36 para 6].

Cash generating units are comparable to income-generating units (IGUs). [FRS 11 para 27].

The recoverable amount of an individual asset cannot be determined if:

- the asset's value in use cannot be estimated to be close to its fair value less costs to sell (for example, when the future cash flows from continuing use of the asset cannot be estimated to be negligible); and

- the asset does not generate cash inflows that are largely independent of those from other assets.

Similar. FRS 11 says that, in practice, it is not normally possible to estimate the value in use of an individual fixed asset. [FRS 11 para 25]. However, it specifies that an asset to be disposed of forms an income generating unit of its own. [FRS 11 para 31].

In such cases, value in use and, therefore, recoverable amount, can be determined only for the asset's cash-generating unit. [IAS 36 para 67].

For the purpose of impairment testing, goodwill acquired in a business combination should, from the acquisition date, be allocated to one or a group of cash-generating units. Each of these units or group of units should represent the lowest level at which goodwill is monitored for internal management purposes and should not be larger than a reportable segment determined in accordance with IAS 14. [IAS 36 para 80].

Similar. Capitalised goodwill should be allocated to income-generating units or groups of similar units. [FRS 11 para 34]. However, FRS 11 does not specify the minimum and maximum levels.

Timing of impairment reviews

At each reporting date an entity should assess whether there is any indication that an asset may be impaired. If any such indication exists, the entity should estimate the asset's recoverable amount. [IAS 36 para 9].

Similar. [FRS 11 para 8].

Impairment indicators include the following:

Similar. [FRS 11 para 10].

- Significant decline in an asset's market value.

- Significant changes with an adverse effect on the entity that have or will shortly occur in the technology, market, economic or legal environment in which the entity operates.

- Market interest rates have increased.

- The carrying value of net assets exceeds the entity's market capitalisation.

- Evidence of physical damage/obsolescence.

- Significant adverse change in the operation of an asset.

- Economic performance of asset is, or will be worse than expected.

[IAS 36 paras 12 to 14].

Annual impairment tests are required for goodwill and intangible assets with indefinite useful lives (or those not yet available for use). The annual impairment review should take place at the same time each year (not necessarily the year end), but if subsequent to the test, further goodwill or intangible assets are acquired then these should be tested for impairment before the end of the current period. [IAS 36 paras 10, 96]. Also, if there is a trigger event subsequent to an annual impairment test then the impairment test must be updated. [IAS 36 para 8].

Goodwill and intangible assets amortised over more than 20 years (or not amortised) should be reviewed for impairment at the end of each period. [FRS 10 para 37]. Also, FRS 10 requires a review of other goodwill and intangible assets at the end of the first full year after acquisition and in other periods if events or change in circumstances indicate that the carrying value may not be recoverable. [FRS 10 para 34].

Full impairment tests for intangible assets with indefinite useful lives do not need to be performed each year, subject to strict criteria. [IAS 36 para 24].

In many cases a detailed value in use calculation will not be necessary because a simple estimate will be sufficient to show that value in use is higher than carrying value. [FRS 11 para 18].

Acquired business merged with existing business

There is no specific guidance in IAS 36. Thus, there is no requirement to calculate any notional internally generated goodwill.

FRS 11 requires that the notional carrying amount of the internally generated goodwill is estimated at the time of merging an acquired business with an existing business. This is done by deducting the fair values of the net assets and purchased goodwill within the existing income-generating unit from its estimated value in use before combining the businesses. Any impairment identified subsequent to the merger should be allocated pro-rata to the existing and the acquired businesses; only that relating to the acquired goodwill should be recognised in the financial statements. [FRS 11 paras 50 to 52].

Measurement

Fair value less costs to sell

Fair value less costs to sell is the amount obtainable from the sale of an asset (or cash-generating unit) in an arm's length transaction between knowledgeable, willing parties, less the costs of disposal. [IAS 36 para 6].

Similar, although FRS 11 uses the terminology 'net realisable value'. [FRS 11 para 23].

Costs of disposal include incremental costs directly attributable to disposal, but do not include termination or reorganisation costs. [IAS 36 para 28].

Same. [FRS 11 para 23].

Value in use

Value in use is the present value of the future cash flows expected to arise from the continuing use of an asset and from its disposal at the end of its useful life. [IAS 36, paras 6, 39].

Similar. [FRS 11 para 2].

Future cash flows should be reasonable and supportable. [IAS 36 para 33(a)].

Similar. [FRS 11 para 36].

Cash flow projections should be based on most recent budgets approved by management and should not exceed five years, unless a longer period can be justified. [IAS 36 para 33(b)].

Similar. [FRS 11 para 36].

Forecasts should be based on assumptions using steady or declining growth rates, unless an increasing rate can be justified. This growth rate should not exceed the long-term rate for the products, industries or countries in which the company operates, unless a higher rate can be justified. [IAS 36 para 33(c)].

FRS 11 restricts relevant long-term growth rates to those of the country rather than products, industries or countries – this can be overridden only in exceptional circumstances and this requires disclosure. [FRS 11 para 36(b), 37].

Future cash flows should be estimated for the asset in its current condition and should not include estimated cash flows from:

Similar, but there is an exception for newly acquired income generating units (see below). [FRS 11 para 38, 39].

- A future restructuring to which the entity is not yet committed.

- Future expenditure that will improve or enhance the asset.

[IAS 36 para 44].

No equivalent exception to that in FRS 11 for the cost of future reorganisations and capital expenditure in respect of a newly acquired subsidiary.

In assessing the value in use of a newly acquired subsidiary, costs and benefits of future reorganisations and capital expenditure may be taken into account in impairment reviews if they were anticipated at the time of performing the impairment review in the first full year after acquisition and were consistent with plans and budgets at that time. [FRS 11 para 39].

Estimates of future cash flows should not include cash flows from financing activities or income tax receipts or payments. [IAS 36 para 50].

Similar. [FRS 11 para 36].

The value in use calculation should take account of the time value of money and the uncertainty or risk inherent in the future cash flows. The risk adjustment can either be applied to the future cash flows or to the discount rate used to calculate the present value of non-risk adjusted cash flows. [IAS 36 paras 30, 32].

Similar. [FRS 11 para 45].

The discount rate should be a pre-tax rate that reflects current market assessments of the time value of money and the risks specific to the asset for which the future cash flow estimates have not been adjusted. [IAS 36 para 55].

Similar. [FRS 11 para 41].

Management are required to assess the reasonableness of the assumptions in the current cash flow projections by examining the causes of differences between past cash flow projections and actual cash flows. However, there is no requirement to recognise losses that would have arisen in the past (but which have since reversed). [IAS 36 para 34].

For the five years following an impairment test, there should be subsequent monitoring of actual cash flows against those included in the forecast – any impairment that should have been recognised at the time should be recognised immediately, unless it has since reversed (and reversal of the loss is permitted to be recognised), in which case the reasons for the reversal should be disclosed. [FRS 11 paras 54, 71].

Presentation

Impairment losses should be recognised in profit or loss immediately. [IAS 36 para 60]. However, an impairment loss on a revalued asset is recognised against any revaluation surplus first, and only in profit or loss if it exceeds the revaluation surplus relating to that asset. [IAS 36 para 61].

FRS 11 requires impairments that have been caused by the clear consumption of economic benefits to be charged to the profit and loss account regardless of whether the asset has been revalued. [FRS 11 para 63].

Impairment losses for cash-generating units are allocated first to goodwill allocated to the unit and then pro-rata to intangible assets and other assets in the unit. [IAS 36 para 104].

Impairment losses are allocated first to goodwill, then to intangible assets and then to other tangible fixed assets. [FRS 11 para 48].

Reversals of impairment losses for goodwill are not permitted. [IAS 36 para 124].

Impairment losses on goodwill and intangible fixed assets are reversed if there is an external event reversing the impairment in an unforeseen way or the loss arose on an intangible with a readily ascertainable market value. [FRS 11 para 60].

Reversals of impairment losses for intangible assets and tangible fixed assets are permitted. An impairment loss recognised for an asset in prior years should be reversed if, and only if, there has been a change in the estimates used to determine the asset's recoverable amount. [IAS 36 para 114].

Similar for tangible fixed assets. [FRS 11 para 56]. Reversals of impairment losses for intangible fixed assets are restricted (see above).

Disclosures

Disclosures required by IAS 36 are much more detailed than FRS 11. The main differences are:

Detailed disclosures for each class of assets impacted by impairments or their reversals. [IAS 36 para 126].

The same level of detail is not required.

Detailed disclosures for each reportable segment based on the entity's primary reporting format. [IAS 36 para 129].

The same level of detail is not required.

Detailed disclosure for each material impairment loss recognised or reversed in the period for an individual asset (including goodwill) or a cash-generating unit and for aggregate impairment losses and reversals where these are not individually material. [IAS 36 paras 130, 131].

The same level of detail is not required.

If recoverable amount is value in use, the discount rate(s) used in the current estimate and previous estimate (if any) of value in use. [IAS 36 para 130].

If an impairment loss is measured by reference to value in use, the discount rate used should be disclosed. [FRS 11 para 69].

Additional disclosures (including disclosure of the key assumptions used to determine the recoverable amount) are required for each cash-generating unit(s) for which the carrying amount of goodwill or intangible assets with indefinite useful lives allocated to that unit(s) is significant in comparison to the entity's total carrying amount of goodwill or intangible assets with indefinite useful lives. [IAS 36 paras 134, 135].

No equivalent requirement.

Disclosure of the key assumptions used to determine the recoverable amount of other assets (cash-generating units) is encouraged. [IAS 36 para 132].

For cash-generating unit(s) where the carrying amount of goodwill or intangible assets with indefinite useful lives is significant, disclosure should be given of the growth rate used in cash flow projections beyond the period covered by the most recent forecasts and the justification for using any growth rate that exceeds the long-term average growth rate. [IAS 36 para 134(iv)].

Disclosure of key assumptions not specifically mentioned in FRS 11.

If the impairment test assumptions have assumed growth rates greater than the relevant country average growth rate, then these rates and the reasons for assuming the higher rates, must be disclosed. [FRS 11 paras 72, 73]

IAS 37 and FRS 12 – Provisions, contingent liabilities and contingent assets

IAS 37, Provisions, contingent liabilities and contingent assets	FRS 12, Provisions, contingent liabilities and contingent assets
Effective for accounting periods beginning on or after 1 July 1999.	*Effective for accounting periods ending on or after 23 March 1999.*

Related pronouncements

IFRIC 1, Changes in existing decommissioning, restoration and similar liabilities	–
IFRIC 6, Liabilities arising from participating in a specific market - Waste electrical and electronic equipment	–

Overview

In this summary, references to IAS 37 include consequential amendments in subsequent standards. IAS 37 and FRS 12 were developed at the same time and there are no significant differences between the two. FRS 12 deals with the circumstances in which an obligation recognised as a provision results in the recognition of an asset. IAS 37 does not deal with this in the standard, but there is an illustrative example that is consistent with the FRS 12 guidance. Also, FRS 12 includes more guidance than IAS 37 on the discount rate to be used in determining the present value of a provision.

Convergence

IAS 37 is being reconsidered as part of the IFRS/US convergence project and in June 2005 the IASB published proposed amendments. It is proposed that it would require entities to recognise all obligations that satisfy the IASB framework's definition of a liability, unless they cannot be measured reliably. Uncertainty about the amount or timing of the obligation would no longer affect whether or not a liability should be recognised, but would be reflected in the obligation's measurement. There are also proposed amendments to accounting for restructuring provisions and termination benefits (in IAS 19).

In July 2005, the ASB published FRED 39, 'Amendments to FRS 12 Provisions, contingent liabilities and contingent assets and Amendments to FRS 17 Retirement benefits', based on the IASB's proposals.

First-time adoption of IFRS

There are no specific rules in IFRS 1 in respect of IAS 37 and so the general rule of retrospective application will apply. There is an exemption from retrospective application of IFRIC 1, but this should not be relevant to UK companies as UK practice would normally be in line with IFRIC 1.

Summary of main points

IAS 37 excludes executory contracts (except where onerous) and provisions covered by another standard (for example, contingent liabilities assumed in a business combination, construction contracts, income taxes, leases, employee benefits and insurance contracts). [IAS 37 paras 1, 5].	Similar. [FRS 12 para 3].
IAS 37 does not apply to financial instruments (including guarantees) that are within IAS 39's scope. [IAS 37 para 2].	For companies not applying FRS 26, FRS 12 excludes financial instruments that are carried at fair value. For companies applying FRS 26, FRS 12 does not apply to financial instruments (including guarantees) that are within FRS 26's scope. [FRS 12 para 5].
Provisions relating to depreciation, impairment of assets and doubtful debts are not covered in this standard. [IAS 37 para 7].	Same. [FRS 12 para 9].

Recognition

Provisions

A provision should be recognised when an entity has a present obligation (legal or constructive) as a result of a past event and it is probable that an outflow of resources embodying economic benefits will be required to settle the obligation and a reliable estimate of that obligation can be made. [IAS 37 para 14].	Similar, but refers to the transfer of economic benefit rather than an outflow of resources embodying economic benefits. [FRS 12 para 14].
Only liabilities that exist at the balance sheet date can be recognised.	Same.
A provision is defined as a liability of uncertain timing or amount. [IAS 37 para 10].	Same. [FRS 12 para 2].
A constructive obligation derives from an entity's actions where the entity has indicated to other parties that it will accept certain responsibilities, or where the entity has created a valid expectation that it will discharge those responsibilities. [IAS 37 para 10].	Same. [FRS 12 para 2].

Contingent liabilities

Contingent liabilities should not be recognised. [IAS 37 para 27].	Same. [FRS 12 para 27].
A contingent liability should be disclosed unless an outflow of resources embodying economic benefits is remote. [IAS 37 para 28].	Similar, but refers to the possibility of a transfer of economic benefit being remote. [FRS 12 para 28].

Contingent assets

Contingent assets should not be recognised. [IAS 37 para 31].	Same. [FRS 12 para 31].
A contingent asset should be disclosed where an inflow of economic benefits is probable. [IAS 37 para 34].	Same. [FRS 12 para 34].

Measurement

Best estimate

The amount recognised as a provision should be the best estimate of the expenditure required to settle the present obligation at the balance sheet date. [IAS 37 para 36].	Same. [FRS 12 para 36].
Risks and uncertainties should be taken into account in reaching the best estimate of a provision. [IAS 37 para 42].	Same. [FRS 12 para 42].

Discounting

Where the effect of the time value of money is material, the amount of a provision should be the present value of the expenditures expected to be required to settle the obligation. [IAS 37 para 45].	Same. [FRS 12 para 45].

The discount rate should be a pre-tax rate that reflects current market assessments of the time value of money and the risks specific to the liability. It should not reflect risks for which future cash flow estimates have been adjusted. [IAS 37 para 47].

Same. [FRS 12 para 47].

The unwinding of the discount is recognised as a borrowing cost. [IAS 37 para 60].

The unwinding of the discount should be shown as 'other finance costs' adjacent to interest. [FRS 12 para 48 as amended by FRS 17].

Future events

Future events that may affect the amount required to settle an obligation should be reflected in the amount of the provision where there is sufficient objective evidence that they will occur. [IAS 37 para 48].

Same. [FRS 12 para 51].

Disposal of assets

Gains from the expected disposal of the assets should not be taken into account in measuring a provision. [IAS 37 para 51].

Same. [FRS 12 para 54].

Reimbursements

A reimbursement relating to a provision should only be recognised when its recovery is virtually certain and it should not exceed the amount of the provision. It should be treated as a separate asset. [IAS 37 para 53].

Same. [FRS 12 para 56].

Utilisation of provisions

Provisions should be reviewed at each balance sheet date and adjusted to reflect the current best estimate. Provisions should be reversed if no longer required. [IAS 37 para 59].

Same. [FRS 12 para 62].

A provision should be used only for expenditures for which it was originally recognised. [IAS 37 para 61].

Same. [FRS 12 para 64].

Recognition of related assets

No specific guidance in the standard, but example 3 in Appendix C is consistent with FRS 12. Also, IAS 16 includes dismantling and restoration costs recognised as a provision as examples of directly attributable costs that are capitalised as part of the cost of an asset. [IAS 16 para 16(c)].

When an obligation recognised as a provision (for example, decommissioning costs) gives access to future economic benefits then an asset should also be recognised. Otherwise, the provision should be charged immediately to profit and loss account. [FRS 12 para 66].

Application of the recognition and measurement rules

Future operating losses

Provisions should not be recognised for future operating losses (although assets may have to be written down for impairment). [IAS 37 paras 63, 65].

Same. [FRS 12 paras 68, 70].

Onerous contracts

Present obligation under an onerous contract should be recognised and measured as a provision. [IAS 37 para 66].

Same. [FRS 12 para 71].

An onerous contract is one in which the unavoidable cost of meeting the obligations under the contract exceed the economic benefits expected to be received under it. [IAS 37 para 10].	Same. [FRS 12 para 2].

Restructuring

Restructuring provisions should be recognised only if there is an obligation at the balance sheet date. A constructive obligation arises only if the entity has a detailed formal plan and has raised a valid expectation in those affected by it that the restructuring will be carried out (for example, by starting to implement it or by announcing it in sufficient detail). [IAS 37 para 72].	Same. [FRS 12 para 77].
No obligation arises for the sale of an operation until the entity is committed to the sale. [IAS 37 para 78].	Same. [FRS 12 para 83].
The restructuring provision should include only the direct expenditure arising from the restructuring and should not include costs associated with ongoing activities (such as relocation or retraining costs). [IAS 37 para 80].	Same. [FRS 12 para 85].

Disclosure

The disclosures required by IAS 37 and FRS 12 are similar and include tabular disclosure of the movements on provisions and narrative disclosure of the nature, timing of outflows and uncertainties related to provisions and contingent liabilities.

In extremely rare cases, disclosure need not be given if it can be expected to prejudice seriously the position of the entity in a dispute with other parties. However, disclosure is required of general nature of the dispute and the reasons why the information has not been disclosed. [IAS 37 para 92].	Similar, but FRS 12 makes the point that if disclosure is required by law then it must be given. [FRS 12 para 97].

IAS 38 and FRS 10/SSAP 13 – Intangible assets

IAS 38, Intangible assets	FRS 10, Goodwill and intangible assets SSAP 13, Accounting for research and development
Effective for accounting periods beginning on or after 1 January 1999.	*FRS 10 – effective for accounting periods ending on or after 23 December 1998.*
The revised standard (2004) applies for intangible assets acquired in business combinations for which the agreement date is on or after 31 March 2004 and to the accounting for all other intangible assets prospectively from the beginning of the first annual period beginning on or after 31 March 2004.	*SSAP 13 – effective for accounting periods beginning on or after 1 January 1989.*

Related pronouncements

SIC 32, Intangible assets – web site costs.	UITF 24, Accounting for start-up costs.
	UITF 27, Revision to estimates of the useful economic life of goodwill and intangible assets.
	UITF 29, Website development costs.

Overview

In this summary, references to IAS 38 relate to the revised standard issued in March 2004. A wider range of intangible assets are recognised under IFRS, particularly in respect of business combinations (see IFRS 3 summary).

Under both IFRS and UK GAAP, an intangible asset is an identifiable non-monetary asset without physical substance. Under IAS 38, an asset is identifiable when it is separable (that is, capable of being sold separate from the entity) or arises from contractual or other legal rights. Under FRS 10, the assets have to be capable of being disposed of separately from the business.

FRS 10 requires an internally generated intangible to have a readily ascertainable market value before it can be recognised. IAS 38 allows internally generated assets to be recognised provided they meet criteria similar to those contained within SSAP 13 for development costs. Internally generated brands, mastheads, publishing titles, customer lists and similar items cannot be recognised, as they cannot be distinguished from the development of the business as a whole.

IAS 38 does not contain a rebuttable presumption that the useful economic life of an intangible asset is less than 20 years, whereas FRS 10 does, although both standards state that an intangible asset can have an indefinite life and if this is the case they need not be amortised.

Both IFRS and UK GAAP require annual impairment reviews for intangible assets with an indefinite life. The requirements differ for intangible assets with a finite life. IAS 38 only requires an impairment review if there is an indication of impairment, whereas under FRS 10, an annual impairment review is required where the 20-year useful life presumption is rebutted. IAS 38 also requires an annual impairment review for an intangible asset that is not yet ready for use.

Under IAS 38, research costs must be written off as incurred, whereas development costs should be capitalised where particular criteria are met. This contrasts with SSAP 13 where an entity may choose to capitalise development costs.

Convergence

In July 2005, the ASB published FRED 37, 'Intangible assets (IAS 38)', proposing to replace FRS 10 and SSAP 13 with IAS 38. However, a new UK standard has not yet been issued and this now forms part of the wider debate on convergence to IFRS.

First-time adoption of IFRS

There are no specific transitional rules in IFRS 1 in respect of the revised version of IAS 38 and so the general rule of retrospective application will apply. However, if the business combinations' exemption is used, any assets that were not recognised in the UK GAAP fair value exercise (which will include most intangibles that IAS 38 requires to be separately recognised on an acquisition) are recognised in the opening IFRS balance sheet only if they would be recognised in the acquired entity's separate opening IFRS balance sheet.

Summary of main points

Scope

IAS 38 applies to accounting for intangible assets, but scopes out the following: those that are covered by another standard; financial assets as defined in IAS 39; the recognition and measurement of exploration and evaluation assets (IFRS 6 applies); and expenditure on the development and extraction of minerals, oil, natural gas and similar non-regenerative resources. [IAS 38 para 2].	The scope of FRS 10 in respect of intangible assets is similar. [FRS 10 para 64]. SSAP 13 deals with research and development expenditure.

Definition

An asset is a resource controlled by an entity as a result of past events and from which future economic benefits are expected to flow to the entity. [IAS 38 para 8].	An asset is a right or other access to future economic benefits controlled by an entity as a result of past transactions or events. [FRS 5 para 2].
An intangible asset is an identifiable non-monetary asset without physical substance. [IAS 38 para 8].	An intangible asset is a non-financial fixed asset that does not have physical substance, but is identifiable and is controlled by the entity through custody or legal rights. [FRS 10 para 2].
'Controlled by an entity' is included in the definition of an asset. [IAS 38 para 8].	The definition of an intangible asset includes a reference to control. [FRS 10 para 2].

Identifiability

An intangible asset is identifiable when it is separable (that is, capable of being sold, transferred, licensed, rented or exchanged, separate from the entity) or it arises from contractual or other legal rights (regardless of whether those rights are separable from the entity). [IAS 38 para 12].	An intangible asset is identifiable when it can be disposed of separately from the revenue earning activity to which it contributes. [FRS 10 para 2].
Therefore, separability is not a necessary condition if the asset can be identified by contractual or other legal rights. [IAS 38 para 12].	Separability is a necessary condition for identifiability. [FRS 10 para 2].

Control

An entity controls an asset if the entity has the power to obtain the future economic benefits flowing from the underlying resource and to restrict the access of others to those benefits. Control normally stems from enforceable legal rights. In the absence of legal rights, it is more difficult to demonstrate control. [IAS 38 para 13].	Control is normally secured by legal rights. In the absence of legal rights, it is more difficult to demonstrate control. [FRS 10 para 2].

Recognition criteria

For an intangible asset to be recognised, it must meet the definition of an intangible asset (see above) and the recognition criteria (see below). [IAS 38 para 18].

Not specifically stated, but the same applies under FRS 10.

An intangible asset should be recognised if, and only if, it is probable that the expected future economic benefits that are attributable to the asset will flow to the entity and the cost of the intangible can be measured reliably. [IAS 38 para 21].

FRS 10 does not set out general recognition criteria, but deals with intangible assets acquired as part of a business combination and those that are acquired separately (see below).

An intangible asset should be measured initially at cost. [IAS 38 para 24].

Similar. [FRS 10 para 9].

Separate acquisition

For a separately acquired intangible asset, the effect of probability of expected future economic benefits is reflected in the cost of the asset. Therefore, the probability recognition criterion is always considered to be satisfied for separately acquired intangible assets. [IAS 38 para 25].

Not specifically stated, but a similar assumption is made as separately acquired intangible assets are capitalised at cost. [FRS 10 para 9].

The cost of a separately acquired intangible asset can usually be measured reliably, particularly when the purchase consideration is in the form of cash or other monetary assets. [IAS 38 para 26].

Not specifically stated, but similar applies.

Cost comprises purchase price and directly attributable costs of preparing the asset for its intended use, including legal and professional fees. If payment is deferred, cost is the cash price equivalent (with an interest cost imputed). [IAS 38 paras 27 to 32].

Capitalise at cost. There is no elaboration on what cost includes. [FRS 10 para 9].

Expenditures that are not part of the cost of an intangible asset include costs of introducing a new product or service (including advertising and promotional activities), costs of conducting business in a new location (including staff training costs) and administration costs. [IAS 38 para 29].

Part of business acquisition

For an intangible asset acquired in a business combination, the effect of probability of expected future economic benefits is reflected in the fair value of the asset. Therefore, the probability recognition criterion is always considered to be satisfied for intangible assets acquired in business combinations. [IAS 38 para 33].

No similar assumption.

The fair value of intangible assets acquired in business combinations can normally be measured with sufficient reliability to be recognised separately from goodwill. If an intangible asset acquired in a business combination has a finite useful life, there is a rebuttable presumption that its fair value can be measured reliably. [IAS 38 para 35].

Judgement is required to determine whether cost (that is, fair value) can be measured sufficiently reliably for the purpose of separate recognition. [FRS 10 para 10].

IAS 38 identifies possible techniques for estimating the fair value where no active market exists. [IAS 38 paras 39 to 41].

FRS 10 indicates the techniques that are used to value intangibles. [FRS 10 para 12].

The fair value of an intangible asset is not restricted where there is negative goodwill.

An intangible asset must have a readily ascertainable market value before negative goodwill can be created or increased. [FRS 10 para 10].

An active market is defined as "a market in which all the following conditions exist:

a) *the items traded in the market are homogeneous;*

b) *willing buyers and sellers can normally be found at any time; and*

c) *prices are available to the public".*

[IAS 38 para 8].

Readily ascertainable market value is defined as "the value that is established by reference to a market where:

a) *the asset belongs to a homogeneous population of assets that are equivalent in all material respects; and*

b) *an active market, evidenced by frequent transactions, exists for that population of assets".*

[FRS 10 para 2].

Subsequent expenditure on an acquired IPRD project

Subsequent expenditure on an in-process research and development project that was acquired separately or in a business combination (and recognised as an intangible asset) is accounted for in accordance with the requirements for internally generated intangible assets (see below). [IAS 38 para 43].

Not dealt with in FRS 10 or SSAP 13, but similar would apply.

Exchange of assets

The cost of an intangible asset acquired in exchange for a non-monetary asset is measured at fair value, unless the exchange transaction lacks commercial substance or the fair value of neither the asset received nor the asset given up is reliably measurable. If the acquired asset is not measured at fair value, its cost is measured at the carrying amount of the asset given up. [IAS 38 para 45].

Not dealt with in FRS 10.

Internally generated goodwill

Internally generated goodwill should not be recognised as an asset. [IAS 38 para 48].

Same. [FRS 10 para 8].

Internally generated intangibles

IAS 38 distinguishes between the research phase and the development phase of internally generated intangibles. These phases have a broader meaning than 'research' and 'development' as defined. [IAS 38 para 52].

SSAP 13 applies to research and development expenditure as defined in that standard. FRS 10 does not make a similar distinction for other internally generated intangible assets as in IAS 38.

No intangible asset arising from research (or from the research phase of an internal project) should be recognised and expenditure should be expensed when incurred. [IAS 38 para 54].

Research expenditure should be expensed when incurred. [SSAP 13 para 24].

An internally generated intangible asset arising from development (or from the development phase of an internal project) must be recognised if detailed criteria are met. [IAS 38 para 57].

SSAP 13 allows an option to capitalise development expenditure provided similar detailed criteria are met. [SSAP 13 para 25]. Otherwise, an internally developed intangible asset may be capitalised only if it has a readily ascertainable market value. [FRS 10 para 14].

The detailed criteria include demonstration of the following:

- The technical feasibility of the project.

- Intention to complete the intangible asset for use or sale.

- Ability to use or sell the intangible asset.

- How the intangible asset will generate probable future economic benefits.

- The adequacy of the resources for completion.

- The ability to measure reliably the development expenditure.

[IAS 38 para 57].

SSAP 13 contains similar criteria. IAS 38's criteria are considered to be more stringent, because there is a requirement to demonstrate future benefits rather than to have a reasonable expectation of future benefits under SSAP 13.

IAS 38 prohibits recognition of internally generated brands, mastheads, publishing titles, customer lists, and similar items. [IAS 38 para 63].

Not specifically mentioned, but prohibited by the criteria for recognising internally generated intangibles.

The cost of an internally generated intangible asset is the sum of expenditure incurred from the date when the intangible asset first meets the recognition criteria. Reinstatement of expenditure previously recognised as an expense is prohibited. [IAS 38 paras 65, 71].

Not specifically stated in FRS 10, although a similar principle would apply (for example, as in UITF 34).

SIC 32 rules that a web site developed by an entity for its own use (for internal or external access) is an internally generated intangible asset that is subject to the requirements of IAS 38. The SIC addresses the accounting treatment for internal expenditure.

UITF Abstract 29 deals with the costs incurred by companies in developing websites for their own use. It rules that website development costs should be capitalised as a tangible fixed asset, subject to specific criteria being met for the capitalisation of design and content costs.

Recognition of an expense

IAS 38 specifies costs that should be expensed as incurred. These include certain start-up costs, training costs, advertising/promotional costs and relocation/ reorganisation costs. [IAS 38 para 69].

Similar under UK GAAP. UITF Abstract 24 deals with start-up costs.

Expenditure on an intangible item that was initially recognised as an expense should not be recognised as part of the cost of an intangible asset at a later date. [IAS 38 para 71].

Not specifically stated in FRS 10, although a similar principle would apply (for example, as in UITF 34).

Subsequent measurement

An entity should choose either the cost model or the revaluation model as its accounting policy. [IAS 38 para 72].

Similar. [FRS 10 para 43].

Under the cost model, an intangible asset is carried at cost less amortisation and/or impairment. [IAS 38 para 74].

The treatment for most intangible assets under FRS 10 will be similar to the cost model in IAS 38.

Under the revaluation model, fair value is determined by reference to an active market (few in practice). If an intangible asset is accounted for using the revaluation model, all other assets in its class should also be accounted for using the same model, unless there is no active market for those assets. [IAS 38 paras 72, 75].

Similar. FRS 10 allows revaluation if there is a readily ascertainable market value (also few in practice). [FRS 10 para 43].

Useful life

An entity should assess whether an intangible asset's useful life is finite or indefinite (note this does not mean infinite). IAS 38 sets out factors to be considered in determining an intangible asset's useful life. [IAS 38 paras 88, 90].

There is a rebuttable presumption that useful economic life does not exceed 20 years, but a longer, or indefinite, life, is permitted. [FRS 10 para 19]. Criteria are provided for rebuttal of the presumption, being the demonstration of durability and the ability to continue to measure for impairment.

Amortisation

The depreciable amount of an intangible asset with a finite useful life should be allocated on a systematic basis over its useful life. [IAS 38 para 97].

Similar. [FRS 10 para 15].

The amortisation method used should reflect the pattern in which the asset's future economic benefits are expected to be consumed by the entity. If that pattern cannot be determined reliably, the straight-line method should be used. There will rarely, if ever, be persuasive evidence to support an amortisation method that results in a lower amount of accumulated amortisation than under the straight-line method. [IAS 38 paras 97, 98].

Similar. [FRS 10 paras 30 to 32].

Residual value of an intangible asset with a finite useful life is assumed to be zero, unless there is an active market or commitment by a third party to purchase the asset. [IAS 38 para 100].

Similar. In practice, there should be a legal or contractual right to receive a certain sum at the end of the period of use or a readily ascertainable market value for the residual asset. [FRS 10 para 29].

The residual value is the estimated amount that an entity would currently obtain if the asset were of the age and in the condition expected at the end of its useful life. [IAS 38 para 8].

Residual values are based on prices prevailing at the date of acquisition (or revaluation) of an asset and do not take account of expected future price changes. [FRS 10 para 2].

The amortisation period and the amortisation method for an intangible asset with a finite useful life should be reviewed at least at each financial year end. Changes should be accounted for as changes in accounting estimates in accordance with IAS 8 (that is, prospectively). [IAS 38 para 104].

Similar. [FRS 10 para 33].

Impairment

An intangible asset with an indefinite useful life is reviewed for impairment annually and whenever there is an indication of impairment. [IAS 38 para 108].

In addition to annual impairment reviews for intangible assets with amortisation periods exceeding 20 years, FRS 10 requires an impairment review for all intangibles at the end of the first full year following their acquisition. [FRS 10 para 34].

Review of indefinite life

The useful life of an intangible asset that is not being amortised should be reviewed each period to determine whether an indefinite useful life is supported. If it is not, the change from indefinite to finite life is accounted for as a change in an accounting estimate in accordance with IAS 8, (that is, prospectively). [IAS 38 para 109].	Similar. [FRS 10 para 33; UITF 27 para 5].

Retirements and disposals

An intangible asset should be derecognised on disposal or when no future economic benefits are expected from its use or disposal. Gains and losses are the difference between the net proceeds and the carrying amount. [IAS 38 paras 112, 113].	Not dealt with in FRS 10.

Disclosure

The disclosure requirements are basically the same as in FRS 10. IAS 38 has some additional disclosures being:	Similar to IAS 38.

- The location of the amortisation expense in the income statement.

- A description, the carrying amount and remaining amortisation period of any individual material intangible asset.

- Intangibles acquired by means of a government grant and initially recognised in the financial statements at fair value.

[IAS 38 paras 118, 122].

For an intangible asset with an indefinite useful life, disclosure should be given of the asset's carrying amount and the reasons supporting the assessment of an indefinite useful life (including the factor(s) that played a significant role in determining that the asset has an indefinite useful life). [IAS 38 para 122(a)].	FRS 10 requires disclosure of the reasons for rebuttal of the 20 year life presumption, including the factors contributing to the durability of the asset. [FRS 10 para 58].

IAS 39 and FRS 26, FRS 4 – Financial instruments: Recognition and measurement

IAS 39 and FRS 26, FRS 4 Financial instruments: Recognition and measurement

FRS 26 derives from IAS 39 although the initial version of the standard did not include the recognition and derecognition material in IAS 39. An amendment to FRS 26 was published in April 2006 implementing IAS 39's recognition and derecognition material. The amendment is effective for accounting periods beginning on or after 1 January 2007.

The flow chart FRS 26 (see next page) will help identify which entities are within the scope of FRS 26 and when they will have to implement it. For listed entities, the original version of FRS 26 applies for accounting periods beginning on or after 1 January 2005. For entities using the fair value accounting rules set out in the Companies Act 1985, FRS 26 applies for accounting periods beginning on or after 1 January 2006. For entities not using FRS 26, an amended version of FRS 4 applies.

Scope and effective date and Companies Act requirements for a UK GAAP reporter

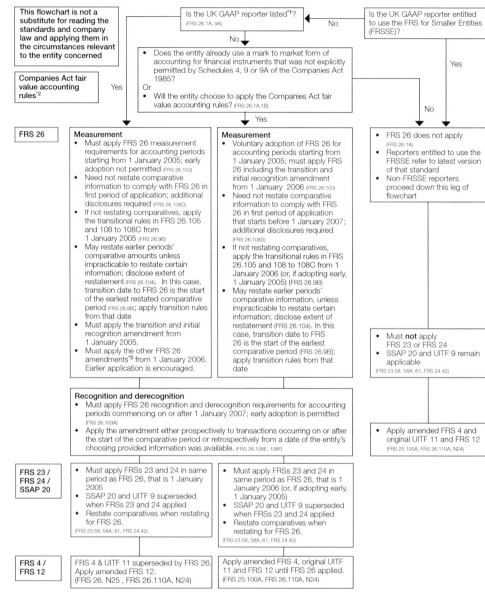

Refer to FRS 25 flowchart for details of FRS 25's presentation and disclosure requirements and FRS 29's disclosure requirements.

*1 A listed entity (FRS 26.9A) is one that has in issue debt, shares or other financial or similar instrument that is traded on a regulated market of any EU Member State. Hence, AIM companies that only have their shares quoted on AIM are not listed nor are entities that have their securities traded only on a market outside of the EU (for example, New York Stock Exchange).

*2 The Companies Act 1985's (the Act) fair value accounting rules are those set out in paragraphs 34A and 34C of Schedule 4, and their equivalents in other schedules. The Act's requirements were inserted by the Companies Act 1985 (International Accounting Standards and Other Accounting Amendments) Regulations 2004.

*3 The amendments referred to here are in relation to 'Cash flow hedge accounting of forecast intra-group transactions'; the fair value option'; and 'Financial guarantee contracts and credit insurance'.

IAS 40 and SSAP 19 – Investment property

IAS 40, Investment property	SSAP 19, Accounting for investment properties
The revised standard (2003) was effective for annual periods beginning on or after 1 January 2005.	*Effective for accounting periods beginning on or after 1 July 1981.*

Related pronouncements

SIC 15, Operating leases – Incentives.	UITF 5, Transfers from current assets to fixed assets.
	UITF 28, Operating lease incentives.

Overview

In this summary, references to IAS 40 relate to the revised standard issued in December 2003 and consequential amendments in subsequent standards. There are significant differences between IAS 40 and SSAP 19 in terms of the measurement bases that may be used and the recognition of gains and losses on revaluation.

Under IAS 40 an entity can choose, for all investment property (with some specified exceptions), between the fair value model and depreciated cost. This differs from the treatment required by SSAP 19, which requires investment properties to be carried at open market value and does not permit such property to be carried at depreciated historical cost.

Under IAS 40, a property interest held by a lessee under an operating lease may be accounted for as an investment property if the property would otherwise meet the definition of an investment property, the lease is accounted for as if it were a finance lease and the fair value model is adopted (for all investment properties).

When the fair value model is applied under IAS 40, the carrying amount is not depreciated. Gains or losses arising from changes in the asset's fair value are recognised in the income statement. Again, this differs from SSAP 19 where a revaluation gain or loss is recognised in the STRGL, unless it is a permanent deficit (or its reversal) that should be recognised in the profit and loss account.

IAS 40 provides detailed guidance on how to account for transfers of assets to and from the investment property category, exchanges of assets and disposals. There is no such guidance in SSAP 19, although properties would be similarly reclassified (but there are some differences in the accounting for transfer values).

The disclosure requirements of IAS 40 are more extensive than the requirements of SSAP 19.

Convergence

The IASB has decided not to remove the present choice in IAS 40 of accounting for investment properties under either a fair value model or a cost model. This issue will be kept under review, with a view to reconsidering the option to use the cost model in due course.

In the UK, the ASB is considering its plans for convergence with IFRS.

First-time adoption of IFRS

Where an entity chooses to use the cost model in IAS 40, IFRS 1 includes an exemption allowing fair value to be used as deemed cost for any item of investment property at the date of transition to IFRS. Also, subject to certain criteria, a revaluation made under previous GAAP may also be used as the basis for deemed cost.

Summary of main points

Scope

Does not apply to:

• Biological assets related to agricultural activity (see IAS 41, Agriculture).	No such scope restriction.
• Mineral rights and mineral reserves such as oil, natural gas and similar non-regenerative resources. [IAS 40 para 4].	

• A property interest held by a lessee under an operating lease may be accounted for as an investment property if the property would otherwise meet the definition of an investment property, the lease is accounted for as if it were a finance lease and the fair value model is adopted (for all investment properties). [IAS 40 para 6].	Properties held by lessees under operating leases can be treated as investment properties and held at valuation.

Definitions

Investment property is property held (by the owner or by the lessee under a finance lease) to earn rentals or for capital appreciation or both, rather than owner-occupied property or property for sale in the ordinary course of business. [IAS 40 para 5].	Similar definition, but: • Any rental income should be negotiated at arm's length. [SSAP 19 para 7(b)]. • Excludes owner occupied properties or properties let to and occupied by other group companies. [SSAP 19 para 8].
Properties being constructed or developed are not investment properties, but IAS 40 does apply to the redevelopment of existing investment properties for continued use as investment properties. [IAS 40 para 9(d)].	• The definition of an investment property requires construction work and development to have been completed. [SSAP 19 para 7(a)]. • No reference to redeveloped properties.
A property that is leased to, and occupied by, a group company does not qualify as investment property in consolidated financial statements, because the property is owner-occupied from the perspective of the group as a whole. However, from the perspective of the lessor, the property is investment property if it meets the definition in IAS 40 paragraph 5. [IAS 40 para 15].	The definition of investment property excludes properties let to and occupied by other group companies. [SSAP 19 para 8(b)].

Recognition

Investment property should be recognised as an asset when, and only when:	No specific recognition criteria in SSAP 19. However, the same general asset recognition criteria are in FRS 5 paragraph 20.
• it is probable that the future economic benefits that are associated with the investment property will flow to the entity; and	
• its cost can be measured reliably.	
[IAS 40 para 16].	

Initial measurement

Investment properties are initially measured at cost, including transaction costs [IAS 40 para 20] – that is, purchase price plus directly attributable expenditure. [IAS 40 para 21].	No mention in SSAP 19, but Companies Act 1985 has similar rules.
The cost of an investment property does not include start-up costs, operating losses incurred before the property achieves the planned level of occupancy or abnormal costs. [IAS 40 para 23].	Not specified in SSAP 19, but similar applies under asset recognition rules.
IAS 16, 'Property, plant and equipment', applies until construction or development is complete. [IAS 40 para 22].	Although not explicit, similarly FRS 15 applies until construction and development is complete.

An investment property interest held under a lease is initially recognised at the lower of its fair value and the present value of the minimum lease payments. [IAS 40 para 25].	Not specified in SSAP 19.
Separate measurement of the land and buildings element is not required when the lessee's interest in both the land and building is classified as an investment property and the fair value model is adopted. [IAS 17 para 18].	No requirement in SSAP 19 or SSAP 21 for separate measurement of leased land and buildings.

Subsequent expenditure

The normal recognition criteria apply (see above). The cost of replacing part of an existing investment property is capitalised when the cost is incurred if the recognition criteria are met. The carrying amount of the replaced parts are dealt with in accordance with IAS 40's derecognition rules. [IAS 40 para 19].	No mention in SSAP 19, but similar treatment would apply.

Measurement subsequent to initial recognition

With the exceptions below, an entity should choose either the fair value model or the cost model as its accounting policy. That policy should be applied consistently to all investment property. [IAS 40 para 30].	No choice of policy under SSAP 19.
Regardless of its choice of policy for all other investment property, an entity may choose either the fair value model or the cost model for all investment property backing liabilities that pay a return linked directly to the fair value of, or returns from, specified assets including that investment property. [IAS 40 para 32A].	Not relevant as there is no choice of policy under SSAP 19.
When a property interest held by a lessee under an operating lease is classified as an investment property, the fair value model has to be applied. [IAS 40 para 34].	Not relevant as there is no choice of policy under SSAP 19.

Fair value model

After initial recognition, an entity that chooses the fair value model should measure all of its investment properties at fair value at the balance sheet date (usually market value, without any deduction for disposal costs), except in the exceptional case where fair value cannot be reliably determined on a continuing basis. [IAS 40 paras 33 to 37 and 53].	Similar, but without the exception. Investment properties should be included in the balance sheet at open market value. [SSAP 19 para 11]. Open market value excludes selling costs (based on RICS PS 4.16).
There is a rebuttable presumption that fair value can be determined reliably. [IAS 40 para 53].	SSAP 19 is silent.
If an investment property has previously been measured at fair value it should continue to be measured at fair value until disposal (or ceasing to be an investment property) even if comparable market transactions become less frequent or market prices less readily available. [IAS 40 para 55].	No equivalent requirement in SSAP 19, as there is no exception where fair values cannot be reliably determined.

Exceptionally, an investment property should be measured under the depreciated historical cost rules in IAS 16 (with a residual value of zero) until disposal, when and only when there is clear evidence on acquisition of the investment property that comparable market transactions are infrequent and alternative estimates of fair value not available. [IAS 40 para 53].

No equivalent.

Entities are encouraged, but not required to use independent professionally qualified valuers to determine fair value. [IAS 40 para 32].

Where investment properties represent a substantial proportion of the total assets of a major enterprise, the valuation would normally be carried out annually by qualified valuers and at least every 5 years by an external valuer. [SSAP 19 para 6].

Revaluation gains and losses should be included in profit or loss for the period in which they arise. [IAS 40 para 35].

Revaluation gains and losses should be recognised in the STRGL, unless it is a permanent deficit (or its reversal) which should be recognised in the profit and loss account. [SSAP 19 para 13]. (With exceptions for investment companies, property unit trusts, insurance companies and pension funds. [SSAP 19 paras 13 and 14].)

No depreciation requirement.

Investment properties are not depreciated, except for properties held on leases, which should be depreciated at least over the period when the unexpired term is 20 years or less. [SSAP 19 para 10]. Non-depreciation involves the use of a true and fair override of the Companies Act.

Cost model

After initial recognition, an entity that chooses the cost model should measure all of its investment properties in accordance with the cost model under IAS 16 (that is, cost less accumulated depreciation and impairment losses), except those that are classified as held for sale under IFRS 5. [IAS 40 para 56].

The cost model is not an option under SSAP 19.

Transfers

Transfers to or from investment property should be made when and only when there is a change in use. [IAS 40 para 57]. Investment property to be disposed of without redevelopment should remain an investment property until disposal. [IAS 40 para 58].

There are no specific rules regarding the transfer of properties to or from investment properties, other than UITF 5.

The fair value (at the date of transfer) of investment property transferred to owner-occupied property or inventories should be treated as the cost of the property for subsequent accounting under IAS 16 and IAS 2. [IAS 40 para 60].

No guidance in SSAP 19.

When owner-occupied property is transferred to investment property under the fair value model, the difference between the carrying amount of the property under IAS 16 and its fair value at the date of transfer should be treated in the same way as a revaluation under IAS 16. [IAS 40 para 61].

No guidance in SSAP 19.

When inventory is transferred to investment property under the fair value model, any difference between the previous carrying amount and fair value at the date of transfer should be recognised in profit or loss for the period. [IAS 40 para 63].	UK GAAP differs. UITF 5 states that the current asset accounting rules should be applied up to the effective date of transfer so that the transfer from current to fixed assets is at the lower of cost and net realisable value. [UITF 5 para 5]. Fixed asset accounting rules apply post transfer. [UITF 5 para 6].
When a self-constructed property is transferred to investment property (carried at fair value) on completion, the difference between previous carrying amount and fair value at the date of transfer should be recognised in profit or loss for the period. [IAS 40 para 65].	No guidance in SSAP 19.

Exchanges

Where an investment property is acquired in exchange for non-monetary consideration, its cost should be measured at fair value, unless the exchange transaction lacks commercial substance or the fair value of neither the asset given up nor the investment property can be determined reliably (in which case the acquired asset is measured at the carrying amount of the asset given up). [IAS 40 paras 27, 28].	No guidance in SSAP 19.

Disposals

Investment property should be derecognised on disposal or when it is permanently withdrawn from use and no future economic benefits are expected from its disposal. [IAS 40 para 66].	No specific guidance in SSAP 19, but general derecognition principles in FRS 5 are similar.
Disposal gains and losses are the difference between net sale proceeds and the carrying amount of the asset and are recognised in profit or loss (unless IAS 17 requires otherwise on a sale and leaseback). [IAS 40 para 69].	Same requirements within FRS 3 and SSAP 21.
Compensation from third parties for investment property that was impaired, lost or given up is recognised in profit or loss when the compensation becomes receivable. [IAS 40 para 72].	Not specified in SSAP 19.

Disclosure

Under either model, disclose:

Whether the fair value model or the cost model is applied. [IAS 40 para 75(a)].	Not relevant.
If the fair value model is applied, whether, and in what circumstances, property interests held under operating leases are classified and accounted for as investment property. [IAS 40 para 75(b)].	No equivalent.
The criteria used to distinguish investment property from owner-occupied property and from property held for sale in the ordinary course of business, when such classification is difficult. [IAS 40 para 75(c)].	No equivalent.

The methods and significant assumptions applied in determining fair value, including a statement whether determination of fair value was supported by market evidence or by other factors. [IAS 40 para 75(d)].

The bases of valuation should be disclosed. [SSAP 19 para 12].

Extent to which fair value is based on a valuation by an independent professionally qualified valuer (or disclosure that there has been no such valuation). [IAS 40 para 75(e)].

The names of persons making the valuation or particulars of their qualifications should be disclosed. Disclose whether the valuer is an employee or officer of the company or group owning the property. [SSAP 19 para 12].

No equivalent.

CA 85 requires disclosure of years in which the assets were valued. [CA85 4 Sch 43].

The amounts recognised in profit or loss for rental income and direct operating expenses. [IAS 40 para 75(f)].

No equivalent in SSAP 19, although SSAP 21 para 60(b) requires disclosure of aggregate rentals receivable.

The cumulative change in fair value recognised in profit or loss on a sale of investment property from a pool of assets in which the cost model is used into a pool in which the fair value model is used. [IAS 40 para 75(f)(iv).

Not relevant under SSAP 19.

The existence and amounts of restrictions on the realisability of investment property or the remittance of income and proceeds of disposal. [IAS 40 para 75(g)].

No equivalent, although CA 85 requires disclosure of charges on any assets and other financial commitments relevant to assessing the company's state of affairs. [CA85 4 Sch 48, 50].

Contractual obligations to purchase, construct or develop investment property or for repairs, maintenance or enhancements. [IAS 40 para 75(b)].

No equivalent, although CA 85 requires disclosure of capital commitments. [CA85 4 Sch 50(3)].

The disclosures above apply in addition to those in IAS 17 for leased properties. [IAS 40 para 74].

The disclosures above apply in addition to those in SSAP 21 for leased properties.

Where the fair value model is adopted also disclose:

Reconciliation of the opening to closing carrying amount of investment property, separately disclosing those items carried at cost due to unreliable measurement. [IAS 40 paras 76, 78].

Reconciliation of fixed assets required by Companies Act [CA85 4 Sch 42] – which, together with FRS 15 implicitly requires separate reconciliation for investment properties.

Investment properties should be disclosed as a separate line item in the balance sheet. [IAS 1 para 68]. There is no requirement to disclose the amount of the investment revaluation reserve.

Carrying value of investment properties and the investment revaluation reserve should be disclosed prominently. [SSAP 19 para 15].

Where an investment property valuation is adjusted, a reconciliation should be given between the investment property valuation obtained and the adjusted valuation included in the financial statements. [IAS 40 para 77].

No equivalent.

Additional disclosure is required in respect of properties not carried at fair value, including an explanation of why there is no reliable fair value and if possible a range of estimates within which fair value is highly likely to lie. [IAS 40 para 78].

No equivalent.

Where the cost model is adopted, also disclose:

• The depreciation methods used.	Not applicable under SSAP 19.
• The useful lives or depreciation rates used.	
• The gross carrying amount and accumulated depreciation at beginning and end of the period.	
• A reconciliation of opening to closing carrying amount.	
• The fair value of investment property.	

[IAS 40 para 79].

IFRS 3 and FRS 6, FRS 7 – Business combinations

Applies to the accounting for business combinations for which the agreement date is on or after 31 March 2004. There are transitional rules for existing goodwill.	*FRS 6 and FRS 7 were effective for accounting periods beginning on or after 23 December 1994.* *FRS 10 was effective for accounting periods ending on or after 23 December 1998.*

Related pronouncements

—	FRS 2, Accounting for subsidiary undertakings. UITF 15, Disclosure of substantial acquisitions. UITF 22, The acquisition of a Lloyds business. UITF 27, Revision to estimates of the useful economic life of goodwill and intangible assets. UITF 31, Exchanges of businesses or other non-monetary assets for an interest in a subsidiary, joint venture or associate.

Overview

Under IFRS 3, merger accounting is prohibited and business combinations are required to be accounted for as acquisitions using the purchase method. Under UK GAAP, merger accounting for business combinations is required in limited circumstances if specified criteria are met. (Merger accounting means that the consideration for the combination and the net assets acquired are not recorded at fair values and, consequently, no goodwill arises.)

IFRS 3 applies to all business combinations, except (i) the formation of joint ventures, (ii) combinations involving entities under common control, (iii) combinations involving two or more mutual entities and (iv) business combinations brought about by contract alone (for example, dual listed companies). FRS 6 does not have scope exclusions.

For acquisition accounting, under both IFRS 3 and UK GAAP, from the date of acquisition an acquirer should incorporate into the income statement the results of the acquiree's operations and recognise in the balance sheet the acquiree's identifiable assets and liabilities (measured at fair values) and any goodwill arising on the acquisition. However, there are some significant differences between IFRS and UK GAAP as follows.

IFRS 3 requires that all the acquiree's intangible assets at the acquisition date should be recognised separately in the consolidated financial statements if they meet the definition of an intangible asset in IAS 38 and if their fair value can be measured reliably. Under IAS 38, there is a rebuttable presumption that the intangible asset's fair value can be measured reliably if it has a finite useful life. UK GAAP is not as stringent as IFRS with regard to identifying intangibles and does not rule out the possibility of many intangible assets being subsumed within goodwill.

Where the acquisition takes place in stages, under IFRS 3, each exchange transaction is treated separately for the purpose of determining the fair values of the identifiable assets and liabilities acquired and for determining the amount of any goodwill on that transaction. Under UK GAAP, the Companies Act 1985 differs as it requires that identifiable assets and liabilities acquired are measured at their fair values at the date the investee becomes a subsidiary. However, FRS 2 notes that, in some circumstances, it may be appropriate to use a true and fair override of the Act's requirements in order to use fair values at the dates of earlier purchases, which would be consistent with IFRS 3.

Under both IFRS 3 and FRS 7, the identifiable assets and liabilities of an acquired business are those that existed at the date of acquisition measured at their fair values at that date. Both standards permit fair values to be initially determined provisionally, but the hindsight periods in which adjustments to fair values/goodwill can be made differ. Under IFRS 3, adjustments to the provisional fair values should be made within twelve months of the acquisition date, with a corresponding adjustment to goodwill. Under FRS 7, adjustments should be made in the financial statements for the first full financial year following the acquisition, which can be a longer period than under IFRS.

Under IFRS 3, adjustments to provisional fair values should be recognised as if the initial accounting had been completed at the acquisition date, that is, comparatives should be restated. Under UK GAAP, the adjustments to provisional fair values are accounted for in the period that the adjustments are made.

Under both IFRS and UK GAAP, goodwill arising on an acquisition is treated as an asset. IFRS 3 prohibits amortisation of goodwill and, instead, subjects it to an annual impairment review. Under FRS 10, there is a rebuttable presumption that the useful life of goodwill does not exceed 20 years, but it permits an indefinite useful life (with annual impairment reviews).

IFRS 3 does not use the term 'negative goodwill' and, instead, terms it as 'excess of acquirer's interest in the net fair value of acquiree's identifiable assets' and requires it to be taken to profit or loss in the year of acquisition. FRS 10 requires that negative goodwill, up to the aggregate fair value of the non-monetary assets acquired should be recognised in the income statement to match the depreciation of those assets. The balance, if any, is recognised in the income statement over the period likely to benefit.

Convergence

Phase II of the IASB's project is being carried out together with the US FASB and in June 2005 the IASB published proposed amendments to IFRS 3, 'Business combinations', and IAS 27, 'Consolidated and separate financial statements'. The proposed amendments are radical and would replace IFRS 3's cost allocation model with a fair value model. This would mean recognising the full fair value of the acquired business, including any minority interest in goodwill; and fair valuing contingent consideration at the acquisition date, with any subsequent changes recognised in profit or loss. The IASB is also proposing that transactions with minority shareholders should be treated as if they are transactions with owners.

In July 2005, the ASB published FRED 36, 'Business combinations (IFRS 3) and Amendments to FRS 2 Accounting for subsidiary undertakings (parts of IAS 27 Consolidated and separate financial statements)'; FRED 37, 'Intangible assets (IAS 38)'; and FRED 38, 'Impairment of assets (IAS 36)'. These propose to introduce UK accounting standards based on IFRS, which will replace SSAP 13, FRS 6, FRS 7, FRS 10 and FRS 11.

First-time adoption of IFRS

A first-time adopter may elect not to apply IFRS 3 retrospectively to business combinations that occurred before the date of transition to IFRS. However, if a first-time adopter restates any business combination to comply with IFRS 3, it has to restate all later business combinations and should also apply IAS 36 (as revised in 2004) and IAS 38 (as revised in 2004), from that same date.

Summary of main points

Scope

A business combination is the bringing together of separate entities or businesses into one reporting entity. It may be structured in a variety of ways. Where it results in a parent-subsidiary relationship, the IFRS applies in the consolidated financial statements. [IFRS 3 paras 4 to 7].	Similar. FRS 6 and FRS 7 apply where an entity becomes a subsidiary of a parent company that prepares consolidated financial statements and where an individual company combines with a business other than a subsidiary undertaking. [FRS 6 para 4; FRS 7 para 4].
IFRS 3 does not apply to business combinations:	FRS 6 and FRS 7 apply to all business combinations.

- In which separate entities or businesses are brought together to form a joint venture.

- Involving entities or businesses under common control.

- Involving two or more mutual entities.

- In which separate entities or businesses are brought together to form a reporting entity by contract alone without the obtaining of an ownership interest (for example, dual listed entities).

[IFRS 3 para 3].

Method of accounting

All business combinations should be accounted for using the purchase method ('acquisition accounting'). [IFRS 3 para 14].

The purchase method views a business combination from the perspective of the acquirer. The acquirer recognises the assets acquired and liabilities and contingent liabilities assumed, including those not previously recognised by the acquiree. [IFRS 3 para 15].

Business combinations not accounted for by merger accounting (see below) should be accounted for by acquisition accounting. [FRS 6 para 20].

The identifiable assets and liabilities to be recognised should be those of the acquired entity that existed at the date of the acquisition. [FRS 7 para 5].

Identifying the acquirer

An acquirer should be identified for all business combinations. The acquirer is the combining entity that obtains control of the other combining entities or businesses. [IFRS 3 para 17].

IFRS 3 includes guidance on identifying an acquirer. All pertinent facts and circumstances should be considered to determine which of the combining entities has the power to govern the financial and operating policies of the other entity (or entities) so as to obtain benefits from its (or their) activities. [IFRS 3 paras 19, 20].

Where a new entity is created to acquire two or more pre-existing entities, one of the pre-existing entities must be designated as the acquirer. [IFRS 3 para 22].

FRS 6 does not require an acquirer to be identified for all business combinations. If no party to the combination, in substance, obtains control over any other, or is otherwise seen to be dominant, merger accounting is required to be used.

FRS 6 sets out specified criteria for determining whether a business combination is a merger. If it does not met these criteria, it is an acquisition.

As above.

Cost of a business combination

The cost of a business combination is the aggregate of the fair values, at the date of exchange, of assets given, liabilities incurred or assumed, equity instruments issued by the acquirer and any costs directly attributable to the business combination. [IFRS 3 para 24].

Similar. The cost of acquisition is the amount of cash paid and the fair value of other purchase consideration given by the acquirer, together with the expenses of the acquisition. [FRS 7 para 26].

The issue costs of shares and debt are not included in the cost of a business combination, but are dealt with in accordance with IAS 32 and IAS 39 respectively. Other directly attributable costs (such as professional fees) are included in the cost of a business combination. General administrative costs are recognised as an expense when incurred. [IFRS 3 paras 29 to 31].

Similar. The issue costs of shares and debt are not included in the cost of acquisition, but are dealt with in accordance with FRS 25 (previously FRS 4). Other incremental costs incurred directly in making an acquisition are included in the cost of acquisition. Internal costs are charged to the profit and loss account as incurred. [FRS 7 para 28].

Adjustments to the cost of combination that are contingent on future events should be included in the cost of the combination at the acquisition date if the adjustment is *probable* and can be measured reliably. [IFRS 3 para 32].

Similar. Where additional consideration is payable at a future date, reasonable estimates of amounts expected to be paid should be added to the cost of acquisition. [FRS 7 para 27].

If the future events do not occur or the estimate needs to be revised, the cost of the business combination shall be adjusted accordingly. [IFRS 3 para 33].

Similar. Estimates should be revised in future years until the final amount is known. [FRS 7 para 27].

When an acquisition is achieved in a single exchange transaction (that is, not in stages), the "*date of exchange*" is the date of acquisition; that is, the date when the acquirer obtains control over the acquiree. [IFRS 3 App A].

UK GAAP does not use the terminology 'date of exchange'

The standard includes rules for determining cost when the business combination is achieved in stages by successive share purchases (see also, 'Business combination achieved in stages' below). [IFRS 3 para 25].

See 'Business combination achieved in stages' below.

Allocating the cost of a business combination

The acquirer should, at the acquisition date, recognise the acquiree's identifiable assets, liabilities and contingent liabilities that satisfy the recognition criteria, at their fair values at that date, except for non-current assets (or disposal groups) that are classified as held for sale, which should be accounted for in accordance with IFRS 5. [IFRS 3 para 36].

The identifiable assets, liabilities and contingent liabilities to be recognised should be those of the acquired entity that existed at the date of acquisition. [FRS 7 para 5].

The acquisition date is the date on which the acquirer effectively obtains control of the acquiree. [IFRS 3 App A].

Similar. [FRS 2 para 45].

For the acquirer to recognise separately the acquiree's identifiable assets, liabilities and contingent liabilities at the date of acquisition, they have to satisfy the following criteria:

Normal asset and liability recognition criteria apply. There are no exceptions for intangible assets and contingent liabilities.

• In the case of assets other than intangibles, it is probable that any associated future economic benefits will flow to the acquirer and the asset's fair value can be measured reliably.

• In the case of liabilities other than contingent liabilities, it is probable that an outflow of resources embodying economic benefits will be required to settle the obligation and the liability's fair value can be measured reliably.

- In the case of intangibles or contingent liabilities, the fair values can be measured reliably.

[IFRS 3 para 37].

The acquirer's income statement should incorporate the acquiree's profits and losses after the acquisition date by including the acquiree's income and expenses based on the cost of the business combination to the acquirer. [IFRS 3 para 38].

Similar. [FRS 6 para 20].

Because the acquirer recognises the acquiree's identifiable assets, liabilities and contingent liabilities at their fair values at the acquisition date, any minority interest in the acquiree is stated at the minority's proportion of the net fair value of those items. [IFRS 3 para 40].

Similar. [FRS 6 para 20].

Fair value of net assets

The fair values attributed to assets, liabilities and contingent liabilities are measured at the acquisition date (see above). They are not affected by the acquirer's intentions.

Similar. Fair values should reflect the conditions at the date of acquisition. They should not be adjusted to take account of changes resulting from the acquirer's intentions or future actions. [FRS 7 paras, 6, 7(a)].

IFRS 3 includes guidance for arriving at the fair values of identifiable assets, liabilities and contingent liabilities. [IFRS 3 para 40, App B paras B16, B17].

FRS 7 includes detailed rules on the application of these principles to determining the fair values of different types of assets and liabilities.

Restructuring provisions and future losses

Liabilities for terminating or reducing the acquiree's activities should only be recognised as part of allocating the cost of the combination when the acquiree has, at the acquisition date, an existing liability for restructuring recognised in accordance with IAS 37. [IFRS 3 para 41(a)].

Similar. Provisions for future reorganisation and integration costs expected to be incurred as a result of the acquisition do not affect fair values at the date of acquisition. [FRS 7 para 7(c)]. Therefore, these are treated as post-acquisition expenses under FRS 7.

Liabilities for future losses or other costs expected to be incurred as a result of the business combination should not be recognised when allocating the cost of the combination. [IFRS 3 para 41(b)].

Similar. [FRS 7 para 7].

Intangible assets

An intangible asset is recognised if it meets the definition of an intangible asset in IAS 38 and its fair value can be measured reliably. To meet the definition, it must be identifiable, which means that it is separable (that is, capable of being sold, transferred, licensed, rented or exchanged, separate from the entity) or it arises from contractual or other legal rights (regardless of whether those rights are separable). [IFRS 3 paras 45, 46].

UK GAAP is not as stringent as IFRS with regard to identifying intangibles and does not rule out the possibility of some 'intangible assets' being subsumed within goodwill.

Acquiree's contingent liabilities

The acquiree's contingent liabilities should be recognised at fair value if this can be measured reliably. Subsequently, contingent liabilities should be measured at the higher of the amount that would be recognised under IAS 37 and the amount initially recognised. [IFRS 3 paras 47 to 50].

Contingent assets and liabilities should be measured at fair values where these can be determined. For this purpose reasonable estimates of the expected outcome may be used. [FRS 7 para 15].

Goodwill acquired in a business combination should be recognised as an asset. [IFRS 3 para 51].	Similar. (FRS 10 para 7).
Goodwill is not amortised. Instead, it is subject to annual impairment tests, or more frequently if there is an indication of impairment. [IFRS 3 paras 54, 55].	Goodwill should be amortised on a systematic basis over its useful economic life. However, where goodwill is regarded as having an indefinite useful economic life, it is not amortised. Goodwill amortised over more than 20 years (or not amortised) should be reviewed for impairment at the end of each period using FRS 11. [FRS 10 paras 15, 17, 37].

Goodwill

Goodwill is the excess of the cost of the business combination over the acquirer's interest in the net fair value of the identifiable assets, liabilities and contingent liabilities. [IFRS 3 para 36].	Similar. [FRS 10 para 2].
Goodwill acquired in a business combination should be recognised as an asset. [IFRS 3 para 51].	Similar. [FRS 10 para 7].
Goodwill is not amortised. Instead, it is subject to annual impairment tests, or more frequently if there is an indication of impairment. [IFRS 3 paras 54, 55].	Goodwill should be amortised on a systematic basis over its useful economic life. However, where goodwill is regarded as having an indefinite useful economic life, it is not amortised. Goodwill amortised over more than 20 years (or not amortised) should be reviewed for impairment at the end of each period using FRS 11. [FRS 10 paras 15, 17, 37].
Not applicable.	There is a rebuttable presumption that the useful economic life of goodwill will not exceed 20 years. [FRS 10 para 19].

'Negative goodwill'

IFRS 3 does not use the term 'negative goodwill'. Instead, it refers to it as 'excess of acquirer's interest in the net fair value of acquiree's identifiable assets, liabilities and contingent liabilities over cost'. It requires that such 'negative goodwill' remaining after reassessing the identification and measurement of assets, liabilities and contingent liabilities and the measurement of the combination's cost should be recognised immediately in profit or loss. [IFRS 3 para 56].	Negative goodwill is recognised as income: • in the periods in which the non-monetary assets are recovered through depreciation or sale (but only to the extent of those assets); and • otherwise, in the periods expected to be benefited. [FRS 10 paras 49, 50].

Business combination achieved in stages

When a business combination is achieved in stages, the distinction between the date of acquisition and the date of the exchange transaction is important. While accounting for the acquisition commences as from the date of acquisition (that is, the date on which control is obtained), it uses cost and fair value information determined as at the date of each exchange transaction. [IFRS 3 para 58].	The calculation of goodwill is based on the fair values of the acquired subsidiary's identifiable assets and liabilities at the acquisition date, that is, the date it becomes a subsidiary. [CA85 4A Sch 9(2); FRS 2 para 50]. However, FRS 2 paragraph 89 notes that, in some circumstances, it may be appropriate to use a true and fair override of the Act in order to use fair values at the dates of earlier purchases, which would be consistent with IFRS 3.

Therefore, where the business combination takes place in stages, each exchange transaction is treated separately for the purpose of determining the fair values of the acquiree's identifiable assets, liabilities and contingent liabilities and for determining the amount of any goodwill on that transaction. [IFRS 3 para 58].

When a group increases its interest in a subsidiary undertaking, the subsidiary's identifiable assets and liabilities should be revalued to fair value and goodwill arising on the increase in interest should be calculated by reference to those fair values. This revaluation is not required if the difference between net fair values and carrying amounts of the assets and liabilities attributable to the increase in stake is not material. [FRS 2 para 51].

Any adjustment to fair values relating to the acquirer's previously held interests is a revaluation and is accounted for as such. This does not signify that the acquirer is applying an accounting policy of revaluing those items under IAS 16. [IFRS 3 para 59].

Similar. However, if the share of tangible fixed assets previously owned is revalued, it has generally been considered that the group would then have to comply with FRS 15 and adopt a policy of regularly revaluing these assets.

Initial accounting determined provisionally

The acquirer should account for the business combination using provisional values if the acquiree's identifiable assets, liabilities or contingent liabilities or the cost of the combination can be determined only provisionally. The acquirer should recognise adjustments to the provisional values within twelve months of the acquisition date, with a corresponding adjustment to goodwill. [IFRS 3 para 62].

Any necessary adjustments to provisional fair values should be made in the financial statements for the first full financial year following the acquisition. [FRS 7 para 25].

The acquirer should recognise adjustments to the provisional values as a result of completing the initial accounting, as if the fair values of the identifiable assets, liabilities, contingent liabilities at the acquisition date had been recognised from that date. Comparative figures should be restated as if the initial accounting had been completed from the acquisition date. [IFRS 3 para 62].

The adjustments to provisional fair values are accounted for in the period that the adjustments are made. [FRS 7 para 25].

Recognising deferred tax assets after the initial accounting is complete

If a deferred tax asset did not satisfy the recognition criteria when a business combination was initially accounted for, but is subsequently realised, the acquirer should recognise the benefit as income in accordance with IAS 12. In addition, the acquirer should reduce goodwill to the amount that would have been recognised if the deferred tax asset had been recognised from the acquisition date and recognise the reduction in the carrying amount of the goodwill as an expense. [IFRS 3 para 65].

No similar rule.

Disclosures

The disclosures required in the financial statements for the period during which the combination has taken place include:

- The names and descriptions of the combining entities or businesses.

Similar. [FRS 6 para 21].

- The acquisition date.

Similar. [FRS 6 para 21].

• The percentage of voting equity instruments acquired.	FRS 2 requires disclosure of the proportion of voting rights held by the parent and its subsidiary undertakings. [FRS 2 para 33].
• The cost of the combination and a description of the components of that cost, including any costs directly attributable to the combination.	Similar. FRS 6 requires disclosure of the composition and fair value of the consideration for the acquisition and details of deferred or contingent consideration. [FRS 6 para 24].
• The number of equity instruments issued or issuable as consideration for the combination and the fair value of those instruments, together with the basis for determining that fair value.	As above. [FRS 6 para 24].
• Details of any operations the entity has decided to dispose of as a result of the combination.	FRS 6 does not require disclosure of operations that the acquirer has decided to dispose of.
• The amounts recognised at the acquisition date for each class of the acquiree's assets, liabilities and contingent liabilities, and, unless disclosure would be impracticable (disclose that fact with explanation), the carrying amounts of each of those classes, determined in accordance with IFRS, immediately before the combination.	FRS 6 requires a table showing for each class of assets and liabilities acquired, the book values, fair value adjustments, fair values at the date of acquisition and the amount of goodwill arising. [FRS 6 para 25].
• The amount of any 'negative goodwill' recognised in profit or loss and the line item in the income statement in which the excess is recognised.	Similar. [FRS 10 para 53(c)].
• A description of each intangible asset that was not recognised separately from goodwill and an explanation of why its fair value could not be measured reliably.	No similar requirement.
• The amount of the acquiree's post-acquisition profit or loss, unless disclosure would be impracticable (disclose that fact, together with an explanation of why this is the case).	FRS 6 requires the post-acquisition operating results of businesses acquired in the year to be disclosed separately for each material acquisition and for other acquisitions in aggregate. [FRS 6 para 23, 28].
[IFRS 3 para 67].	
Not specified by IFRS 3, but see the requirement below for the combined entity's *pro forma* 'annualised results' (in IFRS 3 para 70).	For a material acquisition, the profit after taxation and minority interests of the acquired entity should be given for (a) the period from the beginning of the acquired entity's financial year to the date of acquisition giving the date on which this period began; and (b) its previous financial year. [FRS 6 para 35].
Not specified by IFRS 3.	For substantial acquisitions in the year, FRS 6 requires disclosure of additional information about the pre-acquisition results of the acquired company (for the periods described above). This includes a summarised profit and loss account and statement of total recognised gains and losses. Substantial acquisitions are generally those business combinations in which any of the ratios set out in the Listing Rules for the classification of transactions exceeds 15 per cent. [FRS 6 paras 36, 37].

In addition, there are the following disclosures requirements:

Disclosure of the following information, unless it would be impracticable (disclose that fact with explanation):	No similar requirement.

* The combined entity's revenue for the period as though the acquisition date for all business combinations in the period had been the beginning of that period.

* The combined entity's profit or loss for the period as though the acquisition date for all business combinations in the period had been the beginning of the period.

[IFRS 3 para 70].

Detailed disclosure requirements for goodwill. [IFRS 3 para 75].	FRS 10 includes disclosure requirements for goodwill.
Disclosure of information enabling users to evaluate the financial effects of gains, losses, error corrections and other adjustments recognised in the current period that relate to business combinations that took place in the current or previous periods. [IFRS 3 para 72].	Any exceptional profit or loss in periods following the acquisition that is determined using the fair values recognised on acquisition should be disclosed in accordance with the requirements of FRS 3, and identified as relating to the acquisition. Also, disclosure of the costs incurred in reorganising, restructuring and integrating an acquisition. [FRS 6 paras 30, 31].
Disclosure of the information required by paragraph 67 (see above) for each business combination effected after the balance sheet date but before the financial statements are authorised for issue, unless such disclosure would be impracticable (disclose that fact with explanation). [IFRS 3 para 71].	FRS 21 requires disclosures in respect of non-adjusting post-balance sheet events.

Reverse acquisitions

In a reverse acquisition, the legal subsidiary is regarded as the acquirer if it has the power to govern the financial and operating policies of the legal parent so as to obtain benefits from its activities. [IFRS 3 para 21].	
Guidance on the accounting for reverse acquisitions is given in Appendix B to IFRS 3. The entity issuing the shares is treated as the acquiree and the entity whose existing shareholders receive the shares is treated as the acquirer. [IFRS 3 App B].	Under section 258 of the Companies Act 1985, the issuer is treated as the acquirer and the recipient is treated as the acquiree. A departure from this will involve use of the true and fair override.

Transitional rules

IFRS 3 includes transitional rules for existing users of IFRS. [IFRS 3 paras 79 to 85].These will not apply to first-time adopters. Instead, the exemption for business combinations in IFRS 1 will be applicable.	FRS 10 also included transitional rules when it was introduced.

Merger accounting

Merger accounting (or 'uniting of interests') is not permitted by IFRS 3 for business combinations within its scope.	Merger accounting for a business combination is required if it is not prohibited by companies legislation (CA85 4A Sch 10) and the combination meets the criteria set out in FRS 6 paragraphs 6 to 11. [FRS 6 para 5].
Not applicable.	The criteria for the use of merger accounting are:
	• No party to the combination is portrayed as either the acquirer or the acquired.
	• All parties to the combination participate in establishing the management structure for the combined entity.
	• Based on relative sizes, one party does not dominate the combined entity (normally, not more than 50 per cent larger than the other party).
	• Any non-equity consideration is an immaterial proportion of the fair value of the consideration received by the equity shareholders.
	• No equity shareholders of any of the combining entities retain any material interest in the future performance of only part of the combined entity.
	[FRS 6 paras 6 to 11].
Not applicable.	The Act requires that at least 90 per cent of the nominal value of equity shares must be acquired, in exchange for the issue of equity shares by the parent. Also, any non-equity consideration must not exceed 10 per cent of the nominal value of the equity shares issued. [CA85 4A Sch 10].
Not applicable.	Merger accounting is not appropriate where one of the parties results from a recent divestment by a larger entity. [FRS 6 para 58].
Not applicable.	Under merger accounting, the carrying values of the combining parties' assets and liabilities are not adjusted to fair value on consolidation, although appropriate adjustments should be made to achieve uniformity of accounting policies. Any difference between the amount recorded as share capital issued plus any additional consideration and the amount recorded for the share capital acquired should be adjusted against reserves. [FRS 6 paras 16 to 18].
Not applicable.	Merger expenses should be charged to the profit and loss account at the effective date of the merger, as non-operating restructuring expenses. [FRS 6 para 19].
Not applicable.	FRS 6 sets out disclosure requirements for mergers. [FRS 6 para 22].

Group reconstructions

A business combination involving entities or businesses under common control is defined as a business combination in which all of the combining entities or businesses ultimately are controlled by the same party or parties both before and after the combination, and that control is not transitory. [IFRS 3 para 10].

A *group reconstruction* is defined as any of the following arrangements:

- The transfer of a shareholding in a subsidiary undertaking from one group company to another.

- The addition of a new parent company to a group.

- The transfer of shares in one or more subsidiary undertakings of a group to a new company that is not a group company but whose shareholders are the same as those of the group's parent.

- The combination into a group of two or more companies that before the combination had the same shareholders.

[FRS 6 para 2].

IFRS 3 does not deal with the accounting for business combinations involving entities under common control. Also, these are wider in scope than FRS 6's group reconstructions as the extent of minority interests in each of the combining entities before and after the business combination is not relevant to determining whether the combination involves entities under common control. [IFRS 3 para 13].

A group reconstruction may be accounted for by using merger accounting (even if it does not meet the definition of a merger) provided:

- the use of merger accounting is not prohibited by companies legislation (CA85 4A Sch 10);

- the ultimate shareholders remain the same, and the rights of each such shareholder, relative to the others, are unchanged; and

- no minority's interest in the net assets of the group is altered by the transfer.

[FRS 6 para 13].

IFRS 5 and FRS 3 – Held for sale and discontinued operations

IFRS 5, Non-current assets held for sale and discontinued operations	FRS 3, Reporting financial performance (part)
Effective for annual periods beginning on or after 1 January 2005.	*Effective for accounting periods ending on or after 22 June 1993.*

Related pronouncements

–	–

Overview

IFRS 5 sets out requirements for the classification, measurement and presentation of non-current assets held for sale. There is no equivalent UK standard.

IFRS 5 introduces the concept of a 'disposal group'. Assets classified as held for sale and the assets in a disposal group that is classified as held for sale are presented separately from other assets in the balance sheet. The liabilities of a disposal group classified as held for sale should be presented separately from other liabilities. There is no equivalent UK rule.

An asset held for sale, or included within a disposal group that is held for sale, is not depreciated under IFRS 5. This differs to UK GAAP where depreciation would continue until the asset was actually disposed of.

Under IFRS 5, subsidiaries acquired exclusively with a view to resale that meet the conditions to be classified as held for sale are consolidated, but their results are presented as a single line item. They are presented in the balance sheet as two separate items (that is, assets, including goodwill, and liabilities) measured at fair value less costs to sell. Under UK GAAP, these subsidiaries are exempt from consolidation and are included in the balance sheet as a single asset at fair value based on net proceeds.

The definitions of discontinued operations differ. Under IFRS 5, a discontinued operation is a separate major line of business or geographical area of operations or is part of a single plan to dispose of a major line of business or geographical area of operations or is a subsidiary acquired exclusively with a view to resale. FRS 3 requires the discontinued operation to have a material effect on the nature and focus of the reporting entity's operations.

Under IFRS 5, an operation is classified as discontinued at the date the operation meets the criteria to be classified as held for sale or when the entity has disposed of the operation. 'Held for sale' means that the asset (or disposal group) must be available for immediate sale in its present condition and its sale must be highly probable. To be highly probable, management should be committed to a plan to sell and an active programme to locate a buyer and complete the plan should have begun. The sale should be completed within one year of the date of classification as held for resale (except if this is delayed due to circumstances beyond the entity's control). Operations may qualify as discontinued earlier than they would have done under UK GAAP as FRS 3 specifies a three month cut-off period after the period end.

IFRS 5 requires a single number to be disclosed on the face of the income statement, being the total of (i) the discontinued operation's post-tax profit/loss and (ii) the post-tax gain/loss recognised in the measurement of the fair value less costs to sell or on the disposal of the discontinued operation's assets. A breakdown of this number is required to be given either on the face of the income statement or in the notes. FRS 3 requires disclosure of the split on the face of the income statement.

IFRS 5 requires disclosure of the net cash flows attributable to operating, investing and financing activities of discontinued operations, whereas under UK GAAP, FRS 1 only encourages disclosure of cash flows from discontinued operations.

Convergence

In July 2003, the ASB issued FRED 32, 'Disposal of non-current assets and presentation of discontinued operations', based on the exposure draft that preceded IFRS 5 (ED 4).

First-time adoption of IFRS 1

Entities with a date of transition before 1 January 2005 (this includes all entities applying the EU 2005 Regulation) apply the same transitional provisions that are in IFRS 5. Entities with a date of transition on or after 1 January 2005 apply the standard retrospectively.

Summary of main points

Scope

IFRS 5 applies to all non-current assets (basically assets that are not cash or held for short-term use or trading) and to all disposal groups of an entity. These are groups of assets that are to be disposed of together in a single transaction along with associated liabilities. If the disposal group is a cash generating unit, acquired and allocated goodwill is included. [IFRS 5 para 2].

IFRS 5's measurement rules do not apply to deferred tax assets, assets arising from employee benefits, financial assets within the scope of IAS 39, non-current assets accounted for in accordance with the fair value model in IAS 40 and contractual rights under insurance contracts as defined in IFRS 4. [IFRS 5 para 5].

There is no UK equivalent standard in respect of assets or disposal groups held for sale. FRS 3 includes requirements for the presentation of discontinued operations.

There are no scope restrictions in FRS 3.

Classification of non-current assets or disposal groups

A non-current asset or disposal group should be classified as held for sale if its carrying amount will be recovered principally through sale rather than through continuing use. [IFRS 5 para 6].

No UK GAAP equivalent.

The non-current asset (or disposal group) must be available for sale in its present condition and its sale must be highly probable. To be highly probable management should be committed to a plan to sell and an active programme to locate a buyer and complete the plan should have begun. The sale should be completed within one year of the date of classification as held for resale (except if this is delayed due to circumstances beyond the entity's control). [IFRS 5 paras 8, 9].

No UK GAAP equivalent.

Non-current assets or disposal groups to be abandoned

A non-current asset or disposal group that is to be abandoned should not be classified as held for sale, because it is to be recovered through continuing use. However, where a disposal group meets the definition of discontinued (excepting that it is not held for sale), the income statement and cash flow presentation and disclosure requirements for discontinued operations apply at the date on which it ceases to be used. [IFRS 5 para 13].

There is no UK equivalent standard in relation to non-current assets or disposal groups held for sale. Where a discontinued operation is terminated, it will qualify as discontinued in a period if the termination takes place in the period or before the earlier of three months after commencement of the subsequent accounting period and the date on which the financial statements are approved. The activities must have ceased permanently in this period. [FRS 3 para 4].

Measurement of non-current assets or disposal groups classified as held for sale

A non-current asset or disposal group classified as held for sale should be measured at the lower of its carrying amount and fair value less costs to sell. This measurement should be applied immediately before initial classification as held for sale, but after all assets and liabilities are measured in accordance with applicable IFRSs. [IFRS 5 paras 15, 18].

There is no UK equivalent standard in relation to non-current assets or disposal groups held for sale. However, a non-current asset to be disposed of will form an income-generating unit of its own and should be written down to its recoverable amount (higher of net realisable value and value in use). [FRS 11 paras 31, 14].

Impairment losses may be recognised at this stage. Subsequent gains may be recognised, but only to the extent that those gains reverse previous impairment losses. [IFRS 5 paras 20 to 22].

No UK GAAP equivalent.

Non-current assets classified as held for sale, or that are part of a disposal group classified as held for sale, should not be depreciated. [IFRS 5 para 25].

Non-current assets should be depreciated over their useful economic lives, right up to the point at which an asset is sold. [FRS 15 para 77],

Discontinued operations

A discontinued operation is a component of an entity. It must, therefore, be distinguishable for financial reporting and operational purposes, that is, a cash generating unit (CGU) or a collection of CGUs. To be classified as discontinued it must have been disposed of, or classified as held for sale, and either:

A discontinued operation is an operation that is sold or terminated (see below). The assets, liabilities, results of operations and activities are clearly distinguishable, physically, operationally and for financial reporting purposes. The discontinued operation:

- is a separate major line of business or geographical area of operations;

- has a material effect on the nature and focus of the reporting entity's operations; and

- is part of a single plan to dispose of a major line of business or geographical area of operations; or

- represents a material reduction in its operating facilities resulting either from its withdrawal from a particular market (whether class of business or geographical) or from a material reduction in turnover in the reporting entity's continuing markets.

- is a subsidiary acquired exclusively with a view to resale.

[IFRS 5 paras 31, 32].

[FRS 3 para 4].

Although an operation must be disposed of or held for sale to be discontinued, a disposal group that has been abandoned and meets the conditions in one of the three bullets above has its results and cash flows presented and disclosed in accordance with the requirements for discontinued operations (see below). It will not, however, be measured in accordance with the IFRS 5 requirements for disposal groups held for sale and it will not be presented separately in the balance sheet.

FRS 3 does not distinguish between operations that are sold and those that are terminated, for the purpose of presenting as discontinued operations.

Timing of classification of an operation as discontinued

This is significantly different from the IFRS 5 definition of discontinued. To be classified as discontinued a component must either have been disposed of in the reporting period or it must meet the definition of held for resale. [IFRS 5 App A]. In common with assets held for sale, it must be available for immediate sale in its present condition and its sale must be highly probable. Operations that are to be sold may qualify as discontinued earlier under IFRS than they will under UK GAAP.

Under FRS 3 a sale or termination must have been completed in the reporting period or before the earlier of three months after the start of the subsequent period and the date on which the financial statements are approved. [FRS 3 para 4].

Subsidiaries acquired exclusively with a view to resale

Subsidiaries acquired exclusively with a view to resale that meet the conditions to be classified as held for sale are, by definition, discontinued operations. [IFRS 5 para 32(c)]. These will be consolidated, but their results will be presented in accordance with the disclosure requirements for discontinued operations, that is, as a single line item (see below). They will be presented in the balance sheet as two separate items (that is, assets and liabilities) measured at fair value less costs to sell.

Subsidiaries acquired exclusively with a view to resale should reasonably be expected to be disposed of approximately within one year of the date of acquisition. They are excluded from consolidation and should be accounted for as current assets at the lower of cost and net realisable value. [FRS 2 paras 11, 25].

Disclosure of discontinued operations

The following needs to be disclosed for discontinued operations:

- A single number should be disclosed on the face of the income statement, being the total of (a) profit/loss after tax of the discontinued operation and (b) the gain/loss after tax recognised in the measurement of the fair value less costs to sell or on the disposal of the assets constituting the discontinued operation.

- On the face of the income statement, separately presented from continuing operations, or in the notes to the financial statements, a breakdown of the single number above into (i) revenue, expenses and pre-tax profit or loss, (ii) the related tax, (iii) the gain or loss on measurement to fair value less costs to sell or on the disposal of the assets and (iv) the related tax.

- Net cash flows attributable to the operating, investing and financing activities of discontinued operations, either on the face of the cash flow statement or in the notes.

[IFRS 5 para 33].

The disclosures in the second and third bullet points above are not required for disposal groups that are newly acquired subsidiaries that are classified as held for sale on acquisition. [IFRS 5 para 33].

The following needs to be disclosed for discontinued operations:

- Continuing and discontinued operations should be disclosed separately. On the face of the income statement the minimum that should be disclosed in respect of discontinued operations is turnover and operating profit. [FRS 3 para 14].

- Analysis of other line items between turnover and operating profit may be given on the face of the income statement or in the notes. Tax and interest may be allocated, but the basis should be stated. [FRS 3 para 14].

In addition to the disclosures required by Schedule 5 of the Companies Act 1985, subject to section 231, disclose, for all subsidiaries not consolidated:

- Particulars of the balances between the excluded subsidiary undertakings and the rest of the group.

- The nature and extent of transactions of the excluded subsidiary undertakings with the rest of the group.

- For an excluded subsidiary undertaking carried other than by the equity method, any amounts included in the consolidated financial statements in respect of:

    - Dividends received and receivable from that undertaking.

- Any write-down in the period in respect of the investment in that undertaking or amounts due from that undertaking.

[FRS 2 para 31].

Prior periods should be adjusted in the income statement and cash flow statement so that the disclosures relate to all operations that have been discontinued by the balance sheet date of the latest period presented. [IFRS 5 para 34].	Same, for income statement. [FRS 3 para 30].

Presentation of a non-current asset or disposal group held for sale

A non-current asset held for sale and the assets of a disposal group held for sale should be presented separately from other assets. The liabilities of a disposal group classified as held for sale should be presented separately from other liabilities. The main classes of assets and liabilities classified as held for sale should be disclosed either on the face of the balance sheet or in the notes. The exception to this is where the disposal group is a newly acquired subsidiary, in which case disclosure of the major classes of assets and liabilities is not required. [IFRS 5 paras 38, 39].

No UK GAAP equivalent.

This means that a subsidiary acquired as held for resale should be measured at fair value less costs to sell and presentation on the balance sheet should be split between total assets (including goodwill) and total liabilities. No further split of the major classes of assets and liabilities is required.

The comparative balance sheet should not be re-presented in respect of operations discontinued at the current balance sheet date or in respect of non-current assets or disposal groups held for sale at the current balance sheet date. [IFRS 5 para 40].

Additional disclosures

In the period in which a non-current asset or disposal group has either been classified as held for sale or sold, entities should disclose:

No UK GAAP equivalent.

- A description of the non-current asset or disposal group.

No UK GAAP equivalent.

- A description of the facts and circumstances leading to the sale or expected disposal and the expected manner and timing of the disposal.

No UK GAAP equivalent.

- Any gain or loss recognised on initial classification as described above, and, if it has not been presented separately in the income statement, the income statement caption in which it is included.

No UK GAAP equivalent.

- If applicable, the segment that includes the non-current asset or disposal group.

[IFRS 5 para 41].

Where items are no longer classified as held for sale the entity should disclose the reasons for this and the effect on the results of operations in the current period and any prior periods presented. [IFRS 5 para 42].

If a sale or termination has a material impact on a major business segment, this fact should be disclosed and explained. [FRS 3 para 53].

No UK GAAP equivalent.

Subject index

Key

1	Similar, but minor differences
2	Some differences
3	Significant differences

IFRS and UK GAAP – A comparison